Factory Politics in the People's Republic of China

Rethinking Socialism and Reform in China

Series Editors

Huaiyin Li (*University of Texas, Austin*)
Chongqing Wu (*Sun Yat-sen University*)

Editorial Board

Joel Andreas (*Johns Hopkins University*)
Xiaoping Cong (*University of Houston*)
Alexander Day (*Occidental College*)
Brian DeMare (*Tulane University*)
Han Xiaorong (*Lingnan University*)
William Hurst (*Northwestern University*)
Li Fangchun (*Chongqing University*)
Jack Qiu (*Chinese University of Hong Kong*)
Yafeng Xia (*Long Island University*)
Yan Hairong (*Hong Kong University of Science and Technology*)

VOLUME 5

The titles published in this series are listed at *brill.com/rsrc*

Factory Politics in the People's Republic of China

Edited by

Joel Andreas

BRILL

LEIDEN | BOSTON

Cover image courtesy of Makhnach_M, istock.com

This book is a result of the cooperation between Open Times Press and Koninklijke Brill NV. These articles were selected and translated into English from *Open Times* (Kaifang shidai 开放时代), an academic journal in Chinese.

This book was copyedited by Niu Yunping, Shi Xiaoying, and Wendy Smyer Yu.

Library of Congress Cataloging-in-Publication Data

Names: Andreas, Joel, editor.
Title: Factory politics in the People's Republic of China / edited by Joel Andreas.
Description: Leiden ; Boston : Brill, 2020. | Series: Rethinking socialism and reform in china, 2468-3035 ; vol. 5 | Summary: "Over the past seven decades-since the 1949 Revolution-every aspect of Chinese society has been profoundly transformed multiple times. No sector has experienced more tumultuous twists and turns than industry. The eight articles contained in this volume examine these twists and turns, focusing on those aspects of industrial relations that involve contention and power, that is, factory politics. They were selected from among articles that have appeared in the Chinese journal Open Times (开放时代) over the past decade. Because Open Times has a well-earned reputation for publishing diverse viewpoints, it has been able to attract some of the very best scholarship in China"—Provided by publisher.
Identifiers: LCCN 2019048104 (print) | LCCN 2019048105 (ebook) |
   ISBN 9789004421745 (hardback) | ISBN 9789004421752 (ebook)
Subjects: LCSH: Industrial policy—China—History. | Industrial
   relations—China—History. | Working class—Political
   activity—China—History.
Classification: LCC HD3616.C63 F33 2020 (print) | LCC HD3616.C63 (ebook) |
   DDC 331.0951–DC23
LC record available at https://lccn.loc.gov/2019048104
LC ebook record available at https://lccn.loc.gov/2019048105

Typeface for the Latin, Greek, and Cyrillic scripts: "Brill". See and download: brill.com/brill-typeface.

ISSN 2468-3035
ISBN 978-90-04-42174-5 (hardback)
ISBN 978-90-04-42175-2 (e-book)

Copyright 2020 by Koninklijke Brill NV, Leiden, The Netherlands.
Koninklijke Brill NV incorporates the imprints Brill, Brill Hes & De Graaf, Brill Nijhoff, Brill Rodopi, Brill Sense, Hotei Publishing, mentis Verlag, Verlag Ferdinand Schöningh and Wilhelm Fink Verlag.
All rights reserved. No part of this publication may be reproduced, translated, stored in a retrieval system, or transmitted in any form or by any means, electronic, mechanical, photocopying, recording or otherwise, without prior written permission from the publisher.
Authorization to photocopy items for internal or personal use is granted by Koninklijke Brill NV provided that the appropriate fees are paid directly to The Copyright Clearance Center, 222 Rosewood Drive, Suite 910, Danvers, MA 01923, USA. Fees are subject to change.

This book is printed on acid-free paper and produced in a sustainable manner.

Contents

List of Contributors　VII
List of Figures and Tables　X

Introduction　1

1　From Passion to Deception – Daily Life at the Grassroots under State Control of Production before and after the Great Leap Forward: an Investigation of TY Factory in Guangzhou (1956–1965)　7
　　Jia Wenjuan (贾文娟)
　　Translated by Shayan Momin

2　Research into the Implementation of the Staff and Workers Congress System in State-Owned Enterprises: a 60-Year Case Study of One Factory　33
　　Cai He (蔡禾) *and Li Wanlian* (李晚莲)
　　Translated by Roderick Graham Flagg

3　A Simple Control Model Analysis of Labor Relations in Industrial SOEs　52
　　Tong Xin (佟新)
　　Translated by Roderick Graham Flagg

4　Changes in Production Models within State-Owned Enterprises under the "Double Transformations:" the Rise of Internal Labor Subcontracting in City A's Nanchang Factory (2001–2013)　75
　　Jia Wenjuan (贾文娟)
　　Translated by Shayan Momin

5　Sustaining Production: Spatial Interactions between Han and Uyghur Workers at the Kashgar Cotton Mill　99
　　Liu Ming (刘明)
　　Translated by Heather Mowbray

6　Corporate Social Responsibility in the Global Toy Industry's Supply Chain: an Empirical Study of Walmart Supplier Factories in China　125
　　Yu Xiaomin (余晓敏)
　　Translated by Shayan Momin

7 Direct Labor Union Elections: Lessons from Guangdong   143
  Wen Xiaoyi (闻效仪)
  Translated by Matthew A. Hale

8 Patterns of Collective Resistance among the New Generation of Chinese Migrant Workers: from the Politics of Production to the Politics of Life   165
  Wang Jianhua (汪建华) *and Meng Quan* (孟泉)
  Translated by Matthew A. Hale

Index   187

Contributors

Joel Andreas
is an associate professor of sociology at Johns Hopkins University in Baltimore. He studies political contention and social change in China. His first book, *Rise of the Red Engineers: The Cultural Revolution and the Origins of China's New Class* (Stanford 2009), analyzed the contentious merger of old and new elites following the 1949 Revolution. His second book, *Disenfranchised: The Rise and Fall of Industrial Citizenship in China* (Oxford 2019), traces radical changes that have fundamentally transformed industrial relations over the past seven decades. Currently, he is continuing to investigate changing labor relations and the ongoing transformation of China's rural society.

Cai He (蔡禾)
is a professor at the School of Sociology and Anthropology at Sun Yat-sen University in Guangzhou, where he also directs the Urban Social Research Center and the Social Science Investigation Center. His research areas are urban social studies, economic sociology, social problems and organizational sociology. He is the author of *Civilization and Costs: The Evolution of Marriage*《文明与代价－婚姻的嬗变》(1993), *Unemployed Groups and Unemployment Security*《失业者群体与失业保障》(co-authored, 1998), *Focusing on the Vulnerable: Research on Urban Disability Groups*《关注弱势: 城市残疾人群体研究》(co-authored, 2008), *Migrant Workers in the Process of Urbanization*《城市化进程中的农民工》(co-authored, 2009), and *Sociological Perspectives of Transitional China*《转型中国的社会学透视》(2016).

Jia Wenjuan (贾文娟)
is an assistant professor of sociology at Shanghai University. She specializes in labor sociology. Her doctoral work focused on the change of labor regimes in a Chinese state-owned enterprise in Guangzhou from the Mao era to the present day. From a historical comparative perspective, she researched how workers' protests during the production process in an SOE are shaped by the contradiction between Chinese official ideology and discourse and market-economy practices. Professor Jia is the author of *Selective Indulgence: Workplace Politics and the Making of the Strategy of Labor Control in a Chinese State-Owned Enterprise*《选择性放任: 车间政治与国有企业劳动治理逻辑的形成》(2016). She has published academic papers on the labor process in China's new economy, labor regime change and market reform of China's state-owned enterprises, ideological domination, and urban culture.

Li Wanlian (李晚莲)

is a professor at the School Of Public Administration and Law at Hunan Agricultural University in Changsha. Her research areas are public management and social governance. She has published more than twenty academic papers in key scholarly journals in China.

Liu Ming (刘明)

is an associate professor and doctoral supervisor at the School of International Cultural Exchange at Xinjiang Normal University in Ürümqi. Dr. Liu studies cultural anthropology. He is author of *Theories and Practices of Xinjiang Ethnology and Anthropology*《新疆民族学人类学理论与实践》(2013), *Migration and Adaptation: the Ethnography of the Tajik in the Pamirs*《迁徙与适应: 帕米尔高原塔吉克族民族志》(in Chinese, 2014), *Studio and Field Works of Xinjiang Anthropology and Ethnology*《新疆人类学民族学书斋与田野》(2016), *Transformation and Communication: the Ethnography on Labors in a Textile Plant*《转型与交往: 一个工厂的劳工民族志》(2017).

Meng Quan (孟泉)

is a lecturer at the School of Labor Economics of the Capital University of Economics and Business in Beijing. His research interests focus on labor dispute prevention and resolution, Chinese trade unions, employment relations governance, and employment relations theory. He has published papers in *ILR Review, Industrial Relations Journal, Globalizations, Dongyue Tribune*, and *China Human Resource Development*.

Tong Xin (佟新)

is a professor of sociology at Peking University. Her research interests include labor studies with a focus on labor relations in Chinese state-owned and foreign-invested enterprises, labor ethics, and labor history as well as gender studies, with an emphasis on the care economy, women's careers and the balance of work and family. She is the author or co-author of thirteen books and has served on the Steering Committee for Teaching Sociology Programs of the Ministry of Education, the Chinese Women's Theory Research Association, and as deputy director of the Beijing Women and Children's Committee of the China Democracy Promotion Association.

Wang Jianhua (汪建华)

is an associate professor at the National Institute of Social Development of the Chinese Academy of Social Sciences in Beijing. His research interests include labor movements, regional comparison of labor problems in China, and the urbanization of rural migrant workers. He is author of *Politics of Livelihood:*

A New Perspective on the Transformation of Industrial Relations in World Factories《生活的政治: 世界工厂劳资关系转型的新视角》(2015) and he has published papers in *Sociological Studies, Chinese Journal of Sociology, Open Times, Twenty-First Century*, and other Chinese-language journals.

Wen Xiaoyi (闻效仪)
is a professor at China University of Labor Relations in Beijing. His research areas are trade unions in China, collective bargaining, and strikes. He has published papers in the *Journal of Contemporary China, British Journal of Industrial Relations*, and *Sociological Studies*.

Yu Xiaomin (余晓敏)
is an associate professor and the director of the Corporate Social Responsibility and Social Enterprise Research Center at the School of Social Development and Public Policy at Beijing Normal University. Her research areas include social enterprise, corporate social responsibility, and civil society. Her publications have appeared in a variety of academic journals, including *Journal of Business Ethics, Economic and Industrial Democracy*, and *Social Enterprise Journal*.

Figures and Tables

Figures

2.1	Number of SWC meetings per year, Factory A, 1957–2008	38
2.2	Number of days of the SWC meetings, Factory A, 1957 to 2010	38
4.1	Change in the number of employees in Nanchang from 1950–2013	78
4.2	Nanchang's business distribution	79
4.3	Nanchang's S Branch organization diagram	79
5.1	Changes in the nature of property rights lead to changes in Uyghur-Han spatial interactions in production	107

Tables

2.1	The proportion of ordinary workers and staff, in the SWC	40
3.1	Changing numbers of SOE employees	53
3.2	Gross industrial output value and annual growth rate of state-owned and state-controlled industrial enterprises	53
5.1	Changes in the number of workers by ethnic group and gender in the Kashgar Cotton Mill	110
6.1	Comparison of "codes of conduct" and implementation/monitoring mechanisms for major global brand operators and retailers	130
6.2	Overview of three toy supplier factories	133
6.3	Factory comparisons	137
8.1	Comparison between three patterns of resistance	184

Introduction

Over the past seven decades – since the 1949 Revolution that brought the Chinese Communist Party (CCP) to power – every aspect of Chinese society has been profoundly transformed multiple times. No sector, however, has experienced more tumultuous twists and turns than industry. The eight articles contained in this volume all treat these twists and turns, focusing on those aspects of industrial relations that involve contention and power, that is, factory politics. They were selected from among articles that have appeared in the journal *Open Times* (开放时代) over the past decade. Published by the Guangzhou Academy of Social Sciences, *Open Times* is one of China's two leading social science journals along with *Social Sciences in China* (中国社会科学) published by the Chinese Academy of Social Sciences in Beijing. While articles in the latter journal must hew close to official perspectives, *Open Times* has a well-earned reputation for publishing diverse viewpoints. This has allowed it to attract some of the very best scholarship in China.

The history that has served as the source for these articles has been dramatic. During the CCP's first decade in power, it nationalized or collectivized all private enterprises and launched a massive industrialization drive. Factories were reorganized into work units (单位), with their employees becoming permanent members; these units served not only as production centers, but also as the main sites of welfare distribution, social control, governance, and political participation. The archetypal industrial work unit provided housing as well as facilities for education, medical care, and recreation, and mobilized its employees to participate in incessant production and political campaigns. Some of these campaigns, most prominently the Great Leap Forward and the Cultural Revolution, generated profound disruptions that reshaped social relations within the factory.

While the market reforms of the 1980s brought substantial changes, in some ways they reinforced the work unit system. The industrial restructuring that began in the 1990s, however, destroyed the system, transforming factories into profit-oriented firms. The great majority of industrial enterprises were privatized and the remainder were reorganized as hybrid entities with both state and private investment. Factories shed their social functions in order to focus on maximizing profits. Alongside the remaining state-owned enterprises (SOEs), a massive private industrial sector emerged that specialized in the intensive exploitation of low-cost labor, allowing China – after it joined the WTO – to become the "workshop of the world."

These changes have profoundly transformed the labor force as well as labor processes and labor relations. Members of the older generation, who once made up the membership of industrial work units, have been largely shunted aside, with tens of millions laid off or retired. Those who remain make up a core of veteran workers in restructured enterprises, waiting to retire. Members of the new generation of industrial workers, most of whom were born in the countryside, are much more itinerant and are subjected to far more coercive factory discipline.

All of the articles selected for this volume focus on factory politics in one sense or another. They are concerned with changes in labor processes, labor relations and labor management, factory hierarchies, social cleavages and conflicts, and power and contention for power within industrial enterprises. The articles are all based on extensive empirical research and they each make a substantial contribution to our understanding of a range of issues connected with industrial relations in China. For scholars who do not read Chinese, they also offer a window into the ways these issues are discussed inside China. While the authors engage theories and arguments produced by Western scholars, they also engage Chinese scholarship and intellectual debates that are not as familiar outside of China. They reflect, in different ways, the Chinese intellectual environment and political perspectives. In addition to theoretical interventions and empirical analyses, all of the articles – some more explicitly than others – make normative arguments, and some make concrete policy suggestions, cognizant of the practical realities of China's political and institutional space.

The articles are arranged in rough chronological order. The first two provide detailed accounts of industrial relations during the socialist work unit era. The focus of the next three articles shifts to the post-Mao Reform era, and particularly to the changes wrought by industrial restructuring in the 1990s. Because they discuss state-owned enterprises, however, factory relations during the work unit era continue to serve as the starting point for all three. The last three articles turn our attention to the private- and foreign-invested factories that, over the past two decades, have become the engines of China's export-manufacturing juggernaut.

In the first article, Jia Wenjuan looks back on changes in factory workers' attitudes towards work before and after the Great Leap Forward (1958–60). This is no easy task more than five decades later, but, based on interviews and contemporary documents, Jia does a remarkable job. Contradicting the conventional wisdom that socialist-era factories were intrinsically characterized by slacking, she argues that during the first decade of the Communist era, Chinese workers toiled "with dedication and passion." Things started to change during the Great Leap Forward (GLF), when, because party leaders began to push them too hard, workers began to adopt passive, negative, and deceptive practices to protect themselves. Workers I have interviewed have told the same story, with the GLF as a turning point. Many others, however, have claimed that collectivist dedication endured until it was undermined by the fragmentation of the Cultural Revolution or, more commonly, by widening wage disparities and the "some get rich first" philosophy of the 1980s. Although Jia's account and the causes of disaffection she cites ring completely true, many experienced the erosion of collectivist commitment as a more gradual process.

In the second article, Cai He and Li Wanlian analyze the evolution of staff and workers congresses (SWCs) over six decades, based on a case study of an individual factory. China's SWCs are, like European works councils, based on the principles of representation, participation and labor-management collaboration, although the CCP has kept the Chinese version on a particularly tight leash. Analyzing the content, frequency and length of congress meetings, Cai and Li highlight two trends. The first was cyclical, with high points in SWC activity coinciding with moments when the CCP was particularly concerned about shoring up its legitimacy among industrial workers – during the recovery from the collapse of the GLF in the early 1960s, during the early 1980s, following Mao's death and Deng's ascension to power, and during the most traumatic years of industrial restructuring in the late 1990s. This is an intriguing interpretation that points to the connection between popular participation and legitimacy in the CCP's original workplace-based model of governance. The second trend was a long-term downward trajectory in SWC activity starting in the mid-1980s, as industrial reforms concentrated power in the hands of factory directors.

The next three articles focus on the restructuring of state-owned industrial enterprises starting in the 1990s. In the third article, based on case studies of a machinery factory, a shipyard, a coal mine, and an oilfield, Tong Xin analyzes how restructuring altered social hierarchies and labor management methods. All four enterprises remained state-owned, but changed in fundamental ways. A new, much steeper social hierarchy was created, consisting of four highly differentiated strata. At the top, now wielding complete control, were a small number of politically-appointed leaders. The next stratum consisted of college-educated managers and technicians who benefitted from the opening up of labor markets and competition between state and private enterprises for highly qualified employees. The third consisted of a layer of veteran workers who, after surviving waves of downsizing, occupied skilled and basic-level supervisory positions. The bottom layer was composed mainly of migrant workers hired through subcontractors or on a temporary basis. The growing instability of employment, Tong found, was accompanied by a shift from a labor management model based on ideology and loyalty to one based on "simple control," which relied on the coercive exercise of hierarchical power. Her finding that all four enterprises, despite very different characteristics, ended up with similar hierarchies and management methods, suggests that many large restructured SOEs were coalescing on the same basic model.

The fourth article, also by Jia Wenjuan, provides a step-by-step analysis of how the conversion of a large state-owned machinery factory into a supplier for a German firm producing for global markets prompted radical changes in the plant's labor force and labor process. As the factory was integrated into a global production system based on "flexible accumulation," it no longer required a full range of engineering expertise or workers who possessed multiple skills, and the old model of shop floor self-management by small teams became an obstacle to the managerial control required to cut costs and meet increasingly demanding production deadlines. Jia expertly describes a contentious process through which managers gained full control of the labor process and the existing workforce was gradually replaced by subcontracted teams that provided more flexible and compliant labor.

In the fifth article, Liu Ming describes similar consequences of restructuring, but in this case, a cotton mill in Xinjiang, the changes in class relations are bound together with changes in ethnic relations. Liu's detailed description of the early decades of the Kashgar cotton mill, built in 1958, is filled with paternalistic relationships – between the state and the largely rural Uyghur population, between enterprise leaders and mill workers (Han and Uyghur), and, most intimately, between skilled machine operators, many of them Han workers transferred from established mills in eastern provinces, and the Uyghur apprentices they mentored. Privatization of the mill in 1999 reorganized class and ethnic relations in ways that were more segregated and antagonistic. While in the past the state-owned mill had consciously sought to integrate management and labor and Han and Uyghur employees by promoting Uyghurs to skilled and managerial positions and housing everyone in the same factory residential compound, this has broken down under the private ownership of a series of Han investors. During the restructuring process, veteran Uyghur workers typically left to pursue small business opportunities and the core of skilled veterans who remain, now mainly in supervisory positions, are largely Han. As working conditions have become much more onerous under private ownership, urban Han youth have little interest in working in the mill, and the great bulk of the workforce is now made up of Uyghurs recruited from surrounding villages. Liu describes an increasingly distant and hostile class/ethnic divide, manifested concretely in the physical separation of the old residential compound (now institutionally separated from the mill) and the dormitories built to house the new arrivals. Although the article only briefly refers to the sharp

INTRODUCTION 5

ethnic conflict and repression in Xinjiang today, it provides valuable insights into their origins.

While the above articles all describe the conditions faced by migrant workers hired as a consequence of industrial restructuring, the migrants arrive as outsiders in narratives in which veteran workers are the main protagonists. In the final three articles, the focus shifts to private and foreign-invested firms that are part of China's massive export-oriented manufacturing sector, and migrant workers become the key protagonists.

In the sixth article, Yu Xiaomin provides an excellent overview of the dynamics of supply chains that start with Chinese factories at the bottom and extend to global retail giants at the top. Yu's selected case studies include three Guangdong-based foreign-owned factories that manufacture toys for Walmart, and her main concern is the implementation of corporate social responsibility (CSR) accords and their impact on labor standards. As Walmart eschewed monitoring by outside CSR organizations and carried out its own inspections, the bulk of the article examines the results of such "self-policing." Factories received advance notice of inspections and workers reported that they were instructed to mislead inspectors in order to avoid contract cancellations that would lead to layoffs. Comparing one factory that was subjected to regular inspections with two others that were not, Yu found that inspections seemed to have little impact on wages or living conditions (which seemed to be largely determined by market conditions), but did succeed in limiting overtime. For workers, however, the latter was a mixed blessing, as wages were set so low that they depended on overtime hours. The article was published in 2008, so it does not reflect important changes that have taken place since then, including the explosion of e-commerce, increasing labor unrest, new labor laws, intensified efforts by the All-China Federation of Trade Unions (ACFTU) to establish union branches in private and foreign-invested firms, changes wrought by the 2008 global economic crisis, and Guangdong's efforts to move up the industrial value chain. Nevertheless, it lays out very clearly the fundamental contradiction between succeeding in a highly competitive global production system (which requires driving down labor costs) and responding to pressures to uphold minimal labor standards.

The seventh article, by Wen Xiaoyi, chronicles efforts to reform the ACFTU, focusing on attempts to promote the direct election of enterprise union chairs. The ACFTU, as Wen makes clear at the outset, is controlled by the CCP and its explicit purpose is preventing conflicts between labor and capital, rather than representing workers in such conflicts. Enterprise unions serve functions similar to HR departments, union chairs report to management, and workers have little reason to trust union officials, even as mediators. The goal of party and union reformers has been to make basic-level union leaders more accountable to workers so they might be better able to play the role of mediators. Efforts to make elections of enterprise union chairs more democratic date back to the Mao era, and Wen picks up the story in the early 1980s, but the article focuses on the past decade, as increasing labor unrest has given new impetus to these efforts. The article specifically examines developments in Guangdong Province, the heart of export-oriented manufacturing, the epicenter of strikes by migrant workers, and long a bastion of reform-minded party and union leaders. Wen's account of efforts to promote more democratic elections – and obstacles to these efforts – does not offer strong grounds for optimism. Moreover, since the article was published in 2014, which marked a high point of recent labor strikes and efforts to democratize the ACFTU, conditions have become much more repressive, dampening tentative reform efforts.

In the final article, Wang Jianhua and Meng Quan analyze resistance by migrant factory workers based on case studies of three prominent examples – the 2010 strike at the Nanhai Honda parts plant, the 2012 strike at the Ohm electronics factory in Shenzhen, and the 2012 riot by Foxconn workers in Taiyuan. In each case, they develop a sophisticated analysis of underlying structural factors, focusing on how different factory regimes interacted with the experiences of distinct segments of migrant worker populations to shape the nature of resistance. Although they develop a tripartite typology (one for each case), they advance a single overarching conclusion: Honda's more humane approach to labor relations provided a basis for negotiation, while Foxconn's more repressive approach led to a riot. At the same time, they note that Honda, which controls the entire production chain, had more revenue to work with and could afford to negotiate, while Foxconn and Ohm, which compete to supply global electronics giants, had lower profit margins and, consequently, little room to bargain.

All of the eight articles selected for this volume are based on case studies of one or several factories or a single region, and while some cover many decades, others focus on briefer periods. As such, they cannot provide a complete picture of seven decades of history. The collection, however, provides a series of "snapshots" (and "video recordings"), each of which offers acute insights into a specific aspect of this history. Together, they leave a profound impression of the forces and conflicts that have shaped and reshaped industrial relations in China over the past seventy years.

Joel Andreas
Johns Hopkins University

CHAPTER 1

From Passion to Deception – Daily Life at the Grassroots under State Control of Production before and after the Great Leap Forward: an Investigation of TY Factory in Guangzhou (1956–1965)

Jia Wenjuan (贾文娟)
Translated by Shayan Momin

Abstract

Soon after the founding of the People's Republic, workers' social status and standard of living saw dramatic increases. Ordinary people displayed passion and enthusiasm for their work. However, the state began to ignore the needs of workers as it slowly became committed to plans for modernization and sought to impose control of production through pressure from individual officials, political campaigns, and production targets. In order to protect their own interests, direct producers responded to this pressure in many different ways. In this historical process, labor enthusiasm was slowly replaced by passivity, negativity, cheating, and fraudulent practices. High modernist planners often believed their vision for society was more carefully considered and farsighted than the facts would justify, but their plans often ended up harming the intended beneficiaries and impeding development.

Keywords

industrial production – Great Leap Forward – labor enthusiasm – fraudulent practices

1 Introduction[1]

In the early days of the People's Republic of China (PRC), ordinary people participated in political and production campaigns with dedication and passion under the leadership of the Communist Party. This was the most important factor in the completion of the First Five-Year Plan (1953–1957). During the Great Leap Forward, the Party attempted to mobilize the masses to achieve fixed economic goals. At that time, people seemed to be possessed by a fanatical belief in socialism, with everyone believing that communist goals could be achieved (Perry 2001; Lin 2010). After the Great Leap Forward, this type of passion among ordinary people significantly declined and, despite massive investment in industrial development since the late 1950s, labor productivity remained stagnant (Field 1983, 641–644). Andrew Walder (1986, 215) argued that during the Cultural Revolution, protectionism and a subculture of instrumental personal relations were already relatively developed, and that in production, workers clearly lacked enthusiasm and labor discipline, and managers would often ignore these problems. Scholars have observed high levels of worker enthusiasm in the early period of the planned economy and a decline in enthusiasm in the later periods, but there has been a lack of investigation into the middle years of the planned economy (1956–1965).

This article will focus on analyzing those middle years. In 1956, China's socialist transformation was complete. In 1966, the Cultural Revolution began. The ten year span in the middle was a relatively ordinary period of production, but it was during this period that the behavior of direct producers underwent significant transformation. How did worker passion and enthusiasm degenerate into dishonest trickery and fraud? What are the theoretical and political implications of these changes?

Zhou Xueguang identified a phenomenon of "collective slack" in Chinese society during the late 1980s, in which people lacked enthusiasm for political movements, and workers were disinterested in their own labor efficiency, often took unauthorized leave and ignored their public responsibilities. Zhou pointed out that within state socialism, "collective slack" took on unique political implications. Collective slack emerges when public protest is risky and state control is tight. Almost like an invisible sit-in protest, collective slack pressures the state through its collectivity, challenging the state's legitimacy and making it difficult for the state to implement policies (Zhou 1993, 54–73). This essay argues that collective slack did not suddenly appear, but instead began earlier

---

[1] This article was originally published in Chinese in *Open Times* 2012, no. 10, pp. 5–21. The research was supported by the "Research on Organizational Change of State-Owned Enterprises" project at Professor Cai He's Center of Urban Social Studies at Sun Yat-Sen University.

within production, when, after the Great Leap Forward, fraudulent work practices were already developed and diffused throughout production sites.

Michael Burawoy argued that production is not merely economic, but is also political and ideological. When commodities are produced, certain social relations and experiences within those relations are also produced. "Labor" is not an individual activity. It is also political, and thus can reflect micro-operations of certain power relations (Burawoy 1985). Through an analysis of a large machine factory in Guangzhou that was directly under the control of the central government, we can discover the political implications behind the behavioral changes of direct producers that reflected flexible responses to state control over production.

2 Social Status and Life Experience: the Rise of Labor Enthusiasm in TY Factory

In August 1952, the First Ministry of Machinery of the People's Republic of China (hereafter, "the First Ministry") was established. The First Ministry was in charge of machinery for civilian use, telecommunications, and shipbuilding. In 1953, three steel and machine factories merged to form south China's largest general purpose machinery enterprise, TY Factory.[2] The factory was put under the First Ministry's supervision, and became one of six factories producing general purpose machinery in China.

In the early days of the PRC, TY Factory only produced relatively simple machinery. In 1955, the factory began to develop and produce machines for sugar refining. Soon, it became the country's designated factory for producing sugar refining machines (Guangzhou City Gazetteer Editing Committee 2000a, 685). In 1958, TY Factory was placed under the management of Guangzhou's Economic and Trade Committee. As the Great Leap Forward advanced, TY Factory's production expanded to include equipment for manufacturing steel, fertilizer, and cement and refining oil. The factory also became the backbone of centrifuge production in China, and its products could be found at the Leipzig Trade Fair in Germany (Guangzhou City Gazetteer Editing Committee 2000b,

---

2 TY Factory's predecessors were Guangzhou Steel Mill, previously controlled by the Kuomintang Resources Committee (国民党政府资源委员会), Guangdong Agricultural Machinery Co. LTD, a joint public-private enterprise, and Guangdong Machinery Plant, a factory dedicated to repairing textile machinery. The latter two were set up in June 1948 and the first in February 1949. After the founding of the PRC, the three factories were taken over by the Industrial Department of the People's Government of Guangdong Province. They were renamed Guangzhou Iron and Steel Factories No. 1, No. 2, and No. 3, and belonged to the local government.

66). In 1962, the factory was once again put under the management of the First Ministry. Due to TY Factory's importance in national production and distribution, Mao Zedong, Zhou Enlai, Zhu De, Ye Jianying and other central leaders all personally visited the factory, and Tao Zhu, the First Secretary of Guangdong Provincial Party Committee, went to TY Factory to conduct investigations in 1961 and 1964.³

In TY Factory's early period, workers and cadres both showed extraordinary enthusiasm. In 1956, after the factory began production of machines for sugar refining, it lacked a proper factory building. Workers and managers worked outside in the hot sun and heavy rain. To avoid exposing the sugar refining machines to the elements, the workers agreed to turn the factory cafeteria into an assembly workshop. After seeing the factory, an expert visiting from the Soviet Union said, "The conditions [at TY factory] are not up to standard. In fact, they are terrible." However, in annual production competitions, the technical departments and workshops set new records every day. From February to November 1956, 12,057 workers exceeded their work quotas. In the entire factory, workers were recognized as "advanced producers" (先进生产者) 1,044 times. This amounts to an average of one award for every four workers. Altogether they saved 160,481 man-hours (TY Factory 1956b).

Corroborating stories can be found in oral histories provided by factory workers. Worker LGQ, who had entered the factory in August 1950, recalled the situation in the factory:

> Our workshop had a guy named Master Wang. He had nine kids. He couldn't even remember their names! But if you asked him where to find some spare part or how processing was coming along or when something might be finished or what still remained a problem, he'd give you a straight and clear answer. He used all of his energy for work.
> May 1, 2011

Master Wang was not a special case. Worker SYY started working in 1958 and retired in 2000, having worked at TY Factory his entire career. He vividly remembered when he first entered TY Factory:

> That time was the beginning of the Great Leap Forward. Aside from the regular eight-hour workday, workers often had to do overtime. It was mandatory – we even had to work on Saturdays and Sundays. The workers were all very sincere then. If we had to work overtime, we just did

---

3 Tao Zhu stayed in TY Factory for over one month each time he visited.

it. If we heard from higher-ups that we still had unfinished work, we all worked overtime and didn't complain or say a thing about it.

February 20, 2011

Where, in the early days of the PRC, did this passion for working come from? In contrast to previous research, this essay argues that the enthusiasm of direct producers did not come from their lofty beliefs in socialist ideals or the sophisticated mobilization by their higher-ups, but from their direct experiences in daily life.

First, within daily life and production, direct producers were respected. They understood their own value and experienced improvements in their social position. As a result, they believed they needed to repay a debt to society. Before the establishment of the People's Republic, many workers who ended up at TY Factory had bitter experiences working under foremen. For example, CX worked as an apprentice in a capitalist factory for three years. According to him, before 1949, workers were not even permitted to speak during work. If they spoke, foremen beat them mercilessly. After Democratic Reform, cadres listened to worker complaints and went to participate in labor themselves. This made workers feel that the People's Republic was different from the China before liberation. According to SYY:

> When planning work responsibilities, you couldn't simply order people around. Sometimes, the factory leaders would say something like, "This work needs to be completed by the 20th," and many workers would ask, "What? How is that possible?" We were confident to speak about our problems and didn't buy their nonsense. If you had opinions about production or anything else, you could bring them up through production meetings, team meetings, and workshop meetings. If others thought you were right, then they would follow your suggestions.
>
> February 20, 2011

The respect that workers received during the production process made them feel that they had ascended to the status of "masters of the country" (主人翁). Additionally, under the eight-grade wage system, worker and cadre salaries were basically the same, and wages increased faster for workers than for cadres. At the time, a joke circulating in factories held that when office cadres went to see their girlfriends, they had to find a worker and borrow his uniform.[4]

Outside of production, cadres also actively helped workers resolve other difficulties in their lives. In 1956, the core logistics group of TY Factory's second

---

4 This discussion originates in the interview with LYM, December 23, 2010.

workshop braved heavy winds and rain to visit a worker who was living in a dilapidated home, promising to help him solve his housing problem. This particular worker was at a loss about how to express his gratitude. From that day on, he not only actively took on responsibilities at work, but also took the initiative to help others in his own team (TY Factory 1956a).

Attractive ideologies and advanced mobilization methods were not enough to encourage workers to actively participate in production. Receiving support in everyday life was crucial. Worker LYM recalled:

> Before liberation, older workers had a difficult life. But after liberation, many workers were happy – compared with how it had been in the old China, they felt like they were masters of their own lives. They had social standing and actively participated in production. The mood then was very good, especially during the years right after liberation. The political standing of workers was high, and everyone felt very respected, such that, at that time, using slogans to mobilize workers was effective. But afterwards, talking about politics wasn't very effective.
> December 12, 2010

Second, productive labor and work unit (单位) welfare were closely linked to personal standards of living. The state requirements for socialist construction were in line with individual requirements for raising living standards. Working hard benefited both the country and the individual. The era of the socialist planned economy had the characteristic of "public-private integration" (公私嵌入性). The individual's field of life was nested within the work unit's field of production, and production and reproduction were similarly intertwined. This meant that the welfare of all workers and staff members was connected to production within the factory (Song 2011). In a sense, the work unit functioned as a home for workers. Individual lives improved as production improved.

At TY Factory, everyone knew that there would be bonuses or extra profits if workers met or exceeded production goals. These resources would be used for the welfare of the work unit as a whole or to improve the standard of living of the workers (State Council of China 1958).[5] Even though profit retention

---

5 In 1952, the State Council enacted "Interim Measures on Incentive Funds for State-Owned Enterprises" (国营企业提用企业奖励基金暂行办法). According to this regulation, after national targets were met, enterprises in electric power and machinery industries were able to apply to keep 3.5% of total profits, and could use 15% of excess profits as incentive funds. One part of the incentive fund could be used for welfare. In 1953, another welfare fund was created; this welfare allowance was 2.5% of total salaries and it could be used in conjunction with the enterprise incentive fund. In 1958, the state turned the incentive funds into part of

policies underwent complicated changes, most interviewees insisted that five percent of profits were used for work unit welfare.[6] Workers were willing to work hard to enhance their work unit's welfare fund. Worker CX, who once worked in a cast steel workshop, recalled:

> Five percent of profits had to be spent on welfare. This was fixed, everyone knew it! What was the welfare money used for? For seeing doctors, kitchen equipment, clothing. It's only five percent! It's not much if divided amongst everyone, but it's a lot if used for the entire factory. If profits were big, everyone was really enthusiastic. That's because welfare involved the interests of every single organization [within the factory]. Housing, health care, meals, and so forth were all covered by work unit welfare. The average worker knew that there was hope if production was going well. If there were one million [yuan] in profits, then fifty thousand would be used on welfare. If two million, then one hundred thousand was for welfare … there was more awareness back then. Everyone hoped the factory and country would develop quicker. Improved welfare would follow improved production.
>
> July 9, 2011

During the First Five-Year Plan, TY was a standout factory. By 1957, TY Factory's welfare infrastructure included 19,998 square meters of dormitories, three dining halls, a cafeteria serving nutritious meals, a school for workers' children, a part-time school for workers, an assembly hall, shower rooms, an infant care center, a health center for women workers, a health clinic, a staff sanatorium (in a villa), a barber shop, guesthouses, a lounge, a workers' leisure center, a library, a basketball court with lighting, a soccer and sports field, a volleyball court, and a swimming pool (TY Factory 1957). Outside of work, dances and get-togethers were organized with textile mill workers. This standard of welfare caused people to understand that working for the country and socialism was the same as working for their own benefit. As Worker CX put it, "As for

---

the profits of the enterprise fund that could be retained by individual enterprises. The ratio of retained profits was calculated by individual competent departments. In 1962, the incentive fund was restored. In 1969, medical subsidies, welfare grants and enterprise incentives were merged into the welfare fund for workers and staff. See Guangzhou City Gazetteer Editing Committee (2000c, 372) and Wang (1998).

6 As a machinery plant, TY Factory's profits were relatively high. In addition to keeping 3.5% of total profits, TY was also able to hold onto 18% in excess profits. From 1959 to 1961, while TY was a local enterprise, it had 9% of excess profits. In 1962, TY returned to central management.

'doing' socialism, we hoped we could help society, and afterwards become well off. That was our unified goal."

In the early days of the PRC, the new regime urgently needed to establish its authority within factories and control production. In order to gain the support of workers, production democracy and worker welfare were state priorities. During this time, the concept of labor integrated personal needs and the needs of the country into one. As "masters of the socialist country," workers were respected and enjoyed a clear increase in social status and standard of living. In addition, they contributed their labor to the state's socialist construction. However, as production improved, state policy slowly gravitated towards modernization, which – intentionally or not – ignored the needs of producers. This had a great impact on production practices at the local level. The rest of the article will analyze this problem.

3 Industrial Production: Socialist Construction under State Leadership

In the PRC, government work reports summarize the accomplishments of certain time periods and lay out plans for future development. Through an analysis of such work reports from 1954 to 1964, this article argues that as time went on, state attitudes towards the development of industry, worker demands, and requirements for enterprises underwent a series of changes.

In the early period of the People's Republic, raising the social status and standard of living for direct producers was a central goal of the government as well as the goal behind the building of socialist industry. The State Council's 1954 Work Report emphasized:

> All of our work is for the people. Our economic and financial work – directly or indirectly – is done entirely in the pursuit of improving the people's material and cultural lives ... because the only goal of the socialist economy is to satisfy the people's material and cultural requirements. Developing modern industries is important for the following reasons: Constant increases in the people's material and cultural lives can only be guaranteed through heavy industry ... we can only overcome the poverty of the people, consolidate the victories of the revolution, and have prosperity in the future through scaling up and expanding production.
>
>   Central People's Government of the People's Republic of China (1954)

With the support of national planning and policy, work units and direct producers could benefit from industrial development. Production and living standards developed together. This was an important factor in creating the people's enthusiasm for labor. In subsequent state plans, industrialization became central and increasing living standards for workers became secondary. In 1956, the Government Work Report stated, "In order to develop production and increase labor productivity, we must gradually improve the lives of workers. Only in this way can we encourage workers to work actively and continue the rapid development of production." The state nevertheless remained concerned about workers' welfare and the Work Report went on to propose, "All administrators should strive to improve the lives of workers, the supply of consumer goods [available to workers], and guarantee work safety" (Central People's Government of the People's Republic of China 1956).

The Great Leap Forward, with its goals of rapid industrialization and the comprehensive transformation of society, marked the launch of China's high modernist project.[7] During the Cold War, China began to compete with Western countries in modernization and industrialization. At the time, the state started to evaluate the success of local modernization projects. The 1959 Government Work Report clearly emphasized this point:

> The speed of China's economic development would never be possible under a capitalist system ... Britain spent more than fifty years developing their steel production. China only spent six years. After more than fifty years, in 1907, Britain's coal production only increased to two hundred and seventy million tons. In six years, by 1958, China had also reached this level of production. As our productive industries grow by leaps and bounds, China's consumer goods industry has also increased by 34%. Can it be said that this type of growth has never been seen before in the capitalist world?
> Central People's Government of the People's Republic of China (1959)

However, in the pursuit of numerical growth and lofty ideals, the actual conditions of people's lives and labor were relegated to a subordinate position. Reports and plans about workers' conditions and livelihoods became harder to find in government work reports. This is evident in a report from 1960, during a national campaign to build public canteens across the country.

---

7 Scott (2004, 4) considers high modernism to be a kind of statist ideology that insists on "scientifically understanding the laws of nature to rationally design the social order."

> While developing production, we should pay close attention to the lives of the masses and make sure there is a proper balance between work and rest. The problem of public canteens is addressing a central problem in living standards ... properly handling these welfare programs and the lives of commune members will promote the development of production.
>
> Central People's Government of the People's Republic of China (1960)

This implies that developing production became the central goal of the government, while improving standards of living became an auxiliary goal.

By 1964, the extraordinary speed of China's industrialization still could not keep up with the demands of state planners. China could no longer endure walking "the old path of technological development, crawling slowly behind others." The pursuit of the high modernist project was strengthened and extended in the 1960s. Planners called for "breaking the rules" and the "full adoption of advanced technology within a relatively short period of time" to "turn China into a powerful, modern country with modernized agriculture, modernized industry, strong national defense and modernized technology" (Central People's Government of the People's Republic of China 1964). Any mention of welfare and raising the standard of living for ordinary people disappeared from reports. Instead, "plain living" was heavily promoted.

> Diligence, frugality, and plain living are first-rate characteristics of the proletariat's way of life. Extravagance, waste, and the pursuit of enjoyment are characteristics of the bourgeoisie's corrupt way of life. We promote the proletariat's outstanding way of life and shall turn it into a social atmosphere in order to resist the corruption of bourgeois ideology. This is extremely important for both the socialist revolution and the construction of socialism ... The entire nation should fight for earning every single yuan as well as struggle for its proper allocation (Ibid.).

It is not difficult to understand that a party that relied on the people's efforts for securing victory in the revolution and building a new country would want to improve the quality of people's lives and perhaps see modernization as a way to achieve those goals. As time went on, however, "modernization" became the dominant goal. Against the turbulent background of the Cold War, leaders of non-industrialized countries that won independence harbored deep resentment and hatred of colonial rule and stagnant economies. They attempted to create "a proud people" within their countries, and gradually began to follow the logic of development – a holistic combination of progress in science and technology, improvements in production, and the transformation of nature.

Under the banner of Marxism, the socialist cause became a race to beat the West in industrialization and modernization (Rofel 2006, 24). The difference was that the scale of social transformation programs and the tools used by the state machinery in socialist countries dwarfed those of the West. These countries walked even further on the road of high modernism.

With this kind of comprehensive planning, heavy industrial enterprises were always placed in core positions. Their importance was not simply seen as units for resource distribution. They were the state's key tools in organizing and controlling urban society.[8] Even more importantly, industrial enterprises took responsibility for modernization and industrialization. The country needed to mobilize all forces to increase its production efficiency and output in order to meet fixed production targets.

As a result, all production in work units was placed under the direct control of the state. This type of control was implemented through three strategies.[9] The first was to put pressure on individual officials. Being accountable to superiors is a key characteristic of Chinese bureaucracy. Officials received pressure from superiors to implement important state projects, and they in turn used their considerable power and authority to pressure direct producers to implement their supervisors' demands. The second strategy was employing production targets to manage production. Using production targets to guide production to "totalize" and "simplify" production management made it easier for the state to control industrial output and development speed and also enabled numerical comparisons with the West. The third strategy was to use political movements to increase production. Although political campaigns are usually understood to be in opposition to production, within industrial enterprises, political campaigns were carried out around production with the idea of using political mobilization to speed up production.

4 The Rise of Fraudulent Practices: State Strategies for Production Control and the Responses of Direct Producers

After the Great Leap Forward, the implementation of state programs aimed at increasing production gradually eroded the enthusiasm of direct producers. As labor enthusiasm in TY Factory declined, there was a gradual increase in fraud,

---

8 See Walder (1986); Lu (1989); Li and Li (1999); Li (2000); Perry (2001); Lin (2010); Whyte and Parish (1985); Lü and Perry (1997); and Bray (2005).
9 Although these three methods of control were used simultaneously, there were different combinations and emphases in different periods.

deception, and negative emotions in daily life at the factory. "There was fraud, opportunism, small financial incentives, material incentives for piecework, concealing the truth – it was like anarchy. There were also people looking for handouts, ripping you off, and so on. Nothing was lacking" (TY Factory 1964a). In practice, the state's strategies to control production harmed the interests of direct producers at the local level. The types of fraud employed by workers can be understood as a type of flexible response to state efforts to control production. The next section examines the three strategies the state used to control production as well as the responses by direct producers.

4.1 *Pressure from Individual Officials and "Perfunctory Production"*

In 1958, shortly after the Great Leap Forward was launched, direct producers faced the most pressure not from political movements or production plans, but rather from higher officials. In most cases, high modernists are state officials or leaders with power, and high modernism is compatible with their interests (Scott 2004, 5). Within the Chinese context, the logic of "being responsible to superiors" allowed government officials with power to have lofty goals, and they increasingly saw industrial enterprises as tools with which to transfer pressure to direct producers (Li 2009a). Pressure from individual officials forced direct producers to work excessive hours with a high degree of labor intensity. Their physical strength was totally overspent. Under these conditions, workers had no bargaining power and were no longer "masters of the country."

After 1959, TY Factory was put under the management of the Guangzhou Municipal Electrical and Mechanical Bureau. Leaders at the national, provincial and municipal levels all transferred their own production tasks to TY Factory. For example, a vice-governor required TY Factory to produce water conservation machinery for him as quickly as possible, claiming "this is extremely important to the lives and property of the masses!" A provincial governor in charge of rolling steel demanded that TY Factory "do a good job rolling steel! Steel is the key link!" The industry department head of the municipal Party committee asked TY Factory to promote ultrasonic generators as quickly as possible, and threatened anyone obstructing the promotion of these generators with expulsion from the Party.[10] LYM, who worked in a workshop during the Great Leap Forward, recalled:

> Provincial and city leaders would all take on projects. Every single one said that their project was extremely important – this is very important, that is very important, everything is top priority. As for our factory, we

---

10 From the personal diaries of LZL.

only had so many people, but every program was top priority. Don't you think that's quite difficult?

December 23, 2010

Under this kind of pressure, working hours became excessively long at TY Factory. There was a serious lack of breaks or rest periods, and people's regular lives were greatly affected. Under the "Eating with an Open Belly" watchword, large baskets filled with snacks were placed in the steel converter plant, but since workers were too tired to ask what was available, the food spoiled and had to be thrown into the Pearl River. Some people complained that the "Great Leap brings great anxiety," others said their "bellies were filled with rage," and still others said "the leaders are getting careless and sloppy! They treat people's property as a trifling matter just to fulfill their own work assignments" (TY Factory 1960). A 1959 work report admitted, "Some workers complained about production, they had a lack of energy during work, they were undisciplined. This led to low production efficiency and both visible and invisible waste" (TY Factory 1959). People generally believed that the problem was caused by excessive demands from higher officials. In order to resist production demands and the harm inflicted upon workers, the direct producers of TY Factories came up with the "Push Back, Drag Out, Retreat" strategy. When faced with pressure from higher officials, they would first try to push back. If they were unable to push back, they would drag out their work. If they could not drag out their work, they would retreat. Delivery orders that reached the workshops would be done in a perfunctory way.

At the beginning of the Great Leap, Guangdong was not very active in steel and iron production. Someone in the central leadership called Tao Zhu, the first secretary of the provincial Party committee, and asked him, "Why can't Guangdong blow its own horn for steel and iron production?" So, in November 1958, Guangdong became a big horn blower for steel and iron production (Zheng and Shu 1992, 262). Early in 1959, Chen Yu (陈郁), then governor of Guangdong Province, rushed to the factory to personally declare that the factory would produce three-ton flat-die hammers to be used in tin, steel and iron production. The accompanying anvil for the hammer weighed 50 tons, which far exceeded the capacity of TY Factory. Deputy Director of the production section, LZL, said to Chen Yu, "Comrade Governor, the anvil for this hammer will need to weigh 50 tons. Our forge isn't nearly big enough. We have no way to do this." Chen Yu hurried to find the equipment power engineer, who shook his head and told him that TY Factory could not make the product. The technicians who refused to produce the hammer and anvil were reprimanded with these words: "You intellectuals are classic Rightist conservatives!

Workers – people who actually do the work – all say it's possible! But if we ask you to write anything, to plan anything, to give an order, you won't do it! You people aren't afraid that communism will fail, you're not afraid of revisionism! You're afraid that the masses will rise up!"[11]

Chen Yu marched to the workshop and gave the production order directly to the workers. Under this kind of pressure from a high official, the workers agreed and started production. According to standard sand casting procedures, molten iron is injected into a sand mold to make a solid cast. This way, the iron is turned into a solid object. But the workers' "perfunctory" method was to fill the mold with pig iron ingots before pouring in the molten iron. In this way, it appeared as if the requirements of the higher officials had been met, but in reality, because the molten iron did not melt the ingots, the interiors of the items were hollow, they were only shells. Such products were only made to cope with the demands of higher officials.[12] Deputy Director of the production section LZL explained:

> Why did the workers agree? Not because the workers were bad people, but they had no choice when you pressure them like that. There was no way for them to refuse. Lots of workers didn't want to express their opinions. They couldn't stand the demands, but they also couldn't speak up for themselves. The provincial governor himself came to give the orders. What can you do? This is how machine workers are – this is how they deal with you. They think, 'OK, fine, if this is how you're going to treat me, then I'm going to mess with you.' Then they'll come up with a method like this to deal with you.
>
> November 26, 2010

Under this kind of perfunctory production, there were 1280.89 tons of rejected and waste products in 1959 (TY Factory 1960). In 1964, Tao Zhu came to TY Factory and said that during the Great Leap Forward, TY Factory wasted an amount equivalent to over 180,000 *liang* of gold (9000kg) (TY Factory 1959).[13]

4.2 "Production Target" Management and the Rise of Fraud and Deception

"The planned economy is highly dependent upon target management. Without targets to guide and control the economy, the system cannot function"

---

11 This case comes from LZL's personal materials, "Remembering XYG."
12 Ibid.
13 From LZL's personal materials.

(Li 2009b). State-directed production targets covered all aspects of enterprise production and management.[14] In reality, production management needs directed targets, but during the period of the planned economy, targets for enterprises were not based on an objective consideration of productive capacity. Instead, the targets were based on the state's requirements for different regions in its larger plans to maintain a certain rate of economic development. As the state put forth comprehensive industrial planning, yearly production targets for individual enterprises began to rise and did not conform to their actual productive abilities or capacity. "Production target" management reduces the number of variables that must be considered by officials, improves administrative standardization, and oversimplifies production.

In 1953, TY Factory started to use planned targets to direct production. At that time, the state's national industrial planning was only in its initial stages, so production targets were relatively relaxed. Even though it is quite difficult to perfectly match planning and production, TY Factory was able to meet its targets through revising plans, adjusting production and organizing labor within the factory itself.

In reality, during the planned economy, the real concern for industrial enterprises was that production targets were too high but actual production tasks were too few. Despite the surge in production targets during the Great Leap Forward, TY Factory could still complete planned tasks through perfunctory production. But the problem of "targeted production" became very serious after the Great Leap Forward. In the early 1960s, as economic policies changed, the state withdrew investment from many different enterprises and overall production shrank. At that time, many enterprises were in financial difficulties. By the end of July 1961, TY Factory had 26,040,000 yuan in bank loans with a monthly interest of 150,000 yuan. There was a serious shortage of production tasks, a marked increase in costs, and a large overstock of substandard products. In September of that year, production was stopped. In October, production reached the lowest level of the previous few years, and in November, the enterprise began to operate at a loss (TY Factory 1961d). In 1962, TY Factory received just half of the production target numbers set during the Great Leap

---

14 When the First Five-Year Plan was promulgated, these targets included total output value, output value of main products, new product trials, important technical and economic quotas, rate of cost reduction, cost reduction quotas, number of workers, number of workers at the end of the year, total wages, average wages, labor productivity, and profits. After 1957, there were only 4 targets: total output, main product output, number of workers, total wages, and profits. The other 8 targets were reduced to "non-directive" indicators. Each department could adjust their individual targets. In 1960, the system reverted to the one under the First Five-Year Plan.

Forward, and the productive tasks assigned to the factory only amounted to 28% of its productive capacity. So TY Factory began to look for other production orders: 66% of its output value came from agricultural machinery and light industrial products (TY Factory 1962).

Despite people's working around the clock, it still was not possible to meet production targets. State industrialization and modernization were in conflict with the living needs of the direct producers. If production targets were not met, the work unit received no bonuses, and the entire year of hard work was a waste. The ideal of "production increases one inch, welfare increases one cent" was gone. Moreover, if the reputation of the enterprise declined, it was harder to obtain resources from superior departments. So TY Factory resorted to fraud, deceit and opportunism.

As TY Factory leaders subsequently noted, "superiors setting production targets is like 'a scholar shutting himself up building a boat' (秀才闭门造船);[15] the plan was merely to make up output value" (TY Factory 1961b). So TY Factory's statistics "were falsified – costs, quality, and planning were all exaggerated" (ibid.). LZL described the situation:

> Some people's monthly calendars were 40 days long! Products that should be finished by the tenth of next month were included in the current month's statistics. Products that weren't completed were reported as completed, and work kept getting pushed to the next month. It was like this every month. At the end of the year the work backlog that had piled up was really too much. What do you do if the work isn't finished at the end of the year? You resort to fraud! Just lie and say the work is actually finished. There are many ways to "finish" the work. Some are completed with missing parts – you're short a couple small parts? Just report that it's finished! Products that haven't passed quality inspection or just haven't been completed? Yes, just report those as done too. The total output value was even worse! How did we calculate the total output value? We'd take total commodity value and add the value of products that weren't finished, or "works-in-progress." The "works-in-progress" were products that were not assembled yet. We just estimated the value of the works-in-progress. There were lots of shady facts. If our calculations didn't meet the targets, we would just add some more works-in-progress. So if only 50% of the work was completed, we'd just add it up so it said 60 or 70%

---

15   This idiom implies carrying out one's idea irrespective of external, practical circumstances; to divorce oneself from the masses and from reality and act blindly; to do whatever one likes oblivious of the world; to draw up plans behind closed doors – Ed.

was finished to meet output requirements. So we always met our targets. You see [in the records] that all of that commodity output was estimated. Very little was actually counted.

May 1, 2011

Was fraud committed by whole departments or by just a few individual leaders? What did workers think about this kind of behavior? LZL said:

Everyone knew about this, but the First Machinery Bureau couldn't investigate us – there were tons of ways to cover it up from them! Workers all supported this. Why? Because if you didn't meet your production quotas, the factory didn't get any bonuses. If there were no bonuses, then workers didn't benefit either. So workers all participated. They'd rather commit fraud than report that they didn't complete the work plan.

November 26, 2010

On the other hand, there was also the problem of concealing the factory's quality control problems due to rushed production. For example, in order to keep up with orders and production quotas, workers in the welding and riveting workshop hastily welded the boiler washing tower, which leaked water in the first hydrostatic testing. But in order to avoid delivery delay and to be able to include the product in the calculations for total production output, the head of the quality inspection section was not interested in finding the cause of the defect. Instead, he told the welding team to weld any gaps shut and not to tell the ordering party about the problems.

In 1961, the Light Industry Bureau of Heilongjiang Province ordered three sets of ø 1,250 [mm] centrifuges from TY Factory. Even though part of the centrifuges had not even been produced yet, they were shipped and TY Factory received payment. Three years later, the factory warehouse had accumulated a number of centrifuge accessories that were owed to customers. The value of these accessories was more than 30,000 yuan. In November 1964, the riveting and welding workshop in TY Factory agreed to produce water discharge tubes and covers for ø 105 [mm] ultracentrifuges, but the products did not fit the dimensions laid out in the order plans. In spite of this, the workers and workshop leaders did not want to do the job over again. When the parts were brought to the second machine workshop, the inspectors decided that the covers and tubes could still technically be used, so they were passed on to the finished products storage (TY Factory 1964a). The phenomenon of fraud did not appear out of thin air. "This situation has existed for a long time, but didn't catch our attention earlier. Unfinished products go to the finished products warehouse, products with missing parts go as well. There was a lack of quality control when output value was to be made up, especially when products were tributes to special holidays" (TY Factory 1961c).

Fraud was not the behavior of only one department or of individual leaders. For the factory's unified interests, supervisors, mid-level administrators, and workers all participated in fraud and deception in their own way. Higher supervisors falsified production targets, dealt with pressure from higher officials, and made false threats to downstream manufacturers. Middle supervisors' roles were mainly to smooth over matters within the factory, coordinate communication between different departments, and make sure that what workers were doing was in line with target quotas. As for the direct producers, they were constantly trying to find ways to speed up production and cover the tracks of higher leaders in the factory. Under these conditions, TY Factory wasted about 17,000,000 yuan between 1961 and 1965. The backlog of goods amounted to a value of over 7,000,000 yuan, which was 60% of the factory's fixed assets (TY Factory 1966). At that point, practicing fraud was recognized as a bad practice and criticized as such. But it did not stop – instead, it intensified.

From the perspective of the state, work units were supposed to use all tools at their disposal to achieve production targets, but the creators of these targets rarely had the practical and comprehensive knowledge needed to set reasonable production goals. In turn, this harmed the expected beneficiaries of their production plans (Scott 2004). Using production targets to speed up production was undoubtedly done in the interest of achieving the ideals of socialist industrialization, but when these strategies ignored the realities of the labor process and harmed the interests of direct producers, they responded in various ways. In the final analysis, the state ended up paying the price in fraud and deception.

4.3 Political Campaigns and the Spread of Passive Attitudes toward Work

The "mobilization" mode of production coexisted with the production target management system. At the extreme end of "production simplification," this strategy to use politics to speed up production utilized workers' emotions rather than specific production processes. After the founding of the People's Republic, political movements from the Anti-Rightist Campaign to the Cultural Revolution emphasized the transferring of the enthusiasm of the people into the productive process. From 1956 to 1964, TY Factory went through many political campaigns, including "Elimination of Counterrevolutionaries" (肃反), "Rectification of Incorrect Working Styles," (整风), "Anti-Rightist Movement" (反右), "Struggle Against Waste, Corruption and Bureaucracy" (三反), "Rectification of Incorrect Work Styles in the Factory" (整风整厂),

and the "Struggle Against the Five Evils" (五反). Campaigns organized by the TY Factory's Party committee were relatively mild, while those organized by the municipal Party committee were more militant. But round after round of political movements not only interfered with normal production, they also encouraged direct producers to do whatever they could to get by, making them cautious, suspicious, passive, indifferent and apathetic.

Workers who made mistakes in the production process were suspected of being class enemies and were subject to closer examination. In July of 1964, during the "Elimination of Counterrevolutionary Elements" campaign, a worker committed suicide because he suspected that his organization did not trust him. In 1961, he had mentioned in the workshop that his brother died of starvation in the countryside and had also expressed dissatisfaction with the amount of cotton cloth the work unit provided. From that moment onward, he suspected his leaders no longer trusted him. After the "Struggle against the Five Evils" campaign, he confessed to the Party branch that he had forgotten to register a few *jiao* (0.10 yuan) when he was head of his union group, which caused him to become increasingly worried and anxious. In 1963, when he caused two production quality problems and was criticized by the section foreman and the workshop director, he was afraid they would claim the incidents were intentional. In 1964, in order to take care of his health, the workshop stopped his night shifts and arranged for him to be a fitter. Other workers were told to approach him less, and some meetings were held without notifying him. In the context of the "Elimination of Counterrevolutionary Elements" campaign, this worker felt extreme pressure and hung himself in the bathroom (TY Factory 1964b).

Workers with bad backgrounds often became targets of struggle. In 1958, because her underground [Communist] organization in Hong Kong was exposed, Ah Rong returned to the mainland from the colony. When she arrived in Guangzhou, she was moved to find many people welcoming her at the train station. She entered the factory and worked hard with a positive attitude. In 1961, she applied for a visit to Hong Kong to see her family. She came back three days in advance, and was suspected of meeting with spies. In this way, she became a "campaign target" – whenever there was a political campaign, she was denounced and struggled against. If her relatives in Hong Kong sent her food, she was accused of having relationships with spies. If she went to find a doctor to request sick leave, she was accused of faking her illness. Additionally, she had little chance to receive raises or promotions and became too distressed to work together with others. After the Reform and Opening Up (改革开放), she immediately returned to Hong Kong.[16]

---

16   From interview with LYM conducted on December 23, 2010.

Aside from workers who made mistakes and workers with bad backgrounds, regular workers had four reasons to be anxious during political campaigns: "Afraid of saying the wrong thing, afraid of making a mistake, afraid of being made to 'wear a hat,' and afraid of being sent to farm."[17] Insecurity and other negative emotions spread through the workshop (TY Factory 1961a), but the most pitiful characters during political movements were cadres. Worker LYM recalled:

> Cadres had to study a lot during the week, you know? After studying they had to make a statement. If you didn't speak up, then you weren't doing your job well. If you did speak up, you'd better not say the wrong thing. What a pain, right? When workers studied, it's simple. After work they studied for a short period of time. Workers didn't have much education, so they couldn't really understand that much. It was tougher for the cadres. During political movements, cadres had to constantly review and analyze things. It was a whole ordeal. Some workers said that after they became cadres, they realized that the pen is much heavier than the hammer. After writing for several nights, they couldn't do it anymore. Not to mention that their salaries were lower than workers. No one really wanted to be a cadre.
>
> December 23, 2010

During the "Rectification of Bad Work Styles" in 1960, 170 out of 600 cadres were no longer willing to be cadres. Among workers who were promoted to cadre positions, there was a general feeling that "being a cadre isn't as good as being a worker." Of TY Factory's fifty-eight cadres, twenty-two were dissatisfied with their posts, and seventeen requested to be sent to the workshop. Twelve of those seventeen were previously workers. Eight of nine section foremen in the machine workshop were no longer willing to be cadres, and within the riveting workshop, all five section foremen did not want to be cadres. The main reason was that "cadres have lots of meetings and lots of responsibilities, they face lots of criticism and pressure, their wages go up slowly and they get no bonuses or overtime pay. It's better to be a worker" (TY Factory 1961a). Among them, the deputy director of the cast iron workshop believed he was not educated enough, not competent enough, did not have a good enough grasp of theory, and was in too poor health to be the deputy director, so he requested to become a common cadre. The director of the general affairs section, a Party member, was prepared to intentionally make a small mistake in order to get demoted

---

17   "Being made to wear a hat" referred to being formally criticized and given a derogatory label – Ed.

two ranks. Machine workshop section foremen, who were all Party members, felt, "Cadres are bullied and don't get promoted quickly." Liang Yaohua of the tools section said, "There's no benefit to being a cadre. Lots of meetings, lots of hard work, no overtime pay. Let me resign – I'd do it even if I had to lose over a hundred *yuan*. I'd sign up to be a worker as soon as I resign" (TY Factory 1960). There were even people who said: "Even if there was a gun pointed at my head, I'd still say it's worse to be a cadre" (TY Factory 1963).

In this kind of situation, workers became cautious and careful. Their working attitude turned passive, and cadres did not have the power to effectively manage the factory. Because cadres were afraid of being criticized by workers during political campaigns, they were careful not to offend them, and turned a blind eye to the corrupt practices taking place in the factory. They did not try to succeed in their work, which contributed to negative attitudes toward production. Political campaigns were meant to stimulate production and worker enthusiasm by spurring the emotions of the direct producers, but this strategy gradually became ineffective in practice and had the unintended consequence of negatively affecting the working attitudes of the direct producers.

5 The Decline of Labor Enthusiasm: LeFort's Paradox and the Results of Implementing the State's Vision

Production is political and ideological. Direct producers' transition from enthusiasm to fraudulent practices not only illustrates changes in their relationship with the state, but also the internal contradictions of socialist practice. LeFort's paradox highlights the split between modern ideological enunciation and ideological rule – the former refers to the ideals of the Enlightenment while the latter refers to what state authorities actually pay attention to in practice (LeFort 1986). In socialist countries, the paradox is that the highest goal of communism is to liberate workers and the rest of society, but in practice, the goal of the state is to be achieved by means of total control over workers and society (Yurchak 2005).

LeFort's paradox originates in the dual nature of the ideal of socialism itself. Socialism has been defined as a way to guarantee the highest productivity of social labor as well as the most comprehensive form of human economic development (Engels 1995). It includes both the development of production and the needs of humanity. The liberation of workers requires highly developed productive forces, but third-world socialist countries do not meet these conditions. As a result, from a macro, long-term perspective, these countries believe that temporary sacrifice is needed to guarantee a prosperous future

(Scott 2004, 125–126; Knei-Paz 1994). In the context of the turbulence of the Cold War, the state wanted to use its power to implement utopian reforms to build a modern, socialist country that could provide benefits to all people. To achieve this goal, unrealistic plans for production were laid out, and the actual living conditions were neglected.

For direct producers, socialist ideals should not come into conflict with providing benefits to people. Their labor enthusiasm originated in their life experience – they received respect, various leisure activities, and better benefits through work. Under high modernism, however, accelerated industrialization and modernization became primary goals. Under pressure from individual officials, production targets, and political campaigns, the lives of direct producers were negatively affected. People believed: "The road to socialism is long. It won't be possible to work this hard every day – we should slow down a bit," and "Work will never be finished in our lifetimes, so there's no point in going back and working on Sundays or working overtime at night" (TY Factory 1959). As time went on, these differences became more and more obvious: as the state looked to the future, the common people began paying more attention to the present; as the state pressed higher production targets, the people were more concerned with changes in their daily lives; as the state believed that concerns about daily life should be secondary to planning for the future, the people believed that ideals separated from their actual lives were not credible. In a Faustian dream, as the state became more demanding in its modernization plans, the common people came up with their own ways to cope. In this historical process, labor enthusiasm was slowly replaced by passivity, negativity and fraudulent practices. During the Cultural Revolution, these feelings were expressed as "political opportunism" (Walder 1986), and then by the 1980s this developed into "collective slack" (Zhou 1993, 54–73).

Today, well-intentioned, local modernization projects designed to catch up to the development level in other countries are still in progress. These projects are more or less guided by numerical targets and receive attention from officials at all levels. We need to consider how the implementation of these projects affects the lives of direct producers and community residents at the local level. As people at the grassroots level are both the objects of these projects as well as their participants, the impact of these projects on their labor, lives, and feelings must be taken into consideration in order for these well-intentioned projects to avoid having counterproductive results.

References

Bray, David. 2005. *Social Space and Governance in Urban China: The Danwei System from Origins to Reform*. Stanford: Stanford University Press.

Burawoy, Michael. 1985. *The Politics of Production*. London: Verso.

Central People's Government of the People's Republic of China 中华人民共和国中央人民政府门户网站. 1954. 1954 年政府工作报告 – 1954 年 5 月 23 日在中华人民共和国第一届全国人民代表大会第一次会议上 ["Report on the Work of the Government by the State Council in 1954 – Delivered at the First Plenary Session of the First National People's Congress on May 23, 1954"]. http://www.gov.cn/test/2006-02/23/content_208673.htm. Accessed March 18, 2012.

Central People's Government of the People's Republic of China 中华人民共和国中央人民政府门户网站. 1956. 1956 年国务院政府工作报告: 关于 1955 年国家决算和 1956 年国家预算的报告 – 1956 年 6 月 15 日在第一届全国人民代表大会第三次会议上 ["Report on the 1955 National Final Account and the 1956 National Budget – Delivered at the Third Plenary Session of the First National People's Congress on June 15, 1956"]. http://www.gov.cn/test/2006-02/23/content_208738.htm. Accessed March 18, 2012.

Central People's Government of the People's Republic of China 中华人民共和国中央人民政府门户网站. 1959. 1959 年国务院政府工作报告 – 1959 年 4 月 18 日在第二届全国人民代表大会第一次会议上 ["Report on the Work of the Government by the State Council in 1959 – Delivered at the First Plenary Session of the Second National People's Congress on April 18, 1959"]. http://www.gov.cn/test/2006-02/23/content_208774.htm. Accessed March 18, 2012.

Central People's Government of the People's Republic of China 中华人民共和国中央人民政府门户网站. 1960. 1960 年国务院政府工作报告: 为提前实现全国农业发展纲要而奋斗 – 1960 年 4 月 6 日在第二届全国人民代表大会第二次会议上 ["Report on the Work of the Government by the State Council in 1960: Striving for Fulfilling the National Program for Agricultural Development ahead of Schedule – Delivered at the Second Plenary Session of the Second National People's Congress on April 6, 1960"]. http://www.gov.cn/test/2006-02/27/content_212502.htm. Accessed March 18, 2012.

Central People's Government of the People's Republic of China 中华人民共和国中央人民政府门户网站. 1964. 1964 年国务院政府工作报告（摘要）– 1964 年 12 月 21 日和 22 日在第三届全国人民代表大会第一次会议上 ["Report on the Work of the Government by the State Council in 1964 (Summary) – Delivered at the First Plenary Session of the Third National People's Congress on December 21 and December 22, 1964"]. http://www.gov.cn/test/2006-02/23/content_208787.htm. Accessed March 18, 2012.

Engels, Friedrich. 1995. 社会主义从空想到科学的发展 ["Socialism: Utopian and Scientific"], in 马克思恩格斯全集 [*Complete Works of Marx and Engels*], vol. 19. Edited by 中央编译局编译 [Central Compilation and Translation Bureau]. Beijing: People's Publishing House.

Field, Robert Michael. 1983. "Slow Growth of Labor Productivity in Chinese Industry, 1952–1981." *China Quarterly*, 96: 641–664.

Guangzhou City Gazetteer Editing Committee, ed. 广州市地方志编纂委员会编. 2000a. 广州市志 [*Guangzhou City Gazetteer*], vol. 6 (Part 1). Guangzhou: Guangzhou Press.

Guangzhou City Gazetteer Editing Committee, ed. 广州市地方志编纂委员会编. 2000b. 广州市志 [*Guangzhou City Gazetteer*], vol. 6 (Part 2). Guangzhou: Guangzhou Press.

Guangzhou City Gazetteer Editing Committee, ed. 广州市地方志编纂委员会编. 2000c. *Guangzhou City Gazetteer* (广州市志). vol. 9 (Part 2). Guangzhou: Guangzhou Press.

Knei-Paz, Baruch. 1994. "Can Historical Consequences Falsify Ideas? Or, Karl Marx after the Collapse of the Soviet Union." *Australian Journal of Politics and History*, 40 (1): 72–82.

LeFort, Claude. 1986. *The Political Forms of Modern Society: Bureaucracy, Democracy, Totalitarianism*. Cambridge: MIT Press.

Li Jianjun 刘建军. 2000. 单位中国 – 社会调控体系中的个人、组织与国家 [*Danwei China: Individual, Organization and State during the Process of Reconstruction of Social Regulation System*]. Tianjin: Tianjin People's Publishing House.

Li Lulu 李路路 and Li Hanlin 李汉林. 1999. 资源与交换：中国单位组织中的依赖性结构 ["Resources and Exchange: The Dependency Structure in Chinese Unit Organizations"], 社会学研究 [*Sociological Studies*], 4: 44–63.

Li Ruojian 李若建. 2009a. 折射：当代中国社会变迁研究 [*Refraction: A Study of the Social Change in Contemporary China*]. Guangzhou: Sun Yat-Sen University Press.

Li Ruojian 李若建. 2009b. 指标管理的失败："大跃进"与困难时期的官员造假行为 ["Failure of Indices Management: Officials' Fraudulent Practices during Great Leap Forward and Three-Year Difficult Period"], 开放时代 [*Open Times*], 3: 84–96.

Lin Chaochao 林超超. 2010. 新国家与旧工人：1962 年上海私营工厂的民主改革运动 ["New State and Old Workers: The Democratic Reform Movement of Private Factories in Shanghai in 1962"], 社会学研究 [*Sociological Studies*], 2: 67–86.

Lu Feng 路风. 1989. 单位：一种特殊的社会组织形式 ["Danwei: A Special Form of Social Organization"], 社会学研究 [*Sociological Studies*], 1: 71–88.

Lü, Xiaobo and Elizabeth J. Perry. 1997. *Danwei: The Changing Chinese Workplace in Historical and Comparative Perspective*. Armonk, NY: M. E. Sharpe, Inc.

Perry, Elizabeth 裴宜理. 2001. 重访中国革命 – 以情感的模式 ["Revisiting the Chinese Revolution: The Mobilization of Emotions"], 中国学术 [*China Scholarship*], 4:97–106.

Rofel, Lisa 罗丽莎. 2006. 另类的现代性：改革开放时代中国性别化的渴望 [*Other Modernities: Gendered Yearnings in China after Socialism*]. Translated by Huang Xin 黄新. Nanjing: Jiangsu People's Publishing House.

Scott, James. 2004. 国家的视角: 那些试图改善人类状况的计划是如何失败的 [*Seeing Like a State: How Certain Schemes to Improve the Human Condition Have Failed*]. Translated by Wang Xiaoyi 王晓毅. Beijing: Social Sciences Academic Press.

Song Shaopeng 宋少鹏. 2011. "回家"还是"被回家"？– 市场化过程中"妇女回家"讨论与中国社会意识形态转型 ["'Returning Home' or 'Being Returned to Home'? Debates on 'Women's Returning Home' in Marketization and the Transformation of Social Ideology in China"] in 妇女研究论丛 [*Collection of Women's Studies*], 4: 5–12.

State Council of China. 1958. 国务院关于实行企业利润留成制度的几项规定 ["Regulations of the State Council Concerning the Implementation of the Retention System in Enterprises"], in 中华人民共和国法规汇编 1958 年 1 月 –6 月 [*Compilation of Regulations of the People's Republic of China (January–June 1958)*], Beijing: Law Press.

TY Factory. 1956a. 家访谈心把思想工作做到日常生活中去 – 二机车间家访工作的经验 ["Doing Ideological Work in Daily Life through Home Visiting and Conversations: Experience of No. 2 Machine Workshop"], in TY 厂综合档案, 1956 [*Comprehensive Archives of TY Factory, 1956*], vol. 24.

TY Factory. 1956b. 1956 年工作总结 ["Work Summary of 1956"], in TY 厂综合档案, 1956 [*Comprehensive Archives of TY Factory, 1956*], vol. 1.

TY Factory. 1957. 1953~1957 年我厂有关职工集体福利事业历年发展情况介绍 ["Introduction to Workers' Collective Welfare in Our Factory during 1953–1957"], in TY 厂综合档案, 1957 [*Comprehensive Archives of TY Factory, 1957*], vol. 21.

TY Factory. 1959. 1959 年生产工作总结 ["Summary of Production Work in 1959"], in TY 厂综合档案, 1959 [*Comprehensive Archives of TY Factory, 1959*], vol. 1.

TY Factory. 1960. 反右倾整风运动总结（初稿）["Summary of the Anti-Rightist Campaign (First Draft)"], in TY 厂综合档案, 1960 [*Comprehensive Archives of TY Factory, 1960*], vol. 3.

TY Factory. 1961a. 一个车间党支部工作情况调查 ["Investigation on the Work of the Party Branch in a Workshop"], in TY 厂综合档案, 1961 [*Comprehensive Archives of TY Factory, 1961*], vol. 23.

TY Factory. 1961b. 整风整党鸣放汇集 ["Opinions on Rectification of Incorrect Working Styles and Party Consolidation: A Collection"], in TY 厂综合档案, 1961 [*Comprehensive Archives of TY Factory*], vol. 5.

TY Factory. 1961c. 党委黄书记在二月八日全厂职工代表大会、三级干部联合大会上的报告 ["Speech by Mr. Huang, Secretary of the Party Committee, on February 8th at the Workers' Congress and Joint Conference of the Three-Level Cadres"], in TY 厂综合档案, 1961 [*Comprehensive Archives of TY Factory, 1961*], vol. 5.

TY Factory. 1961d. 1961 年生产工作总结 ["Work Summary of 1961"] in TY 厂综合档案, 1961 [*Comprehensive Archives of TY Factory, 1961*], vol. 1.

TY Factory. 1962. 1962 年大事记 ["Chronicle of Events in 1962"] in TY 厂综合档案 1962 年卷首大事记 [*Comprehensive Archives of TY Factory, 1962*].

TY Factory. 1963. "Summary of the Campaign against Five Evils (五反运动小结)," in TY 厂综合档案, 1963 [*Comprehensive Archives of TY Factory, 1963*], vol. 36.

TY Factory. 1964a. 在干部中检查揭发资本主义经营思想情况的小结 ["Inspection and Tip-off of Capitalist Business Ideas in Cadres: A Brief Summary"] in TY 厂综合档案, 1964 [*Comprehensive Archives of TY Factory, 1964*], vol. 1.

TY Factory. 1964b. 关于XX上吊死亡的调查报告 ["Investigation Report on XX's Suicide by Hanging"], in TY 厂综合档案, 1964 [*Comprehensive Archives of TY Factory, 1964*], vol. 46.

TY Factory. 1966. 关于反浪费斗争工作小结 ["A Brief Summary of the Anti-Waste Struggle"], in TY 厂综合档案, 1966 [*Comprehensive Archives of TY Factory, 1966*], vol. 4.

Walder, Andrew G. 1986. 共产党社会的新传统主义: 中国工业中的工作环境和权力结构 [*Communist Neo-traditionalism: Work and Authority in Chinese Industry*]. Translated by Gong Xiaoxia 龚小夏. Hong Kong: University of Oxford Press.

Wang Haibo 汪海波. 1998. 中华人民共和国工业经济史 [*Industrial Economic History of the People's Republic of China*]. Taiyuan: Shanxi Economy Press.

Whyte, Martin King and William L. Parish. 1985. *Urban Life in Contemporary China*, Chicago: University of Chicago Press.

Yurchak, Alexei. 2005. *Everything Was Forever, Until It Was No More: The Last Soviet Generation*. Princeton: Princeton University Press.

Zheng Xiaofeng 郑笑枫 and Shu Ling 舒玲. 1992. 陶铸传 [*Biography of Tao Zhu*]. Beijing: China Youth Publishing House.

Zhou Xuegang. 1993. "Unorganized Interests and Collective Action in Communist China". *American Sociological Review* 58 (1): 54–73.

CHAPTER 2

Research into the Implementation of the Staff and Workers Congress System in State-Owned Enterprises: a 60-Year Case Study of One Factory

Cai He (蔡禾) and Li Wanlian (李晚莲)
Translated by Roderick Graham Flagg

Abstract

The characteristics of the staff and workers congress (SWC) system at Factory A have differed significantly across different historical periods. This article examines those changes in terms of the organization and structure of the congress, the composition of representatives and how they exercise their powers, the topics addressed by the congress, and also workers' evaluations of its work. It then attempts to explain these changes with a New Institutionalism approach, proposing that tensions between the logic of legitimacy and the logic of efficiency have brought about changes in how the SWC system has been implemented.

Keywords

staff and workers congress – institutional change – logic of legitimacy – logic of efficiency

1   Introduction and Research Questions[1]

There is no doubt that the reform of state-owned enterprises (SOEs) is the most important aspect of China's economic reform and has been a key factor in the success of that reform. But problems arising from the reform of SOEs have become increasingly apparent – infringement of workers' rights and

---

[1] This article originally appeared in *Open Times* 2014, no. 5, pp. 43–53. This project received funding from the Guangzhou Social Services and Management Innovation Key Research Foundation and represents initial findings of the Hunan Social Sciences Foundation's 2011 project "Research into Implementation of Democratic Management in Businesses."

interests is no longer the sole preserve of private companies. This has led some Chinese academics to look at democratic corporate management structures (Feng 2005; Chang 1995; Liu 2004; Bian 2002; Lü 2000; Ni 2006, etc.)

Attention has therefore fallen on the staff and workers congress (职工代表大会) system and the unions, which are key ways in which workers participate in democratic management of a company, with cases in which workers realize their interests via these systems being examined and reported upon (Zhu 2005; Tong 2006.) In most companies, however, democratic participation via these systems is not as positive as in those few case studies.

In the first half of 2010, we started research into the changes in the structure of Factory A, an SOE founded in 1949 in City G. Fortunately, Factory A retains records dating back to 1949, with fairly complete material on the factory's SWC. Apart from the Cultural Revolution years, the factory has had a functioning democratic SWC system since 1950, which continued even after corporate restructuring, and the workings of the SWC and democratic processes appear to have become more standardized. But in interviews, factory workers commonly said they saw less and less democracy in practice.

This leads to the following questions: Why were workers feeling more distant from democratic processes that appeared to be becoming more standardized? And if these structures are failing to fulfill the purpose of allowing the workers to participate in company management, why are they still maintained? To answer these questions we carried out a systematic review of materials on the SWC in the company's archives and interviewed a number of workers, including those who had started work at the plant between the 1950s and the era of Reform and Opening Up (information about the interviewees is provided in an appendix). This article attempts to describe how the SWC was organized and run at different times, how the SWC system has been implemented, and the internal factors that have caused it to change.

2   Changes in Factory A's SWC

2.1   *The Factory's SWC*

The factory was initially three branch factories previously owned by the Kuomintang Resources Commission (国民党政府资源委员会). In 1951, the first and second branches were merged, and the third was merged in 1953. It was renamed Factory A in 1959, and since 1995 it has been called an enterprise group. The factory mainly produces heavy machinery and has had up to 6,000 workers and staff. Currently, the workforce numbers over 1,200.

In July and August of 1950, Factory Production Management Committees were formed in the first two branch factories (which had not yet been merged), marking the start of participation by workers' representatives in management of the company. The first meeting of workers' representatives was held in 1951, right after the first merger, and four more such meetings were held by the end of 1953. Between the end of 1953 and 1957, due to the country entering a period of socialist economic transformation and economic construction, the form of workers' representatives meetings was discontinued and replaced with an "all-factory production meeting system."

In April 1957, the Chinese Communist Party (CCP) Central Committee published "Notice on Some Important Problems Concerning the Working Class,"[2] which formally replaced workers' representative meetings with staff and workers congresses (or in smaller companies, congresses made up of all workers and staff). In June of that year, Factory A held the first meeting of the first session of its SWC. Since then the SWC has met between one and four times every year, except in 9 years: in 1960 and in 8 years during the Cultural Revolution, namely, 1966–1972 and 1976. Between 1957 and 2010, SWC representatives were elected twenty-one times and the congress met ninety times, with records available for seventy-seven of those meetings.

2.2   Four Stages of Factory A's SWC

The implementation of the SWC system at Factory A can be divided into four periods:

2.2.1   Establishment of the Legitimacy and Authority of the New Government (1949–1957)

This period featured factory production management committee and workers' representative meetings, the main tasks of which were to restore orderly production and implement various political campaigns. With the founding of the People's Republic of China, restoring basic order in the cities and restarting and developing production were key. The new state institutions and grassroots organizations were designed to highlight the essential differences between the old regime and the new, and the factory production management committee came into being as a way for workers to participate in management.

In May 1949, the All-China Federation of Trade Unions (中华全国总工会) held a workers' representative meeting in Tianjin, where Liu Shaoqi (刘少奇) spoke and a decision on establishing factory production management

---

2 关于研究有关工人阶级几个重要问题的通知.

committees and workers' representative meetings in state and public enterprises was made,[3] along with rules for implementing that decision.

On February 28, 1950, the State Council and the Finance Commission issued a document on establishing factory production management committees in state and public enterprises (An 1990). In July of that year, Factory A set up its factory production management committee. During that period, two powerful movements – the Democratic Reform Movement (民主改革运动) and the Three Antis Campaign (三反运动) – were launched to eliminate remnants of the old regime, and Factory A was no exception. In October 1951, Factory A established a workers' representative meeting with the primary task of mobilizing grassroots workers (especially activists) to lead and organize these political campaigns.

2.2.2 Socialist Construction and Organized Campaigns (1957–1978)

In April 1957, the CPC Central Committee published "Notice on Some Important Problems Concerning the Working Class",[4] formally deciding to change the existing workers' representative meetings into permanent workers congresses, and setting out their basic functions. The "Notice" also ruled that company union committees were responsible for organizing and holding the SWC, and for overseeing the implementation of its decisions.

Under instructions from the Central Government's Ministry of Industry and Transport and the City G Party Committee, Factory A carried out a pilot program of this new structure and set up a complete SWC system. In late February 1957, the factory established a working group to prepare for the SWC and the first congress meeting was held in June of that year. This marked the start of a period of normalized operations for the SWC. Overall, the main tasks of the SWC during this period were to encourage production and eliminate any barriers holding production back.

2.2.3 Reform and Opening Up (1979–1991)

The economic reform initiated in 1978 restructured the relationship between the state and the company. The rights, responsibilities and interests of the state and the company were redefined, and the changing relationship between workers, the company and the state inevitably affected the organization and operation of the SWC.

---

3 关于在国营公营企业中建立工厂管理委员会与工厂职工代表会议的决定.
4 关于研究有关工人阶级的几个重要问题的通知.

On June 15, 1981, the State Council published "Temporary Regulations for Staff and Workers Congresses in State-Owned Industrial Enterprises"[5] which declared that the SWC was the basic form through which companies implemented democratic management; it listed five official powers of the SWC and affirmed that it was an organ of power through which the workers participated in management, decision making and supervision of cadres.

On April 13, 1988, the First Session of the Seventh National People's Congress passed the "Law of the People's Republic of China on Industrial Enterprises Owned by the Whole People,"[6] which did not refer to SWCs as "organs of power," but used language from the workers' representative meetings which described them as organs through which the workers exercised their democratic right to participate in company management. In March 1982, in line with the "Temporary Regulations for Staff and Workers Congresses in State-Owned Industrial Enterprises," Factory A produced rules for their implementation.

Under these rules, the tasks of the SWC were to follow the principles, policies and orders of the Party, carry out instructions from superior bodies, strengthen democratic management of the company, establish the workers' status as masters of the factory, run a good socialist enterprise, educate the workers about the honor and responsibilities conferred by their status as masters, innovate and ensure the factories' production targets were met, balance the interests of the state, the masses and the individual, and resolve the company's internal conflicts (Factory A Archives 1982, 9:46).

At the second meeting of Factory A's 15th SWC, rules were adopted about the SWC's nature, structure, and delegates' powers and responsibilities, in line with the "Law of the People's Republic of China on Industrial Enterprises Owned by the Whole People" (Factory A Archives 1986, 6:17). During this period the SWC played a definite role in summarizing the interests of grassroots workers, seeking the basis of legitimacy for grassroots cooperation, and overseeing management.

2.2.4 SOE Restructuring and Reduction of Government Involvement (1992 to Present Day)

Since 1992, SOE reform has aimed at establishing the modern enterprise system, with SOEs becoming independently-run corporations rather than government appendages, competing in the market and being responsible for their own profits and losses. There have been profound changes in how state-owned assets are managed and operated. This has seen the "state," which had underwritten

---

5 国营工业企业职工代表大会暂行条例.
6 全民所有制工业企业法.

the high political status of the workers, withdraw from the SOEs, with workers no longer the "masters of the company," but simply hired "labor."

Since the reform period, the political backing for worker participation in company management has weakened, and legislation has either been lacking or poorly implemented, meaning workers have lost the effective organizational arrangements that allowed them to negotiate with the company. The SWC have increasingly become a formality.

2.3 *Characteristics of Several Changes in the Factory A SWC*

2.3.1 Frequency and Length of Meetings

The frequency and length of SWC meetings reflect the degree to which the system is used and respected. At Factory A, both frequency and length have varied significantly across time (see Figures 2.1 and 2.2). The first peak was during the period of recovery (1962–1964) after the Three Years of Natural Disasters. The second was during Reform and Opening Up (1981–1987). The third was when the company was restructured and workers were laid off (1997). Overall, both frequency and length of meetings have declined over time.

FIGURE 2.1 Number of SWC meetings per year, Factory A, 1957–2008

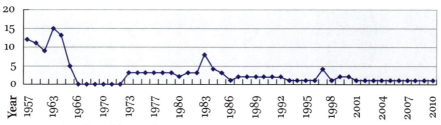

FIGURE 2.2 Number of days of the SWC meetings, Factory A, 1957 to 2010

2.3.2 Changes in Structure and Composition of Representatives

First, there were significant changes in the SWC presidium, which is the SWC's leadership body. Prior to 1986, this group included workers, section heads, managers and the Party committee leaders, with workers occupying at least half of the seats. There were strict procedures for selecting members of the presidium: names were put forward by the representatives of each workshop and these were then passed by a show of hands at the SWC or a preparatory meeting and confirmed by the Party committee.

The presidium was a permanent body, with a clear internal division of labor. Members of the presidium chaired meetings of the SWC, discussed the main issues, agendas, documents and other matters, and examined the decisions of the SWC. When the SWC was not in session, a quarterly rotation of members also handled issues raised by workers, heard reports from special investigation teams, received reports and issued guidance on union work, etc.

After 1986, however, members of the presidium were no longer chosen through elections – often membership was determined by discussions between the union and the relevant departments before being passed by a show of hands at the SWC. Moreover, it was no longer a permanent body; instead its duties were handled by the union when the SWC was not in session. In the lists of presidium members we could find dating from after restructuring [in 1993], not one member was an ordinary worker – all were executives or union leaders.

Second, special monitoring groups that had been set up to carry out the SWC's supervisory functions disappeared after the 17th SWC in 1991. Prior to this, the SWC always had monitoring groups (or working groups), whether to lead the Democratic Reform Movement in 1951 or to promote production during the stage of socialist construction, or to balance differing interests during Reform and Opening Up period. These groups each had their own function – carrying out studies, making suggestions, gathering, checking and compiling proposals to present to the SWC, and overseeing implementation of SWC decisions when the congress was not in session. However, no such groups have existed at Factory A for the last 20 years.

Third, the proportion of ordinary workers in the SWC has fallen. The SWC was established so ordinary workers could participate in the management of the company and oversee its administration, so the effectiveness of the system depends on such questions as: Who is chosen as a representative? and How many of the representatives are ordinary workers? We compiled figures showing that the number of ordinary worker representatives is falling, with an increasing number of representatives drawn from the company administration.

TABLE 2.1 The proportion of ordinary workers and staff, in the SWC

1957	1961	1963	1973	1978	1984	2007
The 1st SWC	The 3rd SWC	The 4th SWC	The 11th SWC	The 12th SWC	The 14th SWC	The 20th SWC
70.6%	70%	80%	70%	74.8%	56%	30%

DATA FROM THE ARCHIVES OF SWC HELD AT FACTORY A

2.3.3 Changes in Topics on the SWC Agenda

During the period of establishment of the legitimacy and authority of the new Chinese Government (1949–1957) the factory production management committee was the company's decision making body, responsible for setting production plans and discussing issues related to production. These issues were decided in advance by the Party committee before being submitted to the factory production management committee, but officially it was the latter committee that made the decision.

As some members holding management and technical posts were from the enterprises under the old regime, army and worker representatives were assigned to the factory production management committee, and during this stage worker representatives can be seen as having participated directly in company decisions. At that time, the workers' representative meetings were not concerned with factory production or welfare, but with the frequent political campaigns that took place during that period, functioning as a locus for the Party to purify the "class ranks" and establish political legitimacy within the company.

For example, the topic of the SWC meeting of 1951 was the organization of Democratic Reform Movement and it later ran the Three Antis Campaign (against waste, corruption and bureaucracy). At that stage, therefore, the SWC was entirely politically oriented.

During the period of comprehensive socialist construction (1957–1969), economic development reached a peak, with "national plans," "increase production and save resources," and "labor competitions" becoming key words at SWC meetings. The SWC became a venue for boosting company output. The "Grassroots Union Work Report" (Factory A Archives 1958, 49:3) stated:

> [We] implemented the mass line, did a good job of holding the SWC, used the SWC to mobilize the masses and reached a new production peak …

> The meeting made clear current key matters and requirements for production, organized representatives to discuss these and pledge their commitment.

Of course, there were always voices within the company that were not entirely in line with achieving state production goals. Therefore the SWC was the venue in which problems with workers' views were resolved and consensus achieved. We can see this in the records of the first meeting of Factory A's First SWC. According to Factory A's "Party Committee Political Work Report" (1957, 18:1–21).

> Higher authorities ordered that in principle in 1957 nobody would be promoted or given a raise, and that apprenticeships would be extended. That conflicted with what the workers wanted and things were quite tense. Some demobilized soldiers and some apprentices sent from the Changsha Technical School, as well as crane drivers and others, expressed objections, with some trying to stir up trouble. Through the SWC we convinced the masses. We discussed the State Council's regulations and reasoned with the workers' representatives, asking them to understand the state's difficulties. Also the labor-capital relations office and the education office criticized themselves for casually granting people's wishes in the past, and they had meetings with the apprentices and crane drivers to gather their opinions, help change their ways of thinking, and bring them into the consensus. Eventually the SWC reached decisions upholding the State Council's decisions.
>   The change from piecework rates to paying bonuses for extra production was in conflict with the economic preferences of the workers ... We submitted the two different opinions to the representatives for discussion, and consensus was reached. Finally the SWC decided to gradually phase out and eliminate piecework rates, to be replaced with a reasonable bonus system.
>   The principle of running a thrifty company conflicted with the workers excessive welfare demands ... We organized discussion among the representatives and used detailed calculations to criticize negative tendencies that overemphasized individual interests, and made a decision on a reasonable company bonus scheme.
>   A request from the cast steel workshop for shorter working hours was in conflict with production requirements. The cast steel workshop works three eight-hour shifts, while circumstances mean the machinery

workshop has three shifts of six and a half hours. The cast steel workers want to adopt the shorter hours, or to receive overtime payments. We passed this on to the SWC for discussion, and the unreasonable request was unanimously rejected ... This discussion greatly educated the cast steel workshop workers.

Between 1979 and 1991, when power and profits were being transferred to SOEs, the main responsibility of the SWC was to examine company plans and welfare allocations. It could be said that during this stage the SWC was an institutionalized venue for workers to participate in democratic management, advance their interests, and get organized. The SWC heard reports from the factory head and the Party secretary, but more important was the wide range of issues that had to be discussed and approved by the SWC. These included the allocation of housing, wage reforms, rules and regulations on bonuses and fines, allocation of welfare, codes of conduct and family planning, development plans and budgets, appraisals and oversight of factory managers and cadres, and even experimental elections of factory leaders.

For example in 1981, at the first meeting of the 13th SWC, matters discussed included "Welfare spending in 1981 and the welfare budget for 1982," "Report on remodeling and expansion of worker housing," "Thoughts on reduction of medical spending in 1981," and "Measures for firmly preventing unplanned births and implementing Province H's family planning rules." The agenda for the following meeting included "Proposed bonus system for Factory A," "Rewards and punishments to strengthen labor discipline," and "Proposal to subsidize water bills." At a subsequent meeting representatives discussed "1983 Factory A housing allocation and adjustments," "System for managing family housing for Family A workers," "Plan for allocation and adjustment of newly built worker housing," "Proposal for establishing a democratic monitoring group for allocation of housing," and "1983 wage changes for Factory A."

Things changed with restructuring in 1993. After that, for the next two decades SWC meetings generally featured restricted and formalized content: reports from the factory head, the union chair, the audit committee and the Party secretary, and then discussion of these reports. There were a few exceptions: a meeting in September 1999 discussed collective contracts and a proposal for more openness in factory affairs, and a June 2008 meeting voted on worker discipline measures, a 20% wage increase, and qualifications for rental housing. But housing was now commercially available and welfare was provided by the state, meaning much of the SWC's major work no longer existed. Some representatives did drift off the topic of the leader's reports to discuss other matters, but with lengthy reports and shorter meetings, there was only minimal time for free discussion.

2.3.4 Workers' Opinions of the Value of the SWC Decreased

Although our research found that the powers and functions of the SWC were never fully exercised, the workers' opinions of the SWC declined, shifting from positive to negative. In interviews with older workers we often heard praise and nostalgia for the democratic management systems in the early years of the People's Republic.

> Q: Could you participate in factory decision-making at that time [of socialist construction]?
> A: Yes, yes, for example, the SWC met several times a year and we could talk about work or our lives. Representatives were chosen proportionally from factory teams. It changed after the Cultural Revolution; then there were lots of restrictions, you had to be a certain age, have a certain level of education, so on and so forth. It was obvious they were restricting it to certain people [laughs]. Before, we'd all have a big meeting and would usually choose someone with a certain amount of knowledge, someone good at their work and ideology, and someone who dared speak up.
> INTERVIEWEE 2

> Q: Do you think the SWC was useful?
> A: Yes, of course. It was very democratic then.
> INTERVIEWEE 1

But in our interviews the most common description we heard about the SWC today was that it was held "for appearance's sake" or "useless, a fraud."

> There aren't any unions in the workshops now. Elected representatives? No, not for over a decade. So who are the representatives? Workshop managers, earning 4,000 or 6,000 yuan a month. Are they going to speak up for the workers? There are some workers among the representatives, one or two, but do they dare speak up? Mr. Lin used to, but now they don't want him there, they don't ask him to go to the meetings.
> INTERVIEWEE 10

> Even if you gave me a vote now, I wouldn't use it. It's useless. Nobody listens to what you say.
> INTERVIEWEE 7

3 Reasons for Changes in the SWC

> In terms of organizational sociology, we find that organizations grow in two different environments: a technical environment and an institutional environment. The technical environmental requires the organization to seek efficiency, while the institutional environment requires it to seek legitimacy.
> CHEN 2009

In this section we attempt to apply organizational sociology to the changes in the SWC system reviewed above.

3.1 The Logic of Legitimacy Motivated SOEs to Implement the SWC System

In New Institutionalism, a field of organizational sociology, legitimacy refers to "the conceptual forces which lead or force organizations to adopt legitimate structures or behaviors" (Zhou 2003). That is, under pressure from the institutional environment the organization will adopt organizational forms and methods that are widely accepted within that environment – regardless of whether or not these forms and methods are efficient choices for the organization.

China is a socialist nation, and the people are the masters of the state, and so naturally also the masters of society and the economy (Wu and Chen 2010). If the state's rule is to be legitimate, there must be a system of guaranteeing the people's rights. However, China is also a Party-led consultative democracy, a system which is appropriate for a country like China – vast, ethnically diverse, with a long history of imperial rule and traditional culture. It is difficult to ensure that every citizen directly enjoys these rights, but the state must try to do so in order to win recognition of the legitimacy of its rule. Grassroots democratic systems, such as rural and urban autonomous governance and the SWC system in SOEs, were chosen to do this.

This means the establishment of SWCs is not something the company itself wants to do – the company is fulfilling a state function, earning workers' recognition of state legitimacy by allowing for their participation in management of the company; this is "a requirement of political ideology" (Zhang 2003). The SWC system in SOEs should, therefore, not be seen only as a way of overseeing and restraining company managers (Li 1995), but as part of a broader democracy.

Clearly, in this institutional environment, SOE managers face greater challenges to their own legitimacy, both from the state and society. The state requires SOEs to make a profit, but also to allow workers to exercise their political rights and to protect the socioeconomic interests of the masses. Meanwhile, the people exercise their political rights through the company, even expecting the company to perform functions that properly belong to the state. If the company fails to deal with these issues, managers may be punished or even removed from their posts by government authorities for failing to manage the company in a way that increases state legitimacy. As one company official we interviewed said:

> I had to follow the [SWC] process, I had to hold one every year, as that was what the policy required. Otherwise even a janitor could have caused me trouble just by writing a letter to our superiors.
> INTERVIEWEE 11

The logic of legitimacy means that implementation of the SWC system varied depending on the degree of pressure on state legitimacy.

3.2 *The Logic of Efficiency Motivates the Company to Restrict Use of the SWC System*

The logic of efficiency here means that company management has, at its heart, economic goals, including profits, as well as efficiency in decision making and management.

Another aim of the SWC system is to balance interests within the company and to restrict internal bureaucracy. This was described by Zhu De in his talk "Several Issues in Union Work:" "Several current problems (conflicts between management and workers) are the result of either a tendency towards higher earnings among the workers, or a tendency towards bureaucracy among the management cadres ... it is therefore very important to democratize management and have mangers act democratically" (Zhu 1949). The SWC therefore aims to provide a system of oversight constraining the managers – which will not necessarily be welcomed by the managers themselves. As one interviewee said: "Democracy makes managing harder" (Interviewee 13).

A company is an organization designed to pursue profit, meaning that, of its own volition, it will only implement structures that will reduce costs or increase income. If the SWC is unable to spur workers to produce more, it will, on the contrary, use up company time and personnel, thus increasing costs. In this case, managers have no reason to support and develop the SWC system. In our interviews we found most managers did not view the SWC system as contributing to efficiency.

Thus, in terms of both economic and decision-making efficiency, managers lack motivation to implement democratic management via the SWC. But as described above, the SWC is a political system embedded within the company – SOEs have no choice in the matter. The rational choice for managers, therefore, is to run the SWC system, but make it subordinate to the logic of efficiency: meetings should be as short as possible, cover as little content as possible, and deliberations should be a simple as possible. Without mandatory external requirements, the managers will do their best to ensure the powers of the SWC exist in appearance only.

> Currently things like wages and safety are decided at joint meetings with the Party officials and administrative officials, although by the book they should be passed by the SWC. [Q: Why isn't that done?]. This is where the problem is. The SWC is fine, the union is fine, and the design of the system itself isn't a problem. Do I think these are good things? I do. But who turns those requirements into actual actions and outcomes? Who covers the cost of implementing this? I think the biggest problem now is that you're required to do this, but the outcomes aren't good enough, and that's what we see now…. An SOE manager isn't the investor himself, but he represents the investor, and if he has to keep on working like that he won't be able to keep going.
> INTERVIEWEE 11

3.3 The Implementation of the SWC System Has Been Determined by the Tension between Legitimacy and Efficiency

As discussed above, due to pressures of legitimacy, company managers hold SWC meetings and go through the SWC's democratic management processes. But, at the same time, efficiency pressures drive them to minimize the actual meaningful work of the SWC, making it exist merely for appearances' sake. The differences in implementation of the SWCs across time are determined by differing degrees of tension between the two different demands. Generally when pressure for legitimacy is greater, the SWC is better implemented; when pressures for efficiency are greater it is more likely to be operated merely for appearances' sake.

There were three peaks in the frequency of SWC meetings. The first peak was during the period of recovery (1962–1964) after the Three Years of Natural Disasters. The second was shortly after the Cultural Revolution and during Reform and Opening Up (1981–1987). The third was when the company was restructured and workers were laid off (1997). During those periods, when there were more SWC meetings, the length of each meeting was also longer. Clearly these were times when the legitimacy of state power was under pressure, and the state transferred this pressure to SOEs.

The Three Years of Natural Disasters (三年自然灾害时期, 1959–1961) were China's hardest economic period, with people thrown into destitution and many starving to death. Factory A had to send workers back to their villages – the archives show it employed 6,141 people in 1959, but only 3,818 in 1961. Subsequently rebuilding faith in socialist construction became the basis of state legitimacy and so there were frequent SWC meetings, which dealt with increasing production.

The ten years of the Cultural Revolution again threw China into turmoil leading to the brink of economic collapse – wages stagnated, company welfare such as housing was not provided, and the quality of workers' lives plummeted. After the end of the Cultural Revolution the rapid restoration of quality of life, welfare and social order was the basis of state legitimacy and so there were frequent SWC meetings, which dealt with welfare and other interests.

The SOE property reforms of the late 20th century reinvigorated companies, but at the cost of laying off many workers. The 1977 Asian financial crisis exacerbated the situation and state legitimacy was dependent on ensuring that discontent arising from restructuring and the economic slowdown did not lead to social unrest; as a result there were frequent SWC meetings, which dealt with ensuring fairness during the restructuring process.

Given that the SWC is a political arrangement embedded within the company, its success is closely linked to the relationship between the company and the state. During the planned economy era the company was not an independent actor – the state controlled its production through a monopoly on resources, and controlled its managers because they were part of the state bureaucracy.

The state was therefore a direct participant in the management of the company and it promoted and oversaw the implementation of the SWC system. But the advent of the market economy saw the state and business separate, with companies becoming increasingly independent market actors. This meant that management behavior was driven more by efficiency concerns, and also that incompatibilities between the SOE system and the new market system appeared.

In 1995, Factory A set up a corporate governance system in line with the Company Law, for the first time forming a board of directors, a board of supervisors, and a shareholders' meeting. Company managers became responsible to directors and shareholders, rather than the workers. Shareholders have a simpler and stronger profit motive than managers, and efficiency became more important than ever before.

Under the new system it was inevitable that the actual capabilities of the SWC to realize democratic participation, oversight, and discussion would be greatly reduced. But at the macro-level, SOEs were still required to embody the socialist principle that the people were the masters of the state and they were still faced with legitimacy pressures from both the state and society, which greatly increased tension between efficiency and legitimacy.

As John Meyer (1977) wrote, when efficiency and legitimacy are opposed within an organization – that is, when there is a conflict between obtaining resources for efficiency and resources for legitimacy – the organization will be forced to disconnect actual practices and structures. This disconnect is demonstrated in China's SWC system – we see SWC procedures and processes becoming more comprehensive, but the actual content of its work becoming more abstract. Thus, the SWC became more ceremonial. Since the changes were adopted in 1995, Factory A's annual SWC meetings (except in 1997) have lasted only a single day – the shortest meetings since 1957.

The SWC system in SOEs is one form of grassroots socialist democracy and it has in the past played a role in the growth of SOEs and in implementing socialist democracy. But with SOEs adopting corporate governance structures, changes in SOE ownership, and with increasing numbers of workers finding themselves in non-state firms, the plight of the SWC system is clear. How can companies again be run democratically under a socialist market economy? How can the rights of workers be protected effectively? How can company governance systems win recognition for the legitimacy of the state? Hopefully the above historical review will help us once more consider these issues.

Appendix: Information about Interviewees

Interviewee 1: Joined the factory in 1950 and retired in 1995. Worked as a worker, workshop Party publicity committee member, workshop union branch head, and workshop union branch chair.

Interviewee 2: Worked as head of the production office and workshop head.

Interviewee 3: Joined the factory in 1949 and retired in 1988. Worked as an apprentice, technician, collective factory head and workshop head.

Interviewee 4: Returned overseas Chinese, joined the factory in 1963. Was a model worker, People's Representative and member of the factory Party committee.

Interviewee 5: Joined the factory in 1951. Was an apprentice, foundry worker, and team leader; in June 1955 was promoted to section chief and in 1961 to technician. In 1967 became a workshop head and head of the quality management department. While a worker, he was a workers' representative, and remained so while a workshop head. Retired in 1989.

Interviewee 6: Joined the factory in 1951. Was a lathe operator. In 1957 and became a cadre, acting as workshop union branch chair and workshop Party secretary, and held posts in the publicity office, statistics department, production section and young intellectuals office. Retired in 1985.

Interviewee 7: Joined the factory 1982. Currently a worker in the riveting and welding workshop.

Interviewee 8: Joined the factory in 1994. Fitter and lathe operator.

Interviewee 9: Joined the factory in 1988. Machinist.

Interviewee 10: Joined the factory in 1972. Fitter and warehouse manager. Currently a workers' representative and union representative.

Interviewee 11: Currently chair of the Factory A board of directors.

Interviewee 12: Currently chair of the Factory A union.

Interviewee 13: Joined the factory in 1957, retired in 1995. Formerly head of the factory office.

References

An Miao 桉苗. 1990. 工人阶级现状与职工代表大会制度研究 [*Research into the Circumstances of the Working Class and the Staff and Workers Congress System*]. Shenyang: Liaoning People's Publishing House.

Bian Rongzhen 卞荣臻. 2002. 职代会制度要与时俱进 ["The Staff and Workers Congress System Must Move with the Times"]. 中国工运 [*Chinese Workers' Movement*], 2: 35.

Chang Kai 常凯. 1995. 劳动关系·劳动者·劳权 – 当代中国的劳动问题 [*Labor Issues in Contemporary China: Labor Relations, the Workers, and Workers' Rights*]. Beijing: China Labor and Social Security Press.

Chen Wenjiao 陈文娇. 2009. 我国大学组织趋同现象研究 – 基于组织社会学的视角 [*Research into the Trend to Uniformity in China's Universities: An Organizational Sociology Approach*]. PhD dissertation, Huazhong Normal University.

China Union Movement Institute Research Group 中国工运研究所课题组. 2007. 我国企业职工民主管理制度和职代会问题研究 ["Research into China's Democratic Company Management and Staff and Workers Congress System"]. 工运研究 [*Labor Movement Research*], 17: 8–20.

Deng Xiaoping 邓小平. 1994. 邓小平文选 第 1 卷 [*Selected Works of Deng Xiaoping Vol. 1*]. Beijing: People's Publishing House.

Feng Tongqing 冯同庆. 2005. 中国经验: 转型社会的企业治理与职工民主参与 [*The Chinese Experience: Corporate Governance and Democratic Worker Participation in a Transforming Society*]. Beijing: Social Sciences Academic Press.

Li Jingpeng 李景鹏. 1995. 权力政治学 [*The Study of Power Politics*]. Harbin: Heilongjiang Education Press.

Li Shuwen 李书文 and Song Tianhe 宋天和. 2009. 中西企业民主管理模式之比较 ["Comparison of Democratic Management Models in Chinese and Western Companies"]. 企业研究 [*Business Research*], 9: 62–65.

Liu Yuanwen 刘元文. 2004. 相容与相悖 – 当代中国的职工民主参与研究 [*Acceptance and Rejection – Research into Democratic Worker Participation in Contemporary China*]. Beijing: China Labor and Social Security Press.

Lü Keqin 吕克勤. 2002. 坚持和完善职代会制度是推进企业改革和发展的原动力 ["Maintaining and Improving the Staff and Workers Congress System is the Driving Force of Company Reform and Development"]. 工会理论与实践: 中国劳动关系学院学报 (*Labor Union – Theory and Practice: Journal of China University of Labor Relations*), 1: 23–25.

Meyer, John 约翰·迈耶 and Brian Rowan 布莱恩·罗恩. 2007. 制度化的组织: 作为神话和仪式的正式结构 ["Institutionalized Organizations: Formal Structure as Myth and Ceremony"], in 组织社会学的新制度主义学派 [*Organizational Sociology's New Institutionalism*], edited by Zhang Yonghong 张永宏. Shanghai: Shanghai People's Publishing House.

Ni Haomei 倪豪梅. 2006. 职工代表大会制度是具有中国社会主义特色的企业民主管理制度 ["The Workers' Representatives Congress System is a Democratic Company Management System with Chinese Socialist Characteristics"]. 中国工运 [*Chinese Workers' Movement*], 4: 15–17.

Tong Xin 佟新. 2006. 延续的社会主义文化传统 – 一起国有企业工人集体行动的个案分析 ["A Continuing Socialist Tradition – Analysis of One Case of Mass Worker Action in a State-owned Enterprise"]. 社会学研究 [*Sociological Studies*], 1: 59–76.

Wang Chidong 王持栋. 1992. 中国企业民主发展史略 [*A Brief History of the Development of Company Democracy in China*]. Beijing: China Workers Press.

Wu Jianping 吴建平 and Chen Ziwei 陈紫葳. 2010. 企业民主管理的实证基础 – 以员工参与与员工满意度相关关系为视角 ["The Evidential Basis for Democratic Company Management: The Relationship Between Worker Participation and Worker Satisfaction"]. 中国劳动关系学院学报 [*Journal of the Chinese Institute of Industrial Relations*], 4: 71–75.

Zhang Yunmei 张允美. 2003. 中国职工代表大会制与职工参与模式的政治学分析 ["A Political Analysis of Chinese Staff and Workers Congress System and Models of Worker Participation"]. 北京行政学院学报 [*Journal of Beijing Administrative College*], 1: 27–33.

Zhang Jing 张静. 2001. 利益组织化单位: 企业职代会案例研究 ["Organizations of Interests: Staff and Workers Congress Case Studies"]. Beijing: China Social Sciences Press.

Zhou Xueguang 周雪光. 2003. 组织社会学十讲 [*Ten Lectures on Organizational Sociology*]. Beijing: Social Sciences Academic Press.

Zhu De 朱德. 1949. 关于工会工作的几个问题 [Speech of Commander-in-Chief Zhu De at the National Trade Union Work Conference on July 23rd, 1949]. 人民日报 [*People's Daily*] July 25, 1949, 1. http://cpc.people.com.cn/GB/69112/73585/74082/5051425.html. Accessed May 31, 2019.

Zhu Xiaoyang 朱晓阳. 2005. "误读"法律与秩序建成: 国有企业改制的案例研究 ["'Misreading' the Law and the Formation of Order: Case Studies of Restructuring of State-owned Enterprises"]. 社会科学战线 [*Social Science Battlefront*], 3: 197–206.

Zhu Xiaoyang 朱晓阳 and Chen Peihua 陈佩华. 2003. 职工代表大会: 职工利益的制度化表达渠道？ ["Staff and Workers Congresses: An Institutionalized Route for Workers to Express their Interests?"]. 开放时代 [*Open Times*], 2: 120–132.

CHAPTER 3

A Simple Control Model Analysis of Labor Relations in Industrial SOEs

Tong Xin (佟新)
Translated by Roderick Graham Flagg

Abstract

Based on case studies of four industrial state-owned enterprises (SOEs), this paper proposes a simple control model of industrial relations in post-reform SOEs. Under this model, the focus of SOE targets has shifted toward efficiency, while labor relations within SOEs have become hierarchical, with managers enjoying political and economic protection from the state and wielding absolute control. Technicians enjoy certain market advantages but compete as isolated individuals. Skilled workers enjoy the traditional protections of the SOE, but are aging and will not be replaced. The use of large quantities of informal labor has taken the hierarchical application of labor to an extreme. The simple control model and informal labor markets are reliant on each other, undercut the role of the union, and divide permanent and temporary workers across different labor markets.

Keywords

state-owned enterprise – industrial restructuring – industrial relations – informal labor – managerial control

1   Sociological Research into SOE Restructuring and Labor Relations[1]

The restructuring of state-owned enterprises (SOEs) started around 1995. Some were shut down or had production halted, others were merged or were shifted

---

[1] This article originally appeared in *Open Times* 2008, no. 5, pp. 61–76. It is one of the outcomes of the "Ministry of Education Financial Aid for Key Humanities and Social Science Research Centers" project 05JJD840143, "Labor Relations during China's Social Transition."

to other sectors. Larger firms were taken under closer state control, while smaller firms were given more freedom. This process is now complete: SOEs are no longer managed under the "work unit organization" of the planned economy era and have become manufacturers or service providers operating in a market environment. Statistics show that the SOE workforce has shrunk significantly, while efficiency has risen somewhat.

The number of SOE employees has fallen rapidly, both in absolute and relative terms. In 2006, SOEs employed 55.28% of the total workforce, 18% less than in 1993. Meanwhile, output of state-owned industrial firms was on the rise. The question looked at here is as follows: what were the labor and power relationships that allowed industrial SOEs to achieve this efficiency boost?

TABLE 3.1 Changing numbers of SOE employees

Year	Number of SOE employees (millions)	Number of employees (millions)	SOE proportion of total employees (%)
1993	109.2	148.49	73.54
1995	109.55	149.08	73.48
2000	78.78	112.59	69.97
2005	62.32	108.50	57.43
2006	61.70	111.61	55.28

DATA COMES FROM THE NATIONAL BUREAU OF STATISTICS, *CHINA STATISTICAL YEARBOOK 2007*, CHINA STATISTICS PRESS, (2007, 138)

TABLE 3.2 Gross industrial output value and annual growth rate of state-owned and state-controlled industrial enterprises

Year	Gross industrial output value (billion yuan)	Annual growth rate (% compared to previous year)
2000	4,055.44	–
2001	4,240.85	4.4
2002	4,517.90	6.1
2003	5,340.79	15.4
2004	6,597.11	19.0

DATA COMES FROM THE NATIONAL BUREAU OF STATISTICS, *CHINA STATISTICAL SUMMARY 2005*, CHINA STATISTICS PRESS (2005, 127)

Sociological study of labor relations in SOEs has taken four main approaches. The first follows up on from Walder's (1996 [1986]) research into loyalty-protection relationships within work units, that was continued by Oi (1986). This research found that these relationships continued to develop somewhat after the beginning of market reforms. Within work units, benefits accrued collectively to the unit, rather than being divided differentially according to social status (Li 1992; Zhang 2001). Although incomes across work units diverged, income within work units remained equitable (Wang et al. 1992). The work unit and its workers remained dependent upon each other (Li and Li 1999). The above research mainly consisted of analysis prior to the 1995 SOE restructuring. Research has also found that the traditional relaxed and personal SOE style of management has in some cases survived the restructuring process (Li 2003).

The second approach uses class formation as an analytical framework. Ching Kwan Lee (1999) argued that [Walder's] "Communist neo-traditionalism" had already passed into history, replaced by "disorganized despotism." This idea referred to factory heads and managers wielding state authority, leading to dictatorial management where both the Party organization and the union submitted to managerial authority. The adoption of contracts, company autonomy and scientific management techniques eliminated the mutually beneficial relationships of the past, and the state failed to implement its own rules, such as providing social insurance. The old system had disappeared and the new was not yet in place, leaving workers stuck in the middle. At the advent of the 21st century, academics talked of the "reconstruction of the Chinese working class" – that is, with China becoming the center of global manufacturing, the country was again becoming home to the world's largest working class population (Shen 2006).

The third approach is research into labor process theory. China, regarded as the "factory of the world," had become a museum of factory regimes. The most primitive despotic regimes and the hegemonic regimes of monopoly capitalism all existed at the same time, highlighting their differing characteristics. The existing relationships between migrant workers were directly absorbed into labor processes, providing a source of both domination and resistance. This special type of hegemony was referred to as *"guanxi* [relationships] hegemony" (Shen 2007, 8). Starting from labor processes, this type of research shows how surplus value is concealed through the division and manipulation of labor.

The fourth and final approach is that of applied sociology. Applied sociology stresses that labor relations in SOEs are constantly forming and have traits both inherited from the planned economy era and resulting from the impact of the market economy – the outcome of various interacting forces. This approach tries to place research in the context of China's particular development path (Tong 2002, 2006).

This paper takes an applied sociological approach to analyze labor relations in contemporary Chinese industrial SOEs through case studies. Starting in August 2008, we carried out an in-depth study of labor relations in SOEs, foreign-invested companies, and private companies, accumulating large quantities of first-hand materials.[2] This paper, based on investigations of four SOEs, analyzes configurations of labor relations, models of authority relations, and the social foundation of these models, as well as the relationship between the state, international capital and labor markets.

2 Restructuring of Industrial SOEs: Remaking Production

By looking at the outcomes of restructuring of four industrial SOEs we see how these companies have been transformed from the work unit organizations of the planned economy era into marketized, modern firms under the enterprise system.

2.1 Introduction to the Case Studies
2.1.1 BR Printing Machinery, Ltd.
BR Printing Machinery, Ltd (BR), China's largest manufacturer of offset printing presses, is located in Beijing and is a subsidiary of the BR Group. The company was founded in 1952, and in 1958, during the Great Leap Forward, it absorbed a number of smaller firms and became a manufacturer of printing machinery subordinate to the municipal machine-building bureau. The company grew steadily after Reform and Opening Up (改革开放) and was initially restructured as a "headquarters factory" (总厂). In 1985 the headquarters factory started contracting out – that is, signing production and profit quota contracts – with its own subsidiaries and branch factories. More detailed targets were then assigned by the factories to individual workshops, which had to deliver the products. The company was listed on the stock market in 1993, becoming one of the first nine Chinese firms to list H-shares in Hong Kong; it thus became a truly marketized modern enterprise.

---

2 Between 2002 and 2005 the "Corporate governance and worker participation during China's social transformation" study group, made up of Zhu Xiaoyang, Tong Xin, Feng Tongqing, Anita Chan (Chen Peihua), Chen Meixia and Dai Jianzhong supervised research, mostly in the form of case studies, by graduate students at Peking University's School of Sociology. Members of the group later formed the Peking University Chinese Workers and Labor Institute, which continued related studies.

That same year, the company stopped setting production targets – now only profit targets were set. Subsidiaries could only record profits once goods had been delivered and payments received, and the headquarters factory continued to control the allocation of those profits. In 1994, the company was also listed on the A-share market in Shanghai and became a group holding company, combining development, design, manufacture, sales and service for 80 different types and sizes of offset presses, with a share of the domestic market that exceeded 60%. In 2000, the company moved from the city center to a technology park on the outskirts. During the move, equipment was upgraded and employees who were unwilling to move were replaced with a cohort of young technical school graduates living near the company's new site.

Our research team visited the company in August 2002, and carried out thirty-five interviews. Of the interviewees, nineteen were managers (including political cadres), five were ordinary staff, seven were workers, one was a technician and three were retired employees (two of whom had been workers). Interviews took between forty minutes and two hours, producing over one million Chinese characters of transcripts. Written surveys were given to another two hundred employees.[3]

2.1.2   DL Shipbuilding Heavy Industry, Ltd.

DL Shipbuilding Heavy Industry, Ltd. (DL) is located in Dalian. The company was founded in 1898 and experienced both Japanese and Russian colonization. After 1949, it received Soviet assistance, becoming China's first modern heavy industrial facility, and was placed under direct state control. Some of its output was military equipment supplied to the armed forces.

After Reform and Opening Up, DL was restructured, which in this case involved reducing government control and increasing output of products for sale on open markets. Currently very little of its output is military in nature. In 2006, the Sixth Ministry of Machine Building (六机部) was converted into the DL Shipping Heavy Industry Group, a huge shipbuilding conglomerate. The company now had a board of directors, a board of supervisors, an executive staff, and twenty departments with sixteen sub-departments (for example the original manufacturing workshop became the No. 2 Sectional Manufacturing Department). The executive staff also managed twenty mainly service-oriented subsidiary firms, such as the DL Steel Structure Manufacturing Center. The group employed a total of about 11,000 people; of these, over 500 served in

---

3 Participants in the August 2002 study included Zhu Xiaoyang, Tong Xin, Feng Tongqing, Anita Chan (Chen Peihua), Chen Meixia, Dai Jianzhong, Long Yan and Zhu Qinghua.

senior technical posts and 1,400 were technicians. DL is home to the Heavy Industry Group's headquarters.

The research team visited DL three times, in the summers of 2003, 2004 and 2005. At the time of the August 2004 visit, DL had 7,000 people on the payroll, with 6,000 at work. Manufacturing workers, auxiliary workers, managers and technicians accounted for one third of that figure. We interviewed forty-seven employees in various roles, with transcripts amounting to over one million Chinese characters.[4]

2.1.3   YC Coal, Ltd.

YC Coal, Ltd. (YC) is part of the YK Group and is based in a city in Shandong Province. It is a large state-owned company with a workforce of almost 100,000. The YK Group, founded in 1976, was formerly the YC Mine Bureau. In 1996, the Group was restructured as a wholly state-owned company.

In 1998, YC was listed on the Hong Kong, New York and Shanghai stock exchanges, becoming one of China's 100 largest listed firms. It holds 800 million metric tons of coal reserves, estimated to be enough for two decades of mining output. To ensure continual growth, the company is buying mines both at home and abroad, including in countries such as Australia, and it is competing internationally. Its management structure is in full accord with China's Company Law.

We visited the company in the spring of 2007, held meetings at three of YC's mines and conducted in-depth interviews with nine people.[5]

2.1.4   JD Oilfields

JD Oilfields, headquartered in a city in Hebei Province, is part of the Northern China Oilfield Management Bureau, which is a unit of PetroChina. Surveying and development of the northern China oilfields started in 1975, with a command center, later to become the management bureau, founded in 1976. In October 1999, the Northern China Bureau was divided into two companies, one listed and one not listed on the stock exchange, in accordance with both State Council instructions on the restructuring of oil and gas firms and with PetroChina's arrangements. JD Oilfields, which we visited, is part of the listed company. This "drilling company" has over 5,000 employees and, in accordance

---

4 Interviews were carried out on August 19, 2004 by Tong Xin, Liang Meng, Wang Di, Wang Shan, Wang Chunlai. Material was compiled by Wang Chunlai. Tan Baogui and others also carried out interviews at other times.

5 YC Mining was visited between April 17 and 21, 2007 by Feng Tongqing, Tong Xin, Hu Yu, Wang Chunlai, Wu Ling and Chen Liang.

with market requirements, its deputy CEO manages JD Oilfields. The company's wells are in Tanghai (唐海), a two hour drive from its offices, and so its 600 staff members are given a single eight-day rest period every month to allow them to travel home. The workforce is entirely male.

In the spring of 2008, we visited the JD drilling site, where we interviewed nine people, including the manager, the Party secretary, the union chair, team leaders, workers and temporary laborers.[6]

2.2 Governance of State-Owned Industrial Enterprises after Restructuring

These four case studies demonstrate that state-owned industrial companies have completed marketization restructuring, thereby becoming production organizations run in the spirit of China's Company Law.[7] We also identified the following characteristics of industrial SOEs:

First, SOE restructuring saw the state take closer control of large firms while divesting from smaller firms. This means that the remaining SOEs tend to be large or medium-sized, and, in strategic sectors such as oil, gas, coal and machinery, they enjoy monopoly positions.

Second, marketization has strengthened state-owned industrial firms and this is particularly the case with exchange-listed firms. The capital markets are now a major source of funds for large SOEs and listed status puts SOEs under the supervision of both the Company Law and shareholders. This bolsters competitiveness in both product and labor markets, and the ideologically-oriented structures of traditional SOEs have been replaced with efficiency-oriented structures.

Third, unions remain relatively intact within state-owned industrial firms. China's Company Law and the traditions of the planned economy era have made China's unions what they are today – all four companies had full-time union officials and structures, with union groups from the company to team levels, and staff and workers' congresses meet at least annually.

---

6 The HD branch was visited between March 4 and 6, 2008, by Tong Xin, Yang Yi and Wang Ye. Seven people were interviewed, including managers, secretaries, union chairs, team leaders, workers and temporary employees.

7 This refers to the "Company Law of the People's Republic of China," (中华人民共和国公司法) adopted at the Fifth Session of the Standing Committee of the Eighth National People's Congress on December 29, 1993. The initial law was amended on December 25, 1999 and on August 28, 2004; it was revised at the 18th Session of the Standing Committee of the Tenth National People's Congress on October 27, 2005 and then amended for the third time on December 28, 2013. http://english.court.gov.cn/2016-04/14/content_24532981.htm. Accessed June 12, 2019. – Ed.

Restructuring has seen state-owned industrial firms adopt corporate structures and become market-oriented – a process of "translative adaptation," a concept proposed by Japanese scholar Ohno Kenichi. Ohno has said that market mechanisms in developing nations are imported, rather than native, and are the product of interaction between domestic and foreign systems (Ohno 2006, 182). The restructuring of China's SOEs did not take place in a purely market environment – it was government-led and carried out by those companies that had done well under the planned economy. Therefore, SOE reform has inevitably had national characteristics and to an extent carries on the traditions of planned economy era SOEs; but it also brings in market rules as appropriate.

3   Hierarchical Nature of Labor Relations in Industrial SOEs

The actors in labor relations within state-owned industrial firms are managers, technicians, skilled workers, and unskilled workers, with these four classes part of different and hierarchical labor markets, which are shaped by state and private employers and the rural/urban divide.

3.1   *Managers – Market-Motivated Cadres*

On October 27, 2000, the State Economic and Trade Commission (国家经济贸易委员) published the *Basic Norms for Establishing Modern Enterprise Systems and Strengthening Management of Large and Medium-Sized State-Owned Enterprises (Trial)*.[8] Under these norms, SOE managers would no longer be government cadres and companies would no longer use Party and government ranks. Remuneration of managers would no longer be set with reference to equivalent posts in Party and government bodies, and company managers would be treated in accordance with the requirements of the modern enterprise system.

Although from this point on SOE managers were no longer given Party or government ranks, our research found that extremely close links with government superiors remain. The selection of company and senior managers is by no means a competitive process – they are selected behind closed doors from a set of "insiders" and assessed and confirmed by the superior Party organization. In this aspect there has been no fundamental change from the days of the planned economy – the bureaucracy still retains control of managers, and managers still rely heavily on the bureaucracy.

---

8   国有大中型企业建立现代企业制度和加强管理的基本规范（试行）.

At the same time, by devolving authority to SOEs and allowing them to control some profits, the government has given managers the ability to seek and benefit from the huge profits to be made through the market. But this is by no means handing power and profits to the workers – only to managers. The *SOE Managers Salary System (Trial)*[9] document issued in 2000 by the state-owned assets commissions, economic commissions, labor bureaus and financial bureaus in various provinces and municipalities awarded material benefits to managers. The salary system applied to managers of SOEs with annual profits of more than one million yuan and set the basic remuneration the company's legal representative, as well as allowed for bonuses according to company performance, including actual profitability and safety performance. The four companies studied all operated annual salary or lucrative annual bonus schemes for senior managers, confirming their right to company surpluses and creating a new form of protection of managers by the company's state owners.

YC Mining and JD Oilfields both pay managers very high annual salaries – much higher than the salaries of other employees. According to a JD manager:

> We oil companies take safety very seriously, with annual safety targets that can't be missed. If they are missed it's very damaging – the company heads are fined. There are annual payouts [if targets are met]. In 2007, we should have gotten payouts of over 200,000 yuan, but just a few hours before the end of the year there was an accident and I was fined 40,000 yuan.[10]

This is just one glimpse of the annual salary system.

The continuation of the traditional allocation of official power means that SOE managers are both accountable to their government superiors and reliant upon them. This political protection means that the political power of the traditional SOE elite has been retained, while their high salaries mean they have also become part of the economic elite. That is, SOE managers are now members of both the political elite and the economic elite. Their powers lie in their management of companies on behalf of the state, making them high-status individuals within the SOE system, and giving them absolute control within the company.

---

9   国有企业经营者年薪制实行办法（试行）.
10 Interviews were carried out on March 5, 2008, by Tong Xin, Yang Yi, Wang Ye. Material was compiled by Wang Ye.

3.2 *Multinational Capital Helps Create an Elite Labor Market with Individual Bargaining*

Under the influence of multinational capital, an elite labor market for professional technicians has formed in China. This determines the bargaining power and status of these employees within China's industrial SOEs.

In our interviews, we found that all four companies had suffered shortages of technicians and had responded by negotiating with these workers individually. The shortage was due to staff being poached by multinational firms working in China, with talented employees often lured away with salaries five to ten times higher than those offered by an SOE. Incomplete statistics show that every year large numbers of technical and management employees leave Chinese SOEs, government bodies and private firms, with over half moving to multinational companies working in China (Luo 2001, 120).

Technical employees are extremely important for BR, a major machinery manufacturer. The company suffered early losses of senior technicians and in 1996 it drew nationwide attention when it started negotiating salaries with these employees, offering increases in order to retain staff. In 2003, the Party secretary of BR's fourth branch factory said:

> There's already a market and the work unit no longer has exclusive ownership of its staff, no matter how hard you try to stop them leaving. In the mid-90s we made technicians sign ten-year contracts that carried big fines if they left, and we refused to pass on their personnel files to future employers. We also had three rules when taking on university graduates: nobody from famous universities, nobody from developed areas, nobody with very good grades – and even then we couldn't keep the people we did take on. We were even scared to go to international printing press exhibitions – the technicians and VPs from the international firms' Chinese offices were all our former employees. At that point, our salaries for scientific and technical staff were half the market rate. The market rate for a graduate with three to five years of experience was 18,000 yuan a year, and in foreign firms it was tens of thousands more. We were only paying 7,000 or 8,000 yuan. Back then it was the practice of "eating from the same pot" (大锅饭) – some members of the same cohort of graduates from three years prior might have become head designers, others might still need to work under supervision, but they had exactly the same salary, with maybe 20–30 yuan difference in bonuses. We'd never have become the firm we are today if we'd kept that up. So, we tried salary negotiations. First, we set salary levels with reference to market rates, to better allocate our overall salary spending, focusing on the key people who would help us survive and grow. Next, negotiating salaries ended a

situation in which salaries were determined entirely by seniority and at that point bonuses were used to reward actual results. Subsequently, salaries reflected employees' contributions, as well as the risks and responsibilities of their work, and that encouraged them to be innovative. Third, there was an end to egalitarianism – it was all down to your abilities and your achievements. It was no longer the case that salaries went up but rarely down, so our spending on salaries was more effective. The outcome of the first round of salary talks in 1997 resulted in salaries being changed for sixty-one technicians, with salaries ranging from 2,100 to 700 yuan per month. Eleven technicians, or 20%, saw increases of 500 yuan a year or more. Thirty-two saw increases between 100 and 500 yuan. Fourteen – more than 20% of the department – received increases of less than 100 yuan and received less than the average salary. One person saw no change and three had their pay cut. The differences in salaries increased from 20–30 yuan to 400–500 yuan, and up to 900 yuan. In the second round of talks in 1998, fifty-four people saw increases of up to 400 yuan. Salaries for our technicians started to approach market levels for our industry, and that solved some problems, but we still couldn't compete with the multinationals. Staff we'd trained would still leave – especially those with good foreign language skills.

DL saw the same issues. The company's human resources head said:

You have to look at the reasons why educated workers leave. Some want a better salary; some feel they're not making use of their talents, and some want a better environment. Some think they aren't taken seriously by management or don't get along with colleagues. In most cases it's salary. So, we started salary reforms and built up our personnel. Talented personnel, in particular, we could pay a bit more, even if not always very much more. Increased salaries helped a bit, but they [foreign firms] still had advantages, and talented people who were able to leave still left.

Starting in the early 1990s, DL only took on 100-plus graduates a year, and never recruited more frontline workers.

The market gave SOE technicians more bargaining power, but their salaries were still below those of managers. A technical employee with YC said:

My managers were salaried and got more. We were also salaried, but we were paid less than managers. If you didn't think that was fair, you could leave. But most people put up with it and didn't bother leaving.

Our study found that young technicians with in-demand skills and good foreign language abilities were most likely to leave, while those over the age of forty tended to stick with stable SOE jobs, which they found more attractive. SOE technicians found themselves on the labor market for skilled technical personnel, but as they competed individually their competitiveness was limited. This group was made up of isolated but highly mobile individuals.

3.3 Aging and Internal Replacement of Skilled Workers

Overall hiring by SOEs has been steadily decreasing, and this has also been the case in the four SOEs studied. There has been virtually no recruitment of formal employees since 2000, outside of the occasional hiring of the children of retired workers on the condition that they have a relevant educational background. Thus, the average age of skilled workers on long-term contracts is increasing.

At DL the majority of skilled workers were employed in 1968, when 1,000 "politically sound" ("根红苗正") employees were taken on. During restructuring, there was initially a recruitment freeze and then various measures were taken to encourage employees to resign. Prior to 1995, the company had 5,000 employees, while at the time of the study in 2004 it had only 2,500. The company's labor and human resources head said:

> In 1995, we started a full labor-contract system. That was a major reform. Apart from the general manager and the Party secretary, every employee signed a labor contract. There were also some management changes. Then, as we became a corporation, we started to cut staff numbers, as the burdens of being an SOE were too heavy. Mainly, people were pensioned off, sent home on reduced pay or they found other jobs within the company or elsewhere. A very small number were simply made redundant ... People weren't worried, as we were offering good settlements. Second-tier (auxiliary) staff might earn 1,300 or 1,400 yuan a month, but could retire on 1,000 and happily stay at home. All they had to do was apply, and some were happy to do that. Some used their pension to start their own small businesses. The youngest female retiree was 48, she went to look after her mother, who was sick, and still got 900 yuan a month. We cut numbers by 1,300 in 2002. Then we carried out salary reform, with big increases for those still at their posts. The average annual salary had been 17,000 or 18,000 yuan, but that went up to 24,000 yuan. We cut staff, but became more efficient.

It was a similar story at JD, as one team leader described:

Our oilfield started up in 1976. There was a big find and all the factories sent experienced employees to work here, just with a bag or two of belongings. There was no concept of home; you just went where you were sent. Workers nowadays don't have that same idea of working for your country, now it's all about personal worth. Anyway, the oil industry does still have its traditions. Up until 2002, any of our children could come and work here, as long as they went to technical school. And we wanted to employ them, since they didn't need any particular encouragement, and they'd have already been taught about love of the Party and country by their elders. They'd grown up around the oilfields, they saw it every day. They'd been immersed in that spirit of sacrifice.

Skilled workers formally employed by the four industrial SOEs all signed long-term contracts (usually five years, but sometimes more than ten years) and most were at least technical school graduates, were union members, and had certain managerial responsibilities, such as being team leader or deputy team leader. They had relatively good salaries, job security and welfare. These people, with close links to the traditional SOE system, are still the backbone of the modern SOE, but this cohort is aging and not being replaced, and the stability and status they enjoy may not be continued.[11]

3.4 Large-scale Use of Cheap Informal Labor by Industrial SOEs

Our research found that industrial SOEs are relying heavily on cheap informal labor, mainly supplied by migrant workers who make up one third or more of total employees and who receive much lower wages and welfare provisions than formal employees. We found at least two methods of using informal labor – subcontracting and temporary employment.

3.4.1 Subcontracting

In the case of subcontracting, the provision of labor is separated from the SOE. A subcontractor-foreman (包工头) organizes teams of qualified manual workers from rural areas and the team takes on production work from the SOE. Short-term contracts are signed between the workers and the subcontractor, usually for a one-year period.

DL used large numbers of subcontracted laborers. In one particularly memorable scene, permanent SOE employees and subcontracted labors

---

[11] Replacement mechanisms are an extremely complex issue. At DJ, long-standing employees objected when the company stopped recruiting the children of existing staff. This topic will be researched in more depth and the findings published at a later date.

were working on one site but under entirely different conditions, and eating and washing in different facilities. Yet subcontracted workers accounted for almost half of the company's output and were doing the most difficult and tiring tasks for half the wages of regular employees. In 2004, DL had 2,500 long-term employees, but it also employed between thirty and forty subcontracted squads of workers, the smallest of which numbered fifty to sixty people, the largest, 200 or 300. In total, there were 1,900 subcontracted workers, making up 43.2% of the total workforce.

Subcontracted labor had become a key part of the company's operations. The company's labor and human resources department had a special section dedicated to the management of subcontracted labor, with staff to oversee the work. The main task of this section was to check the quality of work carried out by subcontracted labor: "We audit the subcontractors every year and almost every year we let some go and bring others up to standard, usually over safety and wage issues." The company worked on the principle that whoever was employing the labor was responsible for the management of the labor, and subcontracted workers were employed in basic-level workshop jobs.

JT Shipping is one of these subcontractors. One team leader, Mr. Liu, was born in 1967 and is originally from Nantong, Jiangsu. After graduating from university in the early 1980s, he was assigned to work at a shipping firm but due to low wages he went into business for himself in the early 1990s. Three years later, his links with the leaders of various shipbuilding firms won him contracts and he started organizing teams of laborers to work at their shipyards. He has continued doing this for over a decade. Initially, his company employed fifty people and, at the time of our interview (2004), the number had increased to over 100. Most of his employees came from rural areas and were unskilled, receiving training on the job. There were a small number of technical school graduates, mostly electricians. The oldest of his employees was forty-five. The average monthly wage was about 1,500 yuan, which was lower than the wages earned by permanent employees. Mr. Liu said: "So in this shipyard (DL) at the moment, you can say it's mostly subcontracted labor, supplemented by SOE employees. Nine subcontractors can build nine boats ... subcontracting is a trend, a natural trend. A lot of SOEs just won't exist in the future."[12]

3.4.2   Temporary Labor

Temporary laborers, also called dispatch workers, are rural workers recruited by the local labor authorities. This recruitment takes two forms: in one, contracts

---

12   Interviewers were Tong Xin and Wang Chunlai; material was compiled by Wang Chunlai.

are signed with a recruitment agency, and in the other, with the SOE itself. These are short-term contracts, usually for one year.

About one third of JD's workers were temporary laborers; some were migrants recruited by a company in Gansu Province who signed contracts with and were paid by the Gansu company. Others were from Hebei and were recruited by an agency, but signed contracts with JD. These workers received compensation that was approximately two thirds that of regular employees (the difference was mainly accounted for by the lack of welfare payments). These workers received industrial accident insurance and basic safety equipment was provided by JD, but they had no other welfare provisions and did not get the holidays given to permanent employees. Despite only offering one year contracts, however, JD hoped to retain these employees for the long term and any worker who stayed for eight years was eligible for formal employment.

It is extremely unfair that workers doing the same job do not receive the same wages and conditions, but this is commonly the case at industrial SOEs and it has become the best way for these firms to reduce labor costs.

Labor relations in industrial SOEs are hierarchical in nature, with managers maintaining close links with the state, receiving both political and economic protection, and enjoying absolute control. Technicians are in market demand, but are isolated individuals. Skilled workers enjoy traditional SOE protections, but are aging and will not be replaced. The use of large quantities of cheap informal labor has taken the hierarchical model of labor to its extreme, and the structure of this model gives rise to a particular form of labor relations.

4   Simple Control Model of Labor Relations

Companies of any type face issues of authority and control. Even if managers view workers purely as commodities, basic rights must be respected and systems of incentives and sanctions must be used to ensure that they work efficiently. Moreover, no matter what kind of control workers are subject to, they retain their own agency and logic and may choose to resist, negotiate, compromise or accede.

Research has found that, thanks to hierarchical labor markets, SOEs use simple control over their employees. The concept of simple control comes from research by Edwards (1979), who identified three stages of control in modern industry. Simple control is the control of manufacturing processes, including planning, allocation of tasks and direction of production. Technical control is achieved through the evaluation of completed work and relies on monitoring technology and the development of the necessary environment and conditions. This form of control arose alongside assembly lines and standardized manufacturing and its most significant outcome was the submission of individual workers to rules set by the employer. Bureaucratic control relies on rewards and punishments and is embedded in the social structures of the company bureaucracy as a whole; it can only be achieved once technical control has been realized. Critics of Edwards stress that these three methods of control can co-exist, rather than proceeding from one to the other. We hold that if the planned economy era saw top-down loyalty and protection relations, today's control methods have been simplified, and while technical and bureaucratic controls may exist, these are not the most common; the most common method we found was managers using their absolute power over workers to manage production. Although incentives and sanctions may exist, the instability of external labor markets means that these are simply supplemental to salaries. This situation suggests that management of SOEs has been degraded, and many valuable SOE traditions are being lost as a generation of employees retires.

4.1   Strong Managerial Control Aimed at Results and Safety

As managers of state assets, SOE managers have shifted from the ideologically oriented control of the planned economy era to focusing on results and safety. Since 1987, managers at the factory level have taken responsibility for their own work, and the ultimate outcome of the state devolution of power and profit has been that managers seek their own benefit. There are many ways to increase efficiency, including technological innovation, expanding markets and reducing labor costs. Managers' short term interests, however, dictate that the simplest measure – controlling labor costs – is used. This means managers adopt a simple control method over workers, with the aim of getting the work done as long as safety is ensured. At YC, the approach is "quasi-military." One mining team leader explained:

> In practice, because we want workers to be fastidious and work exactly by the book, it's military-style management. It's not just when they're working; anywhere on site is the same, whether they're walking somewhere or eating. They walk in formation. There are rules for every single thing – from how you get down into the mine, to how you get to the coalface, to what you do there, it's all pre-decided. In some cases the rules are posted in the workplace – who is responsible for what, how things are to be done, where you work, how you work. There are lots of rewards, but also lots of punishments. For example this year we're using a monthly safety ratio – if there aren't any injuries in a work unit for one month, and no major

> breaches, no red cards or yellow cards – and if the unit maintains that for three months in a row, everyone gets 1,500 yuan. The whole team – 1,500 yuan each. And safety inspectors, site team managers, managers – they can all fine you [for infractions].

The aim of the military-style management and rewards and punishments is not to make labor more efficient – it is more about safety, albeit in a simple and crude manner. Under these basic controls, workers are tools subordinated to processes.

4.2 Union Protections Exist in Name Only

Worker-oriented management systems must have the interests of workers as a foundation. The survey found that although all of the companies had sound union structures, the unions actually functioned only in service of the simple control of workers and rarely acted to protect workers' rights. First, unions were in place only to protect regular employees; second, managers did not see unions as interlocutors, but as tools to help ensure safe production.

DL had a robust union organization, but its tasks consisted primarily of resolving disputes, providing health check-ups and family planning, ensuring maternity protections for female workers, and providing funeral arrangements for deceased workers. The union used unallocated time for cultural activities, such as group exercise and sports competitions. Education, training and safety were also key parts of the union's work and it had an education office that ran a night school, computer training and cultural classes, Party classes, a newsletter, and a small library; it also provided safety education and monitoring. Talking about the role of the union, a recently retired factory union chief said in 2003:

> The union protects the company's interests first, in order to be able to protect the workers' interests. They can't just worry about one side ... the company's interests are production and operations, and the union needs to be part of the production process. That's the only way you keep both the management and the Party happy.... For over ten years, we've been working on production – providing training and competitions, and educating the workers ... At the workshop level, our work is mainly about production and an important part of our role is to work with management, to understand their position, to cooperate. The union doesn't have any real power; we rely on good relations and respect. A lot of the union's work depends on management, approving holidays, disbursing funds, allocating housing, so on. When female workers are pregnant they can

go home and their job stays open, but they only get 300, or maybe 500 yuan; the union has to go and speak on their behalf, but it comes down to how much respect the union chair has. If you're too young, workers won't give you face and you won't get anything done ... A union chair's work relies on relationships, connections, and respect, not power. So, it's better if you're a bit older.[13]

The unions should protect the interests of all workers, but they appear unable to help temporary, mainly migrant, labor. The DL union chair said:

> The people brought by the subcontractor-foreman are building ships as well, but they're just subcontracted. We're responsible for monitoring and checking quality, just like the customer. The subcontractors have technical qualifications but there's a lot of labor turnover. It's just like the people sent to work at our factory by outside [contracting] companies. In terms of relations, they're not our responsibility, but the bosses certainly won't protect their interests, so if we don't, they're helpless. Some come to see us because their wages aren't being paid. They're working at our shipyard, so while they might not be our employees, I still think we should do a little for them. But we can't take responsibility, like we do with SOE employees, so we just do a little bit here and there. We haven't yet asked them to form a union.

One subcontractor-foreman, Mr. Liu of JT Shipping, described his understanding of the unions:

> A proper union would be good for us too, because unions in China aren't the same as those overseas. It's best if the unions aren't too partial towards the workers, but they can play a role in keeping things stable. But the workers haven't asked to form a union; perhaps it's not something they're aware of.

The union acknowledges that market pressures mean that companies must achieve results, and when that is the companies' only target, the union struggles to help protect workers' rights.

---

13   The interviewee served three terms as a union chair, between 1991 and 2003. Interviewers were Tong Xin and Wang Chunlai; material was compiled by Wang Chunlai.

4.3 The Unfairness and Cruelty of the Market toward Cheap Informal Labor

SOEs previously did not employ cheap informal labor, which is now mainly supplied by migrant workers. Such hiring was the sole preserve of private firms and export-oriented factories. But the increasing use of migrant labor by SOEs has shown the unfairness of the market, and how it has an important effect on all workers – the loss of job security.

The combination of segregated urban-rural labor markets and low agricultural incomes has legitimized the exploitation of migrant workers, a situation that helps support the use of the simple control model in industrial SOEs. When SOE technicians start negotiating as individuals to realize the market value of their labor, and the separation of regular and temporary workers strengthens market segregation, migrant workers become the largest labor reserve available to SOEs and the informal labor market encourages fierce competition. When analyzing power relations, Edwards (1979) focused on internal labor markets, regarding social relationships in the workplace as, in part, a labor exchange system, resolving issues such as promotion, exchanging work and setting wages. Burawoy further discussed how internal labor markets promote, hide and protect the ideological basis for the extraction of surplus value (Burawoy 2008, 101). SOEs can use cheap informal labor markets to easily resolve problems of motivating, promoting and replacing workers.

There is fierce competition between subcontracted and temporary workers, which reduces the likelihood of resistance and keeps the cost of labor low. Mr. Liu, a DL subcontractor-foreman, said:

> There are competition issues. If I offer a low salary, the workers change companies. Sometimes, they switch companies over a one yuan difference. Sichuan workers in particular are picky ... Say someone's level of skill means he only gets thirty or forty yuan [a day], say forty is the absolute maximum and thirty is reasonable. Then some other subcontractor-foreman offers sixty – that happens – and so the worker comes to me and says, "Someone else is offering sixty, so you need to pay me twenty more." I can't do that. I know how skilled he is. He's worth forty, so I have to let him go and he switches companies. And for the first month or two he'll get his sixty yuan a day because they need the workers, but once the team is full, the team leader will start letting people go or cutting wages, and if you don't like it, he'll let you go.

The above statement indicates contention between workers and contractor-foremen. The outcome is disappointing and also predictable, as the contractors have the psychological advantage. This encourages collusion between them, making resistance by the workers impossible. At DL, we found subcontracted teams of workers formed on regional lines – a "Sichuan team," an "Anhui team," etc. These teams would sometimes demand increased wages, but these informal organizations were very weak. Meanwhile, the contractor-foremen were colluding, as they feared excessive competition among them. Nine contractor-foremen signed agreements not to take workers from other teams. Although this did not entirely stem the flow of labor among teams, their collusion was backed by DL, weakening the ability of workers to resist and further exacerbating the use of subcontracted labor at the company.

There were also similarities at JD, which used large numbers of migrant laborers on short-term contracts. As mentioned above, this company was located far from residential areas and so its formal employees worked 22 consecutive days followed by eight days of leave. Temporary workers were used to cover those eight days. Large numbers of migrant workers provide SOEs with a cheap and easily managed pool of labor. Mr. Du from Hebei Province was one such contract worker. Thirty-two years old, he had been working at JD for over a year. He told us:

> The recruitment agency back home got over 500 recruits. Over 100 of them went to mines in northern China, and the same number came here. It says in our contract that if we work here for 8 years, we get a regular job. We're not in a union, but the formal employees are. We prefer working for a big SOE, you can be sure you'll get paid. In a good year you can make 20,000 yuan. In a poor year, 14,000 or 15,000, plus another 3,000 if you don't take any trips home. Most people our age at home have left to find work. You can't stay there, what would you do? There's next to no money in agriculture. You farm for a year and you'll make back the money for seeds and fertilizer, but you won't have much left over. And my family doesn't have much land. We only had six *mu* to start with, and then the government wanted to reforest some, so we reforested 1.2 *mu*, leaving less than 5 *mu*, which my wife, back home, farms. We're not all working together [speaking of his colleagues] because we're from the same place. We just ended up together. So, as long as we get along well, it's OK. Another advantage of working for an SOE is that if you are ever in an accident, they will take care of you. We've all got insurance for that. I used to work processing steel at a [private] factory back home. If anything happened there, you'd consider yourself lucky if you got 10,000 or 20,000 yuan. But at an SOE, accidents are less common, and the compensation is better if there is one.

The flexibility and low cost of the informal labor market is the foundation of the simple control model used in industrial SOEs, and it prevents resistance by regular employees, who stay obedient in order to ensure stability of employment. The informal labor market works against both temporary and regular employees, and works in favor of those owning the means of production.

5 Conclusion and Theoretical Discussion

The restructuring of China's industrial SOEs is now effectively complete: companies have been transformed into state-owned firms operating according to modern company law. In these firms, labor relations have taken on a hierarchical nature, with actors operating in different labor markets and acting according to different sets of logic. Managers have been absorbed into a government-oriented bureaucracy and, with government encouragement, work toward result-oriented targets. Managers, technicians, regular employees and temporary employees operate in different labor markets and, therefore, are rewarded differently, receive different levels of welfare provision, are subject to different reward and punishment schemes, and have different training opportunities.

Hierarchies provide the foundation for the simple control model of labor relations found in industrial SOEs. This form of labor relations, however, is not created solely within the company – it relies heavily on the informal labor market, on the rural-urban division of labor and the large pool of available migrant labor, all of which allow for the use of simple control, which is the cheapest option. Meanwhile the simple control model is tacitly accepted by various state forces, undercuts the roles of unions, and splits regular and temporary employees in the labor market.

First, the simple control model is different from the "disorganized despotism" described by Ching Kwan Lee. On one hand, we do not want to use overly Western terms such as "despotism" or "hegemony." On the other hand, the control of labor we witnessed in SOEs was simple and crude – managers were in complete control and they openly and deliberately used cheap, informal labor, which they regarded as a magic bullet allowing them to hit company targets. The existence of a harsh informal labor market allows managers to achieve simple control.

Second, do relations of loyalty and protection exist between the upper and lower strata in SOEs? If so, it is only between the state and company managers – the state empowers managers and offers key material protections. Any state protection of workers has already been devolved to the market. Some older employees still receive state labor protections, but as this cohort retires, the SOEs will look to the market for replacements.

Third, the current state of labor relations in SOEs creates concern for the future of these firms – simple control of labor is aimed at short-term targets, but hampers the accumulation of both the human and social capital that are mainly based on trust. An SOE that relies on the informal labor market will be unable to develop harmonious labor relations based on collective negotiations, and will be subject to various hazards and legitimacy crises. The most important task for SOEs to undertake would be to rebuild human and social capital and unite their employees.

References

Burawoy, Michael. 2008. 制造同意 – 垄断资本主义劳动过程的变迁 [*Manufacturing Consent: Changes in the Labor Process under Monopoly Capitalism*]. Beijing: The Commercial Press.

Edwards, Richard. 1979. *Contested Terrain: The Transformation of the Workplace in the Twentieth Century*. London: Heinemann.

Lee, Ching Kwan 李静君. 1999. "From organized dependence to disorganized despotism: Changing labour regimes in Chinese factories," *The China Quarterly*, 157: 44–71.

Li Erjin 李铒金. 2003. 车间政治与下岗名单的确定 – 以东北的两家国有工厂为例 ["Workshop politics and deciding who gets laid off – examples from two state-owned factories in the north-east"]. 社会学研究 [*Sociological Studies*], 6: 13–23.

Li Hanlin 李汉林 and Li Lulu 李路路. 1999. 资源与交换 – 中国单位组织中的依赖性结构 ["Resources and exchange: structure of reliance in China's work units"]. 社会学研究 [*Sociological Studies*], 4: 44–63.

Li Peilin 李培林. 1992. 转型中的中国企业: 国有企业组织创新论 [*Chinese Companies in Transition: On Innovation in the Organization of State-owned Companies*]. Jinan: Shandong People's Publishing House.

Luo Jin 罗进. 2001. 跨国公司在华战略 [*The China strategies of multinational companies*]. Shanghai: Fudan University Press.

Ohno, Kenichi. 2006. 日本发展之旅的经验 ["Lessons from Japan's path to development"]. 比较 [*Comparative Studies*], 24: 182–183.

Oi, Jean C. 1986. "Peasant Households between Plan and Market: Cadre Control over Agricultural Inputs." *Modern China* 12 (2): 230–251.

Shen Yuan 沈原. 2006. 社会转型与工人阶级的再形成 ["Social change and the reformation of the working class"]. 社会学研究 [*Sociological Studies*], 2: 13–36.

Shen Yuan 沈原. 2007. 市场、阶级与社会 [*Markets, class and society*]. Social Sciences Academic Press.

Tong Xin 佟新. 2002. 社会变迁与工人社会身份的重构 ["Social change and the rebuilding of workers' social identity"] 社会学研究 [*Sociological Studies*], 6: 1–12.

Tong Xin 佟新. 2006. 延续的社会主义文化传统 – 一起国有企业工人集体行动个案分析 ["Continuing socialist traditions: a case study of mass worker action in one SOE"]. 社会学研究 [*Sociological Studies*], 1: 59–76.

Walder, Andrew G. 1996. 共产党社会的新传统主义: 中国工业中的工作环境和权力结构 [*Communist Neo-Traditionalism: Work and Authority in Chinese Industry*], translated by Gong Xiaoxia 龚小夏. Hong Kong: Oxford University Press.

Wang Hansheng 王汉生, et al. 1992. 从等级性分化到集团性分化: 单位制在现阶段城市分化中的作用 ["From differentiating by class to differentiating by group: the role of the work unit in the current stage of urbanization"]. 社会学与社会调查 [*Sociological Studies and Social Survey*], Beijing Society of Sociology, vol. 1.

Zhang Jing 张静. 2001. 利益组织化单位 – 企业职代会案例研究 [*Organised Interests in Work units – Case Studies of Company Workers Representatives Committees*]. Beijing: China Social Sciences Press.

CHAPTER 4

Changes in Production Models within State-Owned Enterprises under the "Double Transformations:" the Rise of Internal Labor Subcontracting in City A's Nanchang Factory (2001–2013)

Jia Wenjuan (贾文娟)
Translated by Shayan Momin

Abstract

This article analyzes the "internal labor subcontracting" production model within a state-owned enterprise through the lens of labor process theory. Analyzing the emergence and development of internal labor subcontracting shows how the rise of transnational labor processes under economic globalization and market transition shaped the practical logic behind the reform of China's state-owned enterprises and helped state-owned enterprises integrate themselves into a local practice of neoliberal globalization characterized by "flexible accumulation." This paper argues that the change in production models was spurred by two logics: (1) the reorganization of production under transnational labor processes and (2) labor substitution under shop floor politics. If Western enterprises shifted from Fordism-Keynesianism to flexible accumulation by "spatial adjustment" strategies, then Chinese state-owned enterprises integrated themselves into a global production system dependent upon flexible accumulation by utilizing an informal labor market to directly transform internal production models.

Keywords

state-owned enterprises – internal labor subcontracting – flexible accumulation

1   State-Owned Enterprises in Transition: Production Models[1]

During the planned economy era, production in state-owned enterprises (SOEs) was organized through the "work unit (单位)-factory" system, which combined political integration, social control and production incentives. Within this production model, the state managed social relations and production within SOEs. Through mandatory production quotas, the state monitored output. Through political campaigns, the state implemented the management methods spelled out in the "Anshan Iron and Steel Constitution" (鞍钢宪法), thus setting fixed rules about social relations within state-owned enterprises. In the 1990s, the "work unit-factory" production model started to change, and researchers found that factory management's power in controlling production dramatically increased. Managers began using many new methods to strengthen management of production. "Disorganized despotism" became a feature of controlling labor in SOEs (Lee 1999). Further reforms completely transformed the "work unit-factory" production model. Through a comparative analysis of two SOEs, Zhao Wei discovered that after reforms, SOEs ended lifetime employment for workers and pursued modern enterprise management systems such as total quality management, total productive maintenance, and the 5S management system to increase labor productivity (Zhao 2010). As Mary Gallagher has pointed out, SOEs tend to be similar to other types of enterprises with regard to labor management and production control (Gallagher 2010). At the same time, the Polanyi-type labor unrest of laid-off SOE workers was gradually absorbed by society, and the once-glorious working class was lost to history. Research on production models within SOEs gradually faded out of view.

The train of history, however, does not simply stop. Today, more than ten years after the reform of SOEs, production models within SOEs have changed dramatically. From 2010 to 2013, I conducted fieldwork in a state-owned heavy machinery manufacturer, Nanchang, located in City A. Through my fieldwork, I found that production in Nanchang was heavily dependent upon on "subcontracting teams" (外协包工队, literally, "externally-coordinated contracting teams"). Under this system, the manager introduces subcontracting teams to the factory workshops and provides them with production materials (boards, space to work, electricity, gas, equipment, etc.) and tools. The subcontractor-foreman (包工头) then recruits laborers and is responsible for part of the production. As contracted production happens in enterprise workshops and not in private workshops, this article will refer to this form of subcontracted labor as an "internal labor subcontracting" (入厂包工, literally "into-the-factory

---

[1] This article originally appeared in *Open Times* 2015, no. 3, pp. 64–77.

subcontracting"), and refer to its production model as the internal labor subcontracting system.

The reappearance of the labor subcontracting system under neoliberalism is not a new issue. Many scholars have already studied the phenomenon of labor contracting in labor-intensive industries such as construction and clothing and toy manufacturing. However, few studies have paid attention to the emergence and operation of this particular production model within SOEs. This article will not only introduce the operation of the labor contract system within SOEs, but will use a case study of a factory to show how the production model within SOEs changed from a "work unit-factory" system to an "internal labor subcontracting" system against the backdrop of globalization and market transformation. Additionally, the practical logic behind the shift in SOE production will be analyzed using an approach based in labor process theory, local particularities, and history.

Research on the change in modes of production within SOEs can help us see that China has moved out of the planned economy era and is integrating itself into a local practice of a global economic system characterized by "flexible accumulation." According to David Harvey, global capitalism underwent a transformation from Fordism-Keynesianism to "flexible accumulation" starting in the 1980s (Harvey 2004). So-called "flexible accumulation" refers to a system of capital accumulation characterized by more malleable labor processes, market and geographic mobility, and rapid changes in consumer practices. Harvey believes that Western capital, with the help of neoliberal globalization, uses spatial adjustment strategies to transfer Western production sites to Third World countries in order to resolve the problem of falling profits and to complete a kind of historical transformation. This article argues that unlike Western enterprises, China's SOEs have incorporated themselves into the flexible accumulation model through direct transformation of production models.

2 Nanchang and Production Organization under the "Internal Labor Subcontracting" Production Model

2.1 *Introduction to Nanchang*

Founded in 1953, Nanchang is a wholly state-owned heavy machinery enterprise located in the heart of the Pearl River Delta in City A. I conducted ethnographic fieldwork in Nanchang's S Branch from November 2010 to July 2011, and once again from July 2013 to November 2013. During the planned economy era, Nanchang was one of six heavy machinery factories affiliated with the First Machinery Department of the First Industrial Bureau of the People's Republic of China (PRC). It was the largest general-use machinery manufacturer in southern China. In the 1990s, Nanchang began diversifying its operations and formed forty-three subsidiaries, each as legal entities. In 2000, Nanchang faced financial hardship and owed 780 million yuan to banks. In order to reduce its burden and revitalize itself, Nanchang laid off more than three thousand workers between 2002 and 2003.[2]

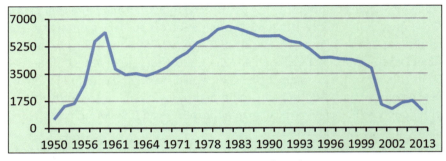

FIGURE 4.1   Change in the number of employees in Nanchang from 1950–2013

In 2001, City A's government was promoting the development strategy of "Opening the Market in Exchange for Technologies" (以市场换技术). That year, Nanchang began cooperating with Germany's H Company, the world's largest tunnel boring machine manufacturer. Before entering the Chinese market, H Company already controlled seventy percent of the European market (Ma 2006). After China joined the WTO, H Company began to make advances within the Chinese market and started cooperating with SOEs in Sichuan and Beijing to establish original equipment manufacturing (OEM) and assembly bases. By 2012, H Company controlled over seventy percent of China's shield tunneling machine market.[3] Cooperating with H Company changed Nanchang's primary business. Nanchang's S Branch was one of the few factories in the Pearl River Delta with an AR1 level qualification that allowed them to manufacture ultra-high-pressure vessels. Before 2001, S Branch mainly focused on designing and producing acid-resistant pumps and other kinds of metal pressure vessels. The factory used machine processing, high-precision welding, heat-forging, welding and riveting. Each step in production – from raw materials procurement, to cutting and blanking, bending, welding, parts production, assembly and painting – was handled by Nanchang factory. After

---

2   Nanchang was formally established in 1953, but its predecessor had been established in 1947. For this reason, figures for the number of employees date back to 1950. These figures include employees in Nanchang's predecessor company.
3   See "The Urban 'Tunnel Warfare' Starring Shield Machines" (《盾构机正在领衔主演城市 "地道战"》), China jijing web (中国机经网): http://www.mei.net.cn/news/2012/01/409307 .html. Accessed September 20, 2013.

CHANGES IN PRODUCTION MODELS WITHIN STATE-OWNED ENTERPRISES 79

beginning cooperation with H Company, production in S Branch changed significantly. It only produced machine bodies, cutter heads, trailers and other parts for manufacturing shield tunneling machines, and became one link in a larger transnational production process. To see more about production in Nanchang factory, see Figure 4.2.

FIGURE 4.2 Nanchang's business distribution

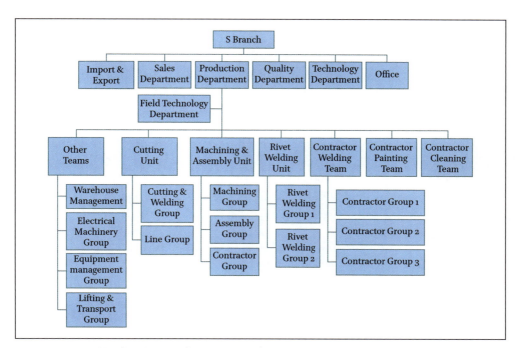

FIGURE 4.3 Nanchang's S Branch organization diagram

2.2   The Operation of the "Internal Labor Subcontracting" System

In 2001, Nanchang's S Branch began to employ a small number of subcontracting teams to help make up gaps in welding work. In 2008, the number of internal labor subcontracting teams increased dramatically. By 2011, Nanchang started to use contractors for cutting and welding during busy periods, and by 2013, Nanchang had four subcontracting teams working in welding, which exceeded the number of regular factory work teams. Currently, under the internal labor subcontracting system, contractors take on one-fourth of the production tasks of S Branch, and two-thirds of the welding tasks. In daily production, welding usually requires eighty to one hundred contracted workers. During rush periods, the total number of subcontracting teams can reach as high as two hundred workers, while factory welders only number around fifty.

2.2.1   The Role of Contractors in Production

In producing shield tunneling machines, the Nanchang purchasing department first procures the necessary plates. Then, lines for cutting blanks are sketched onto the materials, and the cutting and welding teams are responsible for turning large plates into sizes and shapes suitable for production. The workshop scheduler records and allocates the production process, and gives out the work tickets. Then most of the plates go into welding. Welding is the core process in producing machine bodies for shield tunneling machines. The welding teams have to bend and weld large steel plates together in order to produce a machine body. Additionally, plates inside the machine body and those used for auxiliary parts have different specifications, and as other workplaces in the factory require machined steel plates, some of the steel plates enter the machining process. When making the cutter body of the machine, it is necessary for workers to use two hundred boring or milling machines as well as other kinds of large equipment used for processing large pieces. Once these steps are completed, the assembly team assembles the machine. After the machine body is painted, it is checked and prepared for shipment. Nanchang's welding unit uses many subcontracting teams in production. The blanking, machining and assembly units also introduce subcontracting teams into the production processes. These teams use Nanchang's worksites, materials, and tools for production.

From 2001 to 2008, permanent workers who had signed labor contracts directly with Nanchang were considered to be the factory's main production force. Subcontracted laborers were only considered to be auxiliaries. But from 2008 onwards, subcontracting teams became as important to factory production as formal workers. A manager in S Branch told me: "As long as there are admittance systems, check-up systems, and the market, shield machine production does not require our permanent workers." Permanent workers often complained: "Well ... now everything is done by subcontracting teams. Our own tasks have been reduced to basically nothing. It seems like they're the main producers and we're the contract laborers." Using permanent workers to threaten subcontracting teams or using subcontracting teams to threaten permanent workers became an effective management strategy. As a result, both permanent workers and subcontracting teams came to believe they were only marginal to the needs of production.

The perception of their respective positions within production created mutual hostility between permanent workers and subcontracting teams. Permanent workers believed subcontracting team workers were unskilled, shortsighted profit-seekers who were stealing jobs. One permanent worker said: "Contract workers work continuously and they work overtime. The money they get is extra to them. Do you think they're willing to work hard? They don't even have social security! When they're finished, they'll just go home. All the people who get workplace injuries are contract workers!" Conversely, contract workers think permanent workers are all lazy good-for-nothings who are protected by the enterprise. When I asked a contract worker if he wanted social insurance, he replied in a scornful tone: "Who needs that crap? We make double what permanent workers make!"

2.2.2 Subcontracting Team Composition and Salaries

The vast majority of the contract workers we spoke with were migrant workers without urban *hukou* (户口, household registration) in City A. Their education level was mostly junior high school and below, they ranged in age from under twenty years old to over fifty years old, and all were male. Like construction workers, they had all found their jobs through introductions made by friends or family members and they followed a contractor-foreman "like a vine of grapes" into production sites to work. The contract workers often came from the same area and were related in some way. They shared the same dialects, as well as the same eating and dress habits, forming "contractor kingdoms" that could not be fully integrated into Nanchang's work-unit community. Most contract workers were not highly educated. The majority began to work after junior high school. They learned simple welding, oxygen welding and carbon dioxide welding from older workers in the group. They did not sign contracts with the contractor-foreman and did not have any form of social insurance or protection. The rural-urban split caused by the *hukou* system, combined with the split mode of social reproduction of labor and informal labor markets, made for a highly flexible labor force.[4]

---

4 Many rural households are split, with grandparents and grandchildren living in the countryside and young adults living and working in urban areas – Ed.

Technically, wages for contract workers were not paid through a piece-rate system, but instead were paid monthly. However, the specific amount was determined by the foreman in accordance with the labor situation and the skills of the individual worker, with wages sometimes varying greatly. For example, in a subcontracting team from Hubei Province, the wages for workers in the team varied from 2,500 to 6,000 yuan a month. Most had wages between 3,500 and 4,000 yuan a month. Nanchang often paid foremen on time (in accordance with the product contracts), so wage arrears rarely happened. The minimum monthly wage for workers in City A was 1,300 yuan, and the average wage for workers in Guangdong Province was 3,763 yuan. As a result, the income for contract workers was higher than expected.

2.2.3 Subcontracting Team Management

Subcontracting teams generally worked in two shifts, each shift lasting about ten hours. The contractor-foreman usually managed his team as a patriarch manages a family. For example, the foreman of one subcontracting team from Hubei was a forty-year old man. The workers all obeyed him. His salary was 6,000 yuan a month and included full social insurance, a housing stipend and a company car. The foreman went to Nanchang early every morning and made sure his workers clocked in on time. Anyone arriving late would be reprimanded. During working hours, if the foreman was not discussing the job schedule, working drawings, production materials, tools, or worksites with the workshop scheduler, he would be keeping close watch over his workers and production. The foreman set wages for his workers, and also reserved the right to deduct wages as punishment. If workers were lazy, the foreman criticized them harshly. If they did not improve, he docked their wages. If nothing else worked, he fired them. Being put on a "blacklist" was a more severe form of punishment: if a worker slowed down production or caused other trouble, his name would be entered on the blacklist and other contractor-foremen would not hire him.

Use of the "internal labor subcontracting" system allowed for greater flexibility in Nanchang's production. First, it increased the flexibility of labor use. Subcontracting teams and foremen did not sign labor contracts with Nanchang. They were "on call," meaning they could be called to work at any time, which made it easier for Nanchang to manage its labor force. Second, the system increased flexibility in labor control. Controlling contract workers did not go through any sort of bureaucratic system, labor union, party committee, or staff and workers congress. Management was completely in the hands of individual foremen and other subcontractors. Third, it improved labor price flexibility. Enterprise managers and foremen could not only adjust monthly wages according to operating conditions, but also did not have to pay any social insurance to workers. In short, after adopting this production model, enterprise capital turnover time and labor costs were both reduced.

3 The Double Transformations in Chinese Society: the Political-Economic Foundations of the Emergence of "Internal Labor Subcontractors"

Nanchang's "internal labor subcontracting" system was not the result of intentional planning by factory managers, but instead was the result of changes in political-economic conditions and a resulting transformation in SOE management. The "internal labor subcontracting" system was built on the ruins of the old "work unit-factory" system and was developed within the crevices between the old and the new systems. What, then, are the political-economic foundations for this kind of production model within SOEs? From these foundations, how can we understand the practical logic of changing production models within SOEs?

Differing from the "factory system," the "contract system" uses a production contract based on piece-rate payment. It relies on the contractor-foreman, who serves as a mediator between capital and workers, to manage the production process. The foremen usually do not possess the means of production. Some of them can provide a few producer goods. Most of their profits come from the difference between the labor cost that capital pay them and the actual wages that they pay to the workers (Marx and Engels 2004, 636–637). The traditional contractor system is represented by Britain's "middleman system", the United States' "inside contract system," and old Shanghai's contract system. The political-economic foundation for these systems is the separation of rural and urban spheres found in early-stage capitalism.[5] Additionally, in the early period of British industrialization, handicraft producers located in rural areas could only sell their products in urban areas and overseas markets with the help of middlemen. Under these conditions, the rural-urban barriers separating

---

5   For further discussion of Britain's contracting system under early-stage capitalism, refer to Xie (1989). For a detailed description of the inside contract system within the United States, see Englander (1987), Buttrick (1952) and Jones (1982). For a detailed description of the cotton mill contractor system in Shanghai before 1949, see Liu, ed. (2002, 611); for a discussion of contracting in Shanghai's shipbuilding industry before 1949, see Jing Jiang (1981, 17). For a discussion of the "gangmaster and porter system" used on the Shanghai docks before 1949, see Pei (2012, 58–59, 247) and the Committee for the Compilation of Labor Movements in Shanghai, ed. (1997, 104).

producers and consumers allowed middlemen to exist and later develop into production contractors. Before the founding of the PRC and the establishment of the formal labor market, urban enterprises could only find surplus labor from the countryside through contractor foremen with gang backgrounds. In summary, rural–urban segregation encouraged the rise of the contractor system. However, unlike traditional contractor systems, the political-economic foundations of the revival of the contractor system in SOEs are economic globalization and the shift to a market economy.

In the last thirty years, China has been at the intersection of Karl Polanyi's and Michael Burawoy's "great transformations" (Shen 2006). Polanyi's "great transformation" refers to the logic of the market becoming the dominant logic of social life. The economic globalization of the 1980s, however, was more wide-ranging and deeper than the "great transformation" that Karl Polanyi observed. David Harvey has argued that economic globalization follows a strategy that attempts to solve the crises of excessive capital accumulation through geographic expansion. This strategy has helped develop the mechanisms that create uneven geographical development, and "successful" countries have forced others to follow in their footsteps. In an endless stream, every country, region and city has been brought to the front-line of capital accumulation (Harvey 2010). With China's entry into the WTO, SOEs have been forced into the global market and have become OEM factories of transnational capital working to meet the uncertain and rapidly changing needs of the global market. Burawoy's "great transformation" refers to China's shift from a system of planned economic redistribution to a market economy. As Gallagher (2010) has argued, China's market transformation began in the private sector, then gradually penetrated state-owned sectors in the 1990s. During the 14th National Congress of the Communist Party of China (CPC) in October, 1992, the Party claimed "the reform of state-owned enterprises should change from decentralization and the transfer of profits to system transformation and institutional improvement," but this strategy for reform was not formally made until CPC's 15th National Congress in September, 1997. Afterward, to initiate reforms, the state adopted reorganization, alliances, mergers, leasing, contracting and joint-stock cooperatives, in addition to the sale of small-to medium-sized SOEs. The state also attempted to establish a modern enterprise system featuring "clear property rights, clear separation of state and enterprise, clear responsibilities, and scientific management" by "downsizing to increase efficiency" to transform large SOEs. In 1999, the 4th Plenary Session of the 15th CPC Central Committee passed the "Decision of the Central Committee of the Communist Party of China On Several Major Issues Concerning the Reform and Development of State-Owned Enterprises",[6] by which SOEs finally became independent legal entities and market subjects that were self-managing and self-financing. After this change, the goal of SOEs became the increase in both capital accumulation and profit margins, and managers made their own decisions on how to pursue these goals.

If the "double transformations" of Chinese society constitute the political-economic foundations for the change of production modes within SOEs, then widely different local practices determine its actual trajectory and results. Within neo-Marxist theory, labor process theory provides a series of conceptual tools for analyzing changes in industrial production. The labor process refers to "the relationships men and women enter when, facing nature and relying on their imagination, they transform raw materials into commodities" (Burawoy 2005, 130–131). It is made up of two analytically distinct, but actually inseparable, orientations. The first orientation is the technological and practical production process, that is, a series of actions performed by people to turn raw materials into finished products. The second orientation is the social and relational tie within production, that is, the social relations and power relations between workers and managers within the process of production. "Shop floor politics" refers to these kinds of conflict-oriented relationships in the workplace (ibid.). Production model refers to a labor process that is created within a certain political-economic context. Changes in the production process and within relationships of production will bring about changes in the production model. Under the "double transformations" within Chinese society, political economic changes were the primary force pushing SOEs to a labor contract system. But as historical institutionalism claims, the macro-political and economic environments of a system are composed of the consequences of a multitude of events and processes. The development trend of that system is shaped with the passage of time (Thelen 2010, 262). From this perspective, how did structural forces push Nanchang's production from the "work unit-factory" system to the "internal labor subcontracting" system? This can only be understood within the context of the historical practices of the labor process.

---

6 中共中央关于国有企业改革和发展若干重大问题的决定.

4 The Origin of "Internal Labor Subcontracting": the Reorganization of Production under Transnational Labor Processes

Assisted by globalization, Western enterprises adopted "spatial adjustment" strategies. To avoid dealing with powerful domestic trade unions, production was moved to Third World countries without unions. This shift created large, cross-border capital flows (Silver 2012). Transnational capital flows have created major changes in commodity production. "Transnational labor process" refers to "a production process that (1) is affected by transnational capital flows, labor flows and factory organization practices, and (2) is, in the spatial and structural senses, multileveled with transnational and global characteristics" (Ren and Pun 2006, 23). Within the flexible accumulation of capital, one important characteristic of the transnational labor process is the global separation and refinement of the production process. This separation, combined with global inequality, shifts labor-intensive original equipment manufacturing (OEM) production to developing countries. Through the global market, the production of shield tunneling machines was also restructured. H Company's products were split up: core R&D was done in Germany, complex technologies were produced by a joint venture owned by H Company, and the large structural parts of the machines were manufactured by Nanchang's S Branch. As Nanchang's S Branch was swept into the global production process, its own production processes were also transformed.

First, in production technology, OEM factories are the "disassembling link" in the transnational labor process, greatly reducing research and development, production technology and labor requirements. When S Branch was previously conducting independent research and production for pressure vessels, they needed highly-skilled engineers to guide production and workers needed to master a variety of skills to manage the complexities of production. Private contractors and factories do not have these skills or qualifications.[7] The leader of the No. 1 welding and riveting team, said to me: "To do this kind of work, you need both schooling and eight years of relevant experience. Rich experience and diagram recognition abilities are greatly demanded. Math and operational skill requirements for this work are also quite high. You must be both intelligent and energetic." However, cooperation with the German H Company changed the technical requirements of production. For example, upstream brand owners in the production process provided all production diagrams, which had

---

7 Most of Nanchang's welders have mastered manual welding, oxygen welding, vertical welding, automatic welding, carbon dioxide welding, and x-ray welding. Contract workers have only mastered commonly-used welding techniques, but they are quite skilled in them.

been simplified to the extent that engineers and skilled workers were not needed to guide production. Additionally, because there was only one product, the skills required for production were relatively simple. Workers only needed to have basic skills. Even though workers might have mastered advanced welding techniques, the techniques were seldom used in production. As a result, many workers complained that their technical certificates were useless.

Second, in production cycles, Nanchang's production time and turnaround were greatly shortened. When S Branch was producing pressure vessels, shipment time was often late by a month or so. Domestic manufacturers were used to these kinds of delays. But after starting to work with H Company, Nanchang became a link in their "just-in-time" production process. Nanchang needed to meet H Company's requirements for "accelerated production" and "timely production," or they received fines or suffered order cancellations. As a result, tight production schedules became the norm in S Branch. The head of one of S Branch's production teams told me:

> Shield tunneling machines usually take four months to ship. But H Company doesn't give us four months. Take the cutter head of the shield machine, for example – it takes them four and half months to make it themselves, but they only give us three months to make it. Just material procurement alone takes 30 days, so that leaves us only two months to produce one. Many other production tasks are just as difficult as this one.
> HKJ, July 3, 2011

Third, with production coordination, individual processes became the core of production. When Nanchang was producing pressure vessels, it used "group production" to assign work tasks and to organize production and processing among different work units before assembly. At that time, cutting blanks, machining, welding and riveting, and assembly were all of equal importance within the production process, and properly coordinating these tasks was the core task of production. Once S Branch started making shield machines for H Company, there was less of a need to coordinate different production tasks, and the question of how to improve the speed of individual processes – especially in welding – became the core question within production.

The production process at S Branch was originally organized by groups. This "group production" model originated in socialist Soviet factories. It emphasized meticulous production coordination, cohesion between the improvement of workers' skills and the design of the production process. Machines and tools were assigned to groups, clamping equipment was placed in groups, and the assembly process was organized according to groups. Parts were processed separately by different production groups to meet the demands of producing many different kinds of products in relatively small quantities (Zhang 1980). After 2001, the managers of Nanchang realized that if they did not reorganize production and move away from "the group production mode," they would be unable to meet the "flexible" demands of upstream clients. The labor market in the Pearl River Delta had consistently provided welding and riveting subcontracting teams for steel structures. These subcontracting teams used specialized skills and they coordinated labor among experienced workers. With the flexibility to adjust the labor force in accordance with market demands, these subcontracting teams were able to meet the new needs of Nanchang's production. As a result, S Branch began introducing small numbers of subcontracting teams to the factory in 2001.

As for the role of contract-labor teams within production, the head of the welding and riveting team had to admit:

> To be frank, the abilities of those subcontracting teams are not up to snuff. They make acceptable steel structures and common welding parts. For pressure vessels and boilers, usually you have to adhere to some national standards to make them, but these teams don't have the qualifications to do this. No matter how urgent it is to complete the orders, you shouldn't let them do the work. But as far as steel structures, we can't compare with them. People need quality steel structures made quickly and well. Steel structures are needed everywhere, so they make steel structures every single day. We can't really compare with them in this respect.
>
> MHZ, June 30, 2011

It can be seen that "production reorganization under transnational labor processes" was the practical logic that originally pushed SOEs to change their production mode. Most notably, before 2008, subcontracting teams were only used as supplementary labor and the factory's permanent workers were still the main production force. However, the institutional origin of this system cannot explain the system's evolution and development. It developed in accordance with its own surroundings (Thelen 2010, 261). So, why did managers expand the "internal labor subcontracting" system? As previously mentioned, the formation of new production modes depends on changes within the "production process" and the "relations within production." In order to analyze the practical logic of the change of production modes within SOEs, it is necessary to analyze the changes in the relations within productions in SOEs during market transformation.

5 The Development of "Internal Labor Subcontracting:" Labor Substitution under "Shop Floor Politics"

5.1 *Relations of Production before SOE Reform*

Before the reform of SOEs, industrial enterprises were "work units". They were not simply economic organizations, but granted people status, identity, and legitimate rights and interests also. Work units helped people meet various needs and lead secure lives. They functioned as key links of the political and social order (Lü and Perry 1997). Under the work unit system, a type of universal socialist contract existed between workers and the state. The state provided permanent employment and welfare for workers, and workers assumed the identity of "masters of the state" (主人翁) and engaged in production while remaining politically loyal to the state (Lee 2007, 12). "Neo-traditionalism" accurately describes this kind of social relation, which is rooted in patron-client reciprocity. As representatives of "moral-political" authority, workshop leaders had to provide protection to workers in order to receive their cooperation in production. This mutual dependence strengthened the relationship between the two parties (Walder 1996). Older workers at Nanchang claim that during the planned economy era, leaders respected workers. They would often visit the homes of workers to chat and resolve any problems they might be experiencing. In production, leaders would help workers resolve technical problems and discuss coping strategies with them. The salient characteristic of the period's social relations within production was reciprocity between cadres and workers. Conflicts would often occur between different groups of workers, like the conflicts between "activists" and "non-activists" described by Andrew Walder, or conflicts of interest among employees in Nanchang due to wage increases. These conflicts, however, did not affect factory production in a significant way.

5.2 *The Decline of Worker Benefits and the Rise of "Shop Floor Politics"*

The essence of SOE reform was a fundamental change in the relations of production. The goal of changing from "ownership-by-the-whole-people" (全民所有制) to "state ownership" (国家所有制) of the means of production was to turn work units – which in the socialist period had certain social responsibilities – into self-financing market actors. At its core, SOE reform sought to commodify the labor force and absolve SOEs of their social responsibilities. This goal was achieved by laying off workers and establishing a "modern enterprise system." In 2000, Nanchang was selected as one of Guangdong Province's one hundred "key modern enterprises" (Nanchang Archives 2000). From 2000 to 2002, as many as 2,349 workers were dismissed from Nanchang, and a series of "modern enterprise" reforms soon followed.[8] As a result, management power became concentrated at the highest level. Workers, who had been "masters of the state," were turned into a wage-labor force. Soon thereafter, they lost the benefits they had enjoyed during the planned economy era. First, workers lost most of the welfare benefits provided by work units. Second, they lost their social position and status within production and became "resources" to be allocated by managers. Third, wages were extremely low and managers often fined workers.

Permanent workers do not self-identify as "wage laborers" or as part of a class lower than their managers. One female worker said: "How do I say it, we workers aren't stupid. It's just that we've had a few years less schooling than those managers. To put it bluntly, the managers are merely a bit luckier than we workers. But that doesn't mean you should pay no attention to workers." A male technician was also filled with resentment: "Nowadays, leaders just make you work blindly. Work, work, work! They don't care about workers. They don't even say hi to us. They do not pay any attention to us at all." Some of these formal workers fondly recall "the glory years" of the socialist period and have nostalgia for the traditions of socialism. They are dissatisfied with the status quo, and their antipathy toward being exploited serves as the internal motor for their conflicts with management.

In this essay, "shop floor politics" refers to conflict in the relations within production at production sites. Between 2001 and 2013, the political nature of Nanchang's workshops changed dramatically. Between 2001 and 2005, reductions in benefits made workers unhappy, but, due to fear of punishment, they only reacted by complaining to management, using what they perceived as a "weapon of the weak." After 2006, individual conflicts between workers and management started to occur. For example, during a spell of hot weather, Fei

---

8   After downsizing, Nanchang launched a series of measures aimed at managing employees through rules and regulations, such as the "Head Manager Office Meeting System," the "Board of Directors Meeting System," the "Rules and Procedures for Middle-Level Teams," and the "Middle-Level Leaders Communication System." For wage management, Nanchang launched "Measures for Performance Evaluation for Workers in Main Production Workshops," "Measures for Performance Evaluation for Company Staff," "Measures for Performance Evaluation for Sales Department Staff," "Job Responsibilities in Workshops," "Job Responsibilities in Technical Departments," "Code of Conduct for Employees," "Code of Conduct for Employees (revised edition)," "Code of Conduct for Employees (2nd revised edition)," "Rules of Wearing Name Tags at Work and Punch-In Attendance Management System," "6SK Production Management System," "Incentives for Machining and Assembly Employees for Pressure Vessels Implementation Plan," and "Measures for the Management of Comprehensive Performance for Teams and Groups." After SOE reform, Nanchang's salary system changed to a "salary + bonus" system, with monthly salaries ranging from 1,100–2,000 yuan a month, and bonuses given according to performance appraisals.

Zai, a welder, decided to sit on the factory floor after completing his work. A manager saw him and threatened to fine him. Arguing with the manager, Fei Zai picked up a steel bar and chased the manager, threatening to beat him. Many people surrounded them, egging Fei Zai on. Another worker, Master Hou, used a stool to prop up some equipment as he worked. When a manager saw this, he assumed Hou was using the stool to sit down and slack off. As the manager prepared to fine Hou, another worker violently attacked the manager, also attracting a crowd. These kinds of conflicts caused Nanchang's management to soften a bit.

After 2007, labor conflicts in the workshop began to occur more frequently. The workers had several strategies to confront managers. The first strategy was to deliberately break the rules. Welding workers would get together to smoke and tell jokes, sometimes leaving their work stations to gather around the machining team's drinking-water dispenser. Another worker, Master Zhang, would put 20 yuan under his work lamp and then start smoking and playing music. When managers came to his station, he'd point to the lamp and say "The money's right there. Go ahead and take it." The second strategy was to slow down production and refuse to work. One worker was fined after going to the bathroom during work hours. Afterwards, she refused to work, saying "I only make 1,700 yuan a month. Someone as low-class as me can't possibly do such complicated work. Go find someone else to do it." In the welding division – the core of production in Nanchang – workers often said their kids were sick or that they had problems at home in order to skip overtime in the evenings and on weekends. The third strategy was to argue with and provoke management. The managers often threatened workers with dismissal (炒鱿鱼) after SOE reform. But after 2007, this became a way to provoke managers. One worker had an argument with management and when a manager threatened to fire him, he responded, "I was just thinking of retiring early. Give me twenty thousand! Fire me today, and I'll treat you to dinner tomorrow!"

For Beverly Silver, the term "Polanyi-type labor unrest" refers to the backlash from the workers who are harmed by economic transformations and who lose previously-established concessions (Silver 2012, 25). This form of unrest has been strengthened by the political and economic structure of China's transition. Ching Kwan Lee characterized China's political and economic structure as "decentralized accumulation under legal authoritarianism" (Lee 2007, 25).[9]

---

9 With regard to "decentralized legal authoritarianism," "decentralized" refers to "decentralized accumulation" based on local economic decisions within China after market reform; that is, giving local governments more power to manage their own finances and make administrative decisions, increasing their ability to make economic decisions. "Legal authoritarianism" refers to the legitimacy of the state derived from efforts to establish the rule of law instead of utopian ideology, personal authority, and administrative orders.

On the one hand, SOEs have become self-financing market players with independent decision-making power, acting to maximize profits. On the other hand, enterprises are required to implement labor regulations promulgated by the central government to relieve labor problems and achieve social stability.[10] Thus, the political and economic structure causes enterprises to face tensions between capital accumulation and compliance with the law as they balance their own economic interests and state requirements. These structures also allow workers facing layoffs or loss of benefits to strategize against managers by invoking certain policies and laws. With the implementation of the 2008 "Labor Contract Law" (劳动合同法), formal workers, who have enjoyed 20 to 40 years of continuous employment with social benefits, also receive subsidies for working in high temperatures, as well as technical skills allowances, housing subsidies, meal subsidies and other benefits.[11] Under the Labor Contract Law, Nanchang must strictly adhere to an eight-hour workday and cannot require that workers work overtime. Managers also cannot freely fire workers or deduct their wages, or they may be reported. WYX, a former director of Nanchang, said:

> Workers often complain about many different issues, including compensation, overtime pay not being paid on time, length of overtime, holiday wages that are not 300% of their regular wages … they might even complain about the cool drinks we provide during the summertime. Workers understand very well that they can raise a complaint as soon as they see you are out of compliance with the law.
>   WXY, April 8, 2011

---

10   For example, when a State Council SASAC (State-owned Assets Supervision and Administration Commission) director came to inspect the factory in January, 2011, he reminded managers to pay attention to the relationship between supervision and stability: "We must correctly handle the relationship between enterprise management and stability. It is important to push forward scientific development, but we must also adequately address the relationship between development and stability. We should manage historical problems with a high sense of responsibility and in accordance with the law" (Source: 今日南厂 [*Nanchang Today*], 2011).

11   Formal workers in Nanchang are separated into three groups. The first group is made up of older workers who entered the factory around 1972; when I was doing my research, they were beginning to retire. The second group entered the factory around 1991; they were previously the main productive force within Nanchang. The third group is made up of workers from technical schools who were recruited after 2000; these workers tend to move around a lot and many do not stay at Nanchang for long. Workers who entered the factory between 1972 and 1991 survived the layoffs. Their seniority is calculated from the time they entered the factory, so they all have between 20 and 40 years of service.

More importantly, it is difficult for the factory to layoff workers. According to the head of the production department in Nanchang's S Branch, laying off workers requires the approval of the company's human resources and labor departments. As part of the application process for unemployment insurance at the Social Insurance Department, if the factory cannot prove the worker was in violation, workers must be given compensation in accordance with seniority. If workers are about to be fired, they will ask for compensation for all of their deferred holidays. As a result, enterprises are reluctant to go through the trouble of firing workers.

Factory managers have tried to resolve labor shortages by mass recruitment, but younger workers have either been convinced by older workers to leave or taught to slow down production and work passively.[12] Faced with the resistance from permanent workers, managers have discovered that workers' active participation is hard to achieve. Increasing work intensity and working hours to achieve "timely production" and "accelerated production" have faced many obstacles.

5.3 *The Logic of Labor Substitution and the Development of Internal Labor Subcontracting*

Managers decided to deal with intense opposition from permanent workers through tactical "labor substitution." Here, "labor substitution" refers to using temporary, flexible, marginal groups without social insurance to replace core, established employment groups who receive social insurance and other benefits. Within this process, managers do not fire permanent workers, but instead increase their use of subcontracting teams in an effort to marginalize formal workers. As HKJ, the former vice-manager of Nanchang, recounted:

> When workers come to argue with you, it only amounts to not working! "Even though I come here every day, I don't work." Fine! Then I won't give you any work to do. Go stand over there and don't touch your machine tool. I'll find someone else to do it. After the contract workers complete their work, you'll have even less to do, which means you'll earn less money.
> HKJ, July 3, 2011

---

12 Nanchang recruits hundreds of technical school students every year, but no more than twenty end up staying at the factory. Riveting and welding production requires cooperation among many people. In production, older workers often tell younger workers: "I've worked hard for decades and my salary is only 2000 *yuan*. Wages and treatment here are really bad. If you work here for decades, your salaries will also be low. We're too old to leave here, but [you] young people can still go into the private sector and make some money. Otherwise, you won't be able to get married."

The previous director of S Branch's quality control department said:

> You just need two construction teams to complete one- or two hundred million-yuan shield machines. I could even introduce two more construction teams. As long as the price is right, many subcontracting teams are willing to come to work. Just look at the German H Company – the outside workers they contract outnumber their own workers. Look at us – we ourselves are subcontractors for H Company!
> FXF, August 17, 2013

A colleague of mine encountered similar situations in her investigation of SOEs. She discovered if modern enterprise management systems face stiff opposition from workers and if managers are unable to fire workers, subcontracting teams are introduced into the production process. As permanent workers retire, the enterprise introduces harsher management strategies.

After 2008, Nanchang's S Branch began to recruit subcontracting teams on a large scale. In the welding division, the number of subcontracting teams increased to four. More importantly, starting in January 2011, Nanchang abolished its previous fixed wage system and introduced a tonnage piece rate wage system in the riveting and welding and blanking departments. In the machining department, the factory introduced a piece-rate system that also accounted for working hours. After the reform of the wage system, production tasks for formal workers were reduced dramatically, causing their wages to decrease. Afterward, permanent workers felt their livelihoods were actually threatened by the subcontracting teams. As a result, permanent workers rapidly lost their bargaining power in the factory. Their meager wages contributed to a sense of betrayal. But even the most active resisters felt helpless in the face of the status quo. Afterward, in spite of their dissatisfaction, permanent workers had no choice but to speed up production, increase overtime hours and work intensity, and become like a fast-turning gear in the machine of state-owned capital accumulation. After 2013, as permanent workers began to retire, managers basically eliminated the obstacles posed by them and gained total control of production sites. They increased profit margins and fully integrated the factory into circuits of flexible capital accumulation.

6 Conclusion and Discussion: the Political-Economic Significance of the Change in Production Models within SOEs

Changes in production models within SOEs were a result of a fundamental change in enterprise labor processes. Beginning with changes in the labor processes caused by structural, environmental factors, this paper outlines the process of change from the "work unit-factory" system to the "internal labor subcontracting" system of production at Nanchang. This paper also identifies the practical logic behind changes in production at Nanchang – namely, the reorganization of labor under transnational labor processes and labor substitution under "shop floor politics." The reorganization of labor under transnational labor processes refers to state-owned industrial enterprises becoming OEMs and thereby turning into links within a larger transnational labor process, a transformation that took place after China joined the WTO. The simplification of production technologies, the decrease in production times, and the de-emphasizing of production coordination made it difficult for the pre-existing system of "group production" to continue. Managers began to change manufacturing processes to meet the demands of the global market. Under these conditions, Nanchang began to introduce subcontracting teams into the factory, a move that sparked a change in the production mode. Additionally, workers suffered losses due to market transformation and SOE reform, leading to a continuous intensification of "shop floor politics" that threatened enterprise production. Managers then resorted to labor substitution, hiring low-wage subcontracting teams without welfare protection to replace permanent workers. Afterward, managers became dominant within "shop floor politics." Following this logic, Nanchang introduced subcontracting teams to factory production on a large scale, changing Nanchang's production model into one based on "internal labor subcontracting."

As previously noted, the goal in analyzing changes in SOE production models is to help us understand how China's state-owned industrial enterprises left the planned economy and how, through local practices, they incorporated themselves into a system of flexible accumulation. What, then, is "flexible accumulation?" How do Western enterprises and Chinese SOEs incorporate themselves into flexible accumulation?

"Flexible accumulation" refers to a system of capital accumulation that is characterized by a more "flexible" and variable labor process, a more geographically dispersed market, diversified consumer practices, flexible and rapid capital flows, and rapid turnover. According to David Harvey, after the 1980s, flexible accumulation replaced the postwar Fordist-Keynesian system as the dominant path of global capitalism. The Fordist-Keynesian model was a relatively rigid economic model characterized by mass production, standardized mass consumption and social welfare provided by the state. Chinese SOEs had to integrate themselves into the system of flexible accumulation in order to survive. According to Harvey, flexible accumulation is a combination of two traditional capital accumulation strategies. The first strategy is to increase absolute surplus-value by increasing working time, cutting real wages, or reducing welfare. The second strategy is to increase the relative surplus-value through reorganization and technology (Harvey 2004). For Western enterprises, these two accumulation strategies run into two problems. The first is the organized labor force, and the second is state regulations regarding labor practices and social welfare. Research shows that Western enterprises, through neoliberal globalization and "spatial adjustment" strategies (or through reorganizing the geographical organization of production), transferred production to places with weak unions, backward laws, low labor costs, and relaxed regulations to eliminate the aforementioned obstacles. For example, American and European car manufacturing companies moved large numbers of production sites to Brazil, Mexico, South Africa, and China, in order to avoid dealing with powerful trade unions (Silver 2012).

China's SOEs faced similar resistance. On the one hand, large numbers of older workers remained in factories after SOE reform, and these workers refused to comply with strict labor standards. On the other hand, China's labor laws are slowly improving, limiting the exploitative labor practices of enterprises. However, China's SOEs have also found a strategy that is much simpler than "spatial adjustment" to deal with these problems; they rely on the informal migrant labor market. The fact that labor laws and social welfare systems ignore the informal migrant labor force allows SOEs to employ a cheap, tame, flexible workforce. Labor substitution and direct transformation of the production model within SOEs can therefore meet the demands of flexible accumulation.

Nanchang's story is not new. Through substituting labor, transforming production, speeding up production and sales, and reducing capital turnover time, China's SOEs have successfully incorporated themselves into a world economic system characterized by flexible accumulation. However, as SOEs ride the waves of economic growth, they are also moving toward an uncertain future. As David Harvey warns, globalization is capitalism transplanting itself over the surface of the earth, a situation that can only end up as a short-term solution to crises of over-accumulation. In other words, this method can only reorganize the space and time of capitalist crises by transferring the most serious consequences to underdeveloped countries and regions (Harvey 2010, 242). As SOEs are no longer dependent upon skilled workers, they rely on foreign markets and technology, meaning they are placing themselves in a vulnerable situation in the event of global economic crisis. This could mean that when the next global economic crisis hits, China's industrial enterprise production system could suffer a huge blow. Additionally, if the social trust that exists between workers and managers is fully destroyed, it will be difficult for workers and managers to unite to deal with the crisis. They are more likely to pursue their own specific interests, leading to greater social conflict.

References

Burawoy, Michael. 2005. 制造甘愿: 垄断资本主义劳动过程的历史变迁 [*Manufacturing Consent: Changes in the Labor Process Under Monopoly Capitalism*]. Translated by Lin Zonghong 林宗弘 et al. Taipei: Socio Publishing Co., Ltd.

Buttrick, John. 1952. "The Inside Contract System." *The Journal of Economic History*, 12 (3): 205–221.

Committee for the Compilation of Labor Movements in Shanghai, ed. 上海工运志编纂委员会编. 1997. 上海工运志 [*Chronicle of Shanghai Labor Movements*]. Shanghai: Shanghai Academy of Social Sciences Press.

Englander, Ernest J. 1987. "The Inside Contract System of Production and Organization: A neglected Aspect of the History of the Firm." *Labor History*, 28 (4): 429–446.

Gallagher, Mary E. 2010. 全球化与中国劳工政治 [*Contagious Capitalism: Globalization and the Politics of Labor in China*]. Translated by Yu Jianxing 郁建兴 and Xiao Yangdong 肖扬东. Hangzhou: Zhejiang People's Publishing House.

Harvey, David. 2004. 后现代的状况 – 对文化变迁之缘起的探究 [*The Condition of Postmodernity: An Enquiry into the Origins of Change*]. Translated by Yan Jia 阎嘉. Beijing: The Commercial Press.

Jing Jiang 经江. 1981. "解放前上海造船工业中的包工制度" [The Contracting System in Shipbuilding Industry in Shanghai before the Liberation]. 学术月刊 [*Academic Monthly*], 11: 17–21.

Jones, Stephen R. H. 1982. "The Organization of Work: A Historical Dimension." *Journal of Economic Behavior and Organization*, 3: 117–137.

Lee, Ching Kwan. 1999. "From Organized Dependence to Disorganized Despotism: Changing Labour Regimes in Chinese Factories." *The China Quarterly*, 157: 44–71.

Lee, Ching Kwan. 2007. *Against the Law: Labor Protests in China's Rustbelt and Sunbelt*. Los Angeles: University of California Press.

Liu Mingkui 刘明逵, ed. 2002. 中国近代工人阶级和工人运动 第 1 册 [*China's Modern Working Class and Labor Movement*, vol. 1]. Beijing: Party School of the Central Committee of CPC Press.

Lü, Xiaobo and Elizabeth Perry. 1997. *Danwei: The Changing Chinese Workplace in Historical and Comparative Perspective*. New York: M. E. Sharpe.

Ma Wei 马伟. 2006. "盾构机: 正在出炉的大蛋糕？" [Shield Machines: A Newly Baked Cake?]. 中国机电工业 [*China Machinery & Electric Industry*], 6:18–20.

Marx, Karl and Friedrich Engels. 2004. 资本论 第 1 卷 [*Das Kapital* Volume 1]. Translated by Central Compilation & Translation Bureau. Beijing: People's Publishing House.

Nanchang Archives 南厂档案. 2000. 关于下发我省 2000 年建立现代企业制的百户骨干企业名单的通知 [Notice about the List of a Hundred Modernized Enterprises in 2000]. 南厂档案 2000 年（永久）第 1 卷 [Nanchang Archives 2000 (Permanent collection)], vol. 1.

Perry, Elizabeth J. 裴宜理. 上海罢工 – 中国工人政治研究 [*Shanghai on Strike: The Politics of Chinese Labor*]. Translated by Liu Ping 刘平. Nanjing: Jiangsu People's Publishing House.

Ren Yan 任焰 and Pun Ngai 潘毅. 2006. "跨国劳动过程的空间政治: 全球化时代的宿舍劳动体制" [The Politics of Space in Trans-national Labor Process: The Dormitory Labour System in Globalization]. 社会学研究 [*Sociological Studies*], 4: 21–33.

Shen Yuan 沈原. 2006. 社会转型与工人阶级的再形成 ["The Social Transformation and the Reshaping of the Worker Class"]. 社会学研究 [*Sociological Studies*], 2: 13–36.

Silver, Beverly. 2012. 劳工的力量: 1870 年以来的工人运动与全球化 [*Forces of Labor: Workers' Movements and Globalization since 1870*]. Translated by Zhang Lu 张璐. Beijing: Social Science Academic Press.

Thelen, Kathleen. 2010. 制度是如何演化的: 德国、英国、美国和日本的技能政治经济学 *How Institutions Evolve: The Political Economy of Skills in Germany, Britain, the United States, and Japan*. Translated by Wang Xing 王星. Shanghai: Shanghai People's Publishing House.

Walder, Andrew G. 1996. 共产党社会的新传统主义 [*Communist Neo-Traditionalism*]. Translated by Gong Xiaoxia 龚小夏. Hong Kong: Oxford University Press.

Xie Guoxiong 谢国雄. 1989. 外包制度 – 比较历史的回顾 ["Outsourcing System: A Comparative Historical Review"]. 台湾社会研究季刊 [*Taiwan: A Radical Quarterly in Social Studies*] 2 (1): 29–69.

Zhang Zhao 张昭. 1980. "成组技术的发展及其在机床制造业中的应用" [The Development of Group Technology and Its Application to Machinery Manufacturing]. 机床 [*Machine Tools*] 7: 2–6.

Zhao Wei 赵炜. 1980. 工厂制度重建中的工人 [*The Change of Factory Regime in China and Its Impacts on Workers: Case Studies from the White Goods Industry in China*]. Beijing: Social Science Academic Press.

CHAPTER 5

Sustaining Production: Spatial Interactions between Han and Uyghur Workers at the Kashgar Cotton Mill

Liu Ming (刘明)
Translated by Heather Mowbray

Abstract

This paper is based on field research on spatial interactions between Uyghur and Han workers at the Kashgar Cotton Mill [in the Xinjiang Uyghur Autonomous Region]. According to the research, the form taken by working and living spaces has had a role in shaping systemic change and transitional practices. The mill has shifted from being state owned to being privately owned and managed and the formation and disruption of the cultural space in which Uyghur and Han workers interact in work and life are inextricably linked to this transition. In particular, the unbalanced recruitment of Uyghur and Han workers has disrupted an important mentoring relationship between members of the two ethnic groups. In short, an ethnic spatial perspective allows us to better understand the economic and social changes in the transitional period, especially with regard to ethnic and labor relations.

Keywords

ethnic groups – workers – space – work – life

1   Ethnicity as a Labor Issue[1]

Traditional labor sociology revolves around dialogue between labor process theory and class formation theory (Shen and Wen 2012). With China's

---

[1] This article originally appeared in *Open Times* 2015, no. 3, pp. 64–77. This study received financial support in 2014 as part of a regional social science funding project, "Uyghur-Han Labor Interactions in a Transitioning Xinjiang Society" (14BSH060). In 2011, it received funding as part of a national social science project, "Trends and Countermeasures in Urban Ethnic Relations in Xinjiang's Border Areas" (11 & ZD059).

increasing involvement in the process of globalization and the impact of social transformation on the labor force, researchers have gradually brought age and gender (He 2009) and social interaction perspectives (Zhou 2007) into research about labor processes. How to better develop new research areas and forge new research topics is at the forefront of scholars' minds. This study hopes to escape from the labor process perspective and consider labor exchange as part of a spatial culture, thereby enriching the research arena.

Researchers investigating urban social space in Ürümqi, the capital of Xinjiang Province, have combed the history of the past 200 years for changes in the city's structure. From the twin cities of the Qianlong era – the Manchurian city of Gongning and the Han city of Dihua – to the unified city of Dihua in the early Guangxu era, or to the late Qing Dynasty's "one city with four districts," and the Republican era's "one city with two districts," the main context of urban spatial development has been the living patterns of the city's ethnic groups (Huang 2011). Do we have the chance to look again at these residential spatial patterns in our quest for new research horizons? This article hopes to bring an ethnic perspective into labor research, and consider ethnicity as an aspect of labor.

For a long time, researchers have used the seven variables developed by American scholar Milton Gordon (1964) as objective indicators for ethnic relations, namely, assimilation of culture or behavior, social structure, marriage, identity, attitudes and civic affairs. Fei Xiaotong's (1989) analysis of China's historical situation, with a "pluralistic unified" pattern used to describe the coexistence of ethnic groups also has explanatory value. However, in the process of societal change, the theory of pluralistic unity lacks an up-close perspective. It is confined to measuring changes in variables that neither fully nor dynamically acknowledge ethnic developments. The author hopes to understand ethnic relations as ethnic interaction, and specifically, to consider the production and living spaces in which cultural interactions between Uyghur (维吾尔) and Han (汉) workers are shaped and reshaped.

This paper is based on one case study, so it does not aim to discuss differences in labor interactions between ethnic groups in depth; instead, it considers changes and processes involved in the particular situation in light of such differences. In other words, the research question posed by this article is: In the course of national societal transition, how do interactive spaces among members of different ethnic groups working at and living on the grounds of one company form and change?

2 Space as a Location of Action

Space has long been considered to be a critical aspect of the objective, material world and spatial divisions have been shown to be loaded with social differences that are subjectively recognized. Research on Western societies has made the social and political connotations of space well known and has highlighted the power relations implied by knowledge, the body, and subjectivity. Eastern spatial research has also made useful contributions by examining dimensions including the peripheries (Wang 2011), social integration (Pan 2008), and factory dormitories (Ren and Pan 2006).

Space is an important anthropological issue that has been used as a paradigm to analyze daily life, emphasizing interregional social processes of spatial politics and practices, and attaching importance to the knowledge, order and power relations of spatial practices. Henri Lefebvre's (2008) three aspects of space – practices, appearance, and perceptions – have been used in an excellent study of Jinjiang immigrants to Hong Kong (Lin 2006). This paper attempts to combine concrete space and abstract space, and carry out ethnographic research on ethnic working interactions. It employs the concept of space to refer to specific as well as abstract space; specific space is visible and concrete, while abstract space – for instance, institutional space – is invisible.

This study's field investigation site is a cotton mill situated in Kashgar, an oasis town known as the "pearl of the Silk Road" in southwestern Xinjiang Uyghur Autonomous Region in western China. This site was chosen for three reasons. First, Kashgar is a predominantly Uyghur multi-ethnic town. It was the historic capital of the eight southern Xinjiang cities known as the "southern Xinjiang fortress" (Bao 1984). Second, Kashgar serves as the Uyghur center of economic and cultural life in Xinjiang. Scholars believe that the Kashgar region, with its concentrated Uyghur population, is very important to the study of Uyghur-Han relations (Ma 2000). Third, researchers investigated the Kashgar Cotton Mill in the 1980s, and left considerable data, oral case studies and research reports (Liu 1984; Li 1984; Miao 1985; Zeng 1988). Fourth, the author personally experienced a rich and irreplaceable childhood at the Kashgar Cotton Mill.

The decision to establish the Kashgar Cotton Mill as a comprehensive production and living space was made at the Xinjiang Uyghur Autonomous Region Party Committee meeting in September 1957. The government's intention was to build a modern textile printing and dyeing factory in the city, and use its resources to catalyze change in the relative economic backwater of southern Xinjiang. With a long history of traditional handicrafts, Kashgar had begun developing a modern textiles industry in the early Republican period. At that time, in order to export cotton to the Soviet Union, a ginning mill was built outside the east gate of the old city, the only machine-driven industry in town at the time (Gong 1994). Swedish ambassador and scholar Gunnar Jarring (1978) wrote in his memoirs of travel and research in Kashgar:

> Coming to Kashgar in 1929 … The water carriers walked around with their heavy loads of water contained in a sheep or goat skin. Dyers hung their skeins of yarn on rods on top of the flat-roofed mud houses. Their sections of the bazaars were painted blue, yellow, red and mauve, and those cheerful colors were repeated in the clothes they wore.… The imported textiles from Tashkent and other Soviet textile centers were already taking over. Those new fabrics had flowery patterns and glaring colors. Today [1978] they dominate the market and are no longer imported from the Soviet Union, but are manufactured in Kashgar's own textile mills.… Fifty years ago there was no industry in Kashgar. That was the case for the whole of southern Xinjiang, for that matter. Industrial products, mostly in the form of consumer goods, were imported from the Soviet Union and India, and to some extent from central China via Ürümqi. Everything came by caravan. Kashgar was a city of artisans. All of this has changed. Although not yet a significant industrial center, Kashgar is at the beginning of such a development.
> JARRING (1999)

In spatial terms, the establishment of the Kashgar Cotton Mill resulted in several changes. First, there was a transition from traditional handicraft to modern industry. This meant a shift from transportation of water by sheepskin container, and from yarn dyed and spun by craftsmen and other traditional methods to mass machine-driven production. Second, there was a shift from importing textiles to producing them locally for sale in China and for export. The Kashgar Cotton Mill exported printed cloth to the USSR for three consecutive years, and contributed 2,321 rolls (54,600 meters) of *dahua biji* (大花哔叽)[2] to Sino-Pakistani trade (Long 1987). The third change was the first use of the "three works" (industry, factories, workers) concept. The prototype of the industry and the factory started with the construction of a spinning department in January 1958, and after the site's ground-breaking, the new mill established spinning, weaving, printing and dyeing operations, followed by printed cloth

---

2 A serge fabric with a traditional Chinese flower pattern.

production. The mill became one of Xinjiang's earliest medium-to-large scale key enterprises. The establishment of the mill gave rise to Xinjiang's first generation of textile workers. Through the mill, a large number of ethnic minority workers entered the modern industrial workforce. Employment at the mill not only meant gaining production skills, but it also heralded significant changes to social identity and ideas.

3 Change in the Production Space

Changes in the production space took place on a temporal dimension. The Kashgar Cotton Mill developed in nine stages (Liu 2013a): the early years (1958–1966); the Cultural Revolution (1967–1976); recovery and re-emergence (1977–1988); three years under contract management (1989–1991); restructuring (1992–1999); Luxin Textiles (1999–2000); New Mill (2000–2003); New Mill Group (2003–2005); and Youngor Group (2005–2014). In ownership terms, the Kashgar Cotton Mill was state-owned from 1958 to 1999, and was privately owned and run by a succession of contractors since then.

The spatial arrangements between labor and capital felt the impact of the mill's ownership situation. When the mill was a state-owned enterprise, most managers had experience as shop floor workers. For example, Han worker T, who began by riveting and stamping cloth in 1949, went on to become a planning technician (1958), Party office secretary (1961), Party office deputy (1963), dyeing branch Party secretary (1965), mill deputy Party secretary (1974), and finally factory director and deputy secretary of the mill Party committee (1981). Over the course of these seven roles, T gained rich production experience, and rose from an ordinary worker to a senior manager over 32 years.

Uyghur worker H was deputy head of the managerial training group (1958), mill group cadre of the Youth League (1960), general Party branch secretary of the weaving workshop (1961), chief of the mill Party committee's publicity department (1965), head of the mill's political work team (1973), and deputy secretary of the mill Party committee (1974). These six positions gave him varied grassroots leadership experience, turning him from an ordinary worker to state cadre and state-owned enterprise leader in 16 years (Liu 1984). Status shifts like this were the norm not just for leaders but also for middle management.

Social interactions between members of different ethnic groups became increasingly more open. Reflections of the first generation of ethnic minority workers tell us that, first, employees could rise from grassroots workers to senior administrators via production skills development. Second, workers' production initiative increased as a result of the transformation of social identity and values. Specifically, the connection between technical skill level and status was socially important in the mill. Third, mobility in technical positions enabled the first group of ethnic minority workers to study in Qingdao, Xi'an, and Shanghai, and by participating in this training they gained the most sophisticated technical skills. Moreover, a robust apprenticeship system was developed internally at the mill, based on strong relationships between *shifu* (师傅 master) and *tudi* (徒弟 apprentice). From the mill's opening to its bankruptcy in 1999, mentoring was maintained as a long-term part of the production system. The interactive production space between Uyghur and Han workers is best presented in the following case.

> In December 1959, a Uyghur female worker named A and her companions went to study at the No. 1 Zhengzhou State Cotton Mill. She was apprenticed to a Han female worker named G, who was very warm towards her, patiently giving demonstrations. But *Tudi* A did not understand Chinese, and was very anxious as she tried to follow *Shifu* G's example. Once *Tudi* A could not find the toilet and squatted down on the ground anxiously. *Shifu* G thought she was hungry so she gave her a steamed bun, but this just made *Tudi* A cry. Their language barrier gave rise to many humorous incidents. *Tudi* A bought a pencil to write down common phrases and the names of machine parts in a notebook, and set about learning Chinese. *Shifu* G was the production team leader, and in order to cultivate her apprentice's sense of responsibility and overall understanding, she hung a whistle around *Tudi* A's neck and taught her to oversee the whole production. As A progressed quickly, her *shifu* bought her three flower pins to encourage her, explaining that three meant good performance, and one or two meant poor performance. After a period of study, A progressed quickly. One day, she was given three flower pins by her workshop mates, who played gongs and drums in a circle around her. With *Shifu* G's encouragement and help, *Tudi* A not only mastered techniques of production, but left with the seeds of ethnic unity. At the end of the second year, she shed tears of farewell, finding it hard to leave. Afterward, *shifu* and *tudi* kept in touch, and in 1963 *Tudi* A visited again. During the Cultural Revolution period, they were unable to meet, but in 1981, when a delegation of national experts came to the mill, she inquired about her *shifu* at No. 1 Zhengzhou State Cotton Mill. *Tudi* A cried when she heard that her *shifu* was safe after the ten years of chaos in which she had often worried about her. She sent *Shifu* G a hand-embroidered pillowcase. *Shifu* G replied and sent her some clothes. Before Spring Festival 1982, *Tudi* A sent her *shifu* a box of jujubes and a family photo (ibid.).

At the end of the 1950s, there were no other cotton mills in the area from which the Kashgar Cotton Mill could learn. The apprenticeship system it had adopted worked along the lines of the central Chinese model. From the origins of the recruitment and apprenticeship system we can see that first, cadres, workers and technical staff from all over China came to support the border areas. Second, after a trial production period, some college graduates and former military personnel were recruited. Third, regional recruitment was subject to certain conditions and quota restrictions. Kashgar Cotton Mill repeatedly sent new workers to central China to study, making the apprenticeship relationship an important mode of sustained production. Although these apprenticeship relationships were not expressly provided for, they became a link between technical inheritance and interpersonal communication. While the Kashgar Cotton Mill did not originally set up such a system itself, via central China apprenticeships, technical studies and recruitment, it became a part of mill culture.

Among mill workers, apprenticeships were arranged by the workshops. *Shifu* could not pick their *tudi* or vice versa. The main criterion was that *shifu* needed to have good technical production skills. No contract was signed between the two parties, and there was no apprenticeship ceremony. An apprenticeship would last half a year on average. Once the *tudi* was able to do the task independently, they were considered to have graduated and could work as technical workers and even as seasoned workers. In economic terms, the work produced by the *tudi* during the apprenticeship was claimed by the *shifu*, with the *tudi* receiving a fixed salary (Liu and Cui 2006). Older workers recalled that relations between Uyghur and Han workers were very good, and they rarely argued. Regular communication, mutual respect and mutual learning of each other's language were the norm. People participated in each other's festivals, ate together, invited each other into their homes and even slaughtered lambs together.

The opening of this improved spatial channel and apprenticeship system meant everything for Uyghur-Han interactions in production. First, the establishment of the apprenticeship system in the Kashgar Cotton Mill, and especially the participation of Uyghur and Han workers in the system, constituted one of the most important methods of creating an interaction space between the two ethnic groups. The number of apprenticeships directly affected the amount of interaction between the groups, not only in production, but also in their social lives and linguistic exchanges. Harmonious mentorship relations had the knock-on effect of enhancing ethnic unity, alleviating the negative impact of communication impediments, and generating opportunities for mutual understanding so that the two sides could pursue mutual cultural diffusion and share cultural resources (Liu 2013b).

Second, the apprenticeship relationship also reflected the interaction between modern industrial organization and intercultural communication. As a product of modern industrial organization, especially in a multi-ethnic environment such as Xinjiang, apprenticeships served to produce a new multi-ethnic relationship. Mentoring led to more interaction between Uyghur and Han people, and deepened personal relationships between members of the two groups. While this phenomenon had institutional causes, there were also profound cultural factors.

In the fifteen years since bankruptcy, the Kashgar Cotton Mill has gone through several name changes, from Luxin Textiles (2 years) to New Mill (3 years) to New Mill Group (2 years) to Youngor Group (8 years). The ownership structure has also changed profoundly. In private hands, the company was comprised of three groups: first, leaders who took on the responsibilities of capital investors; second, a middle stratum of experienced and skilled veteran employees who have not yet reached retirement age; and third, workers newly recruited into the mill. This created a three-level management structure, consisting of capital, middle level, and new employees.

Under this new structure, the owners took measures to increase production efficiency and reduce production costs. Costs were also reduced by cutting skill development expenditures, workers' health care and other extra responsibilities. Maximizing profits became the private company's main aim. Compared with the state-owned era, in which ethnic relations were more balanced, Uyghur-Han relations became increasingly hierarchical and top-down, as fewer Han workers were represented on the workshop floor. Factors in the recruitment process limited the hiring of Han workers.

Changes in ownership led to changes in Uyghur-Han spatial interactions in production (see Figure 5.1). During the state-owned enterprise period from 1958 to 1999, there were substantial horizontal interactions between the two ethnic groups' ordinary workers, skilled workers and factory managers. From 2000 to 2014, in the era of private ownership, the leadership of the company became comprised of Han Chinese investors from inner China who bought the use of the mill together with the management space. This resulted in a leadership group that lacked talented ethnic minority representatives. Additionally, middle managers were mainly recruited from the original mill's Han retirees who had many years of accumulated textile industry experience. They played the role of intermediary between the leadership and workers. Most of the ethnic minority retirees were looking after their grandchildren or had returned to the countryside to relieve their children's farming pressures. The factory's monthly retirement pay provided a source of income and some also engaged in emerging business activities at the bazaar for additional income. Therefore,

Factory Managers (Uyghur & Han) ↑ Skilled Workers (Uyghur & Han) ↑ Ordinary Workers (Uyghur & Han)	Enterprise Leaders: Investors (non-local Han people) Middle Management: Senior Staff (local Han people) Enterprice Staff: Recruitment (mostly ethnic minorities)

1958–1999 (State-owned Enterprise) 2000–2014 (Private Enterprise) ⟶

FIGURE 5.1 Changes in the nature of property rights lead to changes in Uyghur-Han spatial interactions in production

at the middle level, the private company lacked an experienced group who could pass on skills to newly hired ethnic minority workers. So, the newly recruited employees, most of whom were ethnic minority workers, faced a difficult choice: either gain skills despite poor promotion opportunities or lose their jobs.

How was it that during the era of private ownership, the mill's horizontal employee space came to lack Han workers? To put it another way, why did the number of Han workers drop so dramatically?

First, while the factory was being restructured, the workers had to make a decision about whether to keep their jobs or make a livelihood by other means. The mill was on the verge of bankruptcy, and those who could leave production found a way out via retirement, sick leave or by taking a portion of labor insurance. If they could, many Han workers managed to find employment in downtown Kashgar or switched work units. Only those who could find no other options, and who could not survive at home without working, stayed on at the mill. For those Uyghur workers who lived in the countryside, as long as they found some kind of work in the city, they could get by, getting a day's wage for a day's labor. Rural Uyghurs encountered problems in finding work during this urbanizing period, as their Chinese language skills were poor and this created a barrier to receiving information about opportunities to change their situation or improve their skill sets. Their education had been limited, so they could only find physical labor jobs in the city. Lack of expertise and city registration (*hukou*, 户口) were two key reasons Uyghurs found it hard to integrate into city society. When we interviewed Uyghur workers, we found that they put a lot of value on their hard-to-get employment opportunities. Objectively, rural Uyghurs were in a weaker position than urban Han people to find jobs in a period of urbanizing employment. For that reason, more Uyghurs than Han were hired as workers in the mill during this period.

Second, labor in private enterprises was highly intensive and poorly paid, so it was not appealing to the Han population. According to the author's interviews with female textile workers in 2013, the factory had asked the workers to extend the length of their work day from eight hours to 12 hours, while decreasing the number of shifts from three to two. The goal was to cut the number of employees and reduce production costs. However, this institutional arrangement led to workers' deep discontent and protests. In desperation, the company reintroduced the three shifts of eight hours each, but increased the penalties, through salary deductions, for technical faults. Workers were paid a monthly salary between 1,000 and 2,000 yuan, an amount that was entirely inadequate. One woman told the author that if not for the fact that she was in her thirties, divorced and with children and an elderly father, she would never have stayed in the mill. If she had been under thirty, she would have learned a new skill. Or, if she had been a little older, she would have applied for retirement or early retirement due to illness before the mill went bankrupt. She said frankly to the author, lowering her head, that she had not spent money in a restaurant even once that year.

Regarding income, Han workers' expectations are higher than minority workers. Since the Uyghur workers employed in the mill were mostly from neighboring counties and townships, their salary was better than what could be earned through agricultural labor in their home areas. In the past, workers who remained in the factory expected to receive stable retirement pay; after privatization, without a pension, young Han workers naturally chose not to continue working in a private enterprise for long.

Third, in terms of career planning, Han workers preferred to seek stable jobs with long-term potential, while for the more socially vulnerable young Uyghur villagers leaving the village, the farm, and rural identity was already a bold step. A Uyghur woman described her experience. She had been born in a rural commune in Shule county. Her father felt there was no point in girls studying too much, and he planned to marry her off early to the *tudi* he had adopted. She dropped out of school after finishing primary school and endeavored to enter the mill without informing her parents. After the girl had been working a few days, however, her mother came crying to the factory gate, saying her husband had beaten her and that she had to take her daughter home with her or she could never go home. After the girl returned home, her father slapped her, locked her in a small room and pushed her to marry, not allowing her to go back to the mill. Father and daughter were at a stalemate and had to make concessions. In the end, she married as a condition for returning to the mill (Liu 1984).

Uyghur rural society was very conservative and people were accustomed to rural social arrangements. Encountering industrial society, their ideas and mindset could not be completely changed to adapt. Young people lacked career opportunities and control over their own lives and, having left the countryside, Uyghur workers were happy just to no longer be farmers. For them, hard work in the city and an income greater than could be gained through agriculture already meant a better life. As a result, the number of Uyghur workers at the mill increased, while the number of Han workers decreased.

In the early years of the mill, large-scale recruitment led to the establishment of widespread inter-ethnic mentorships. The number of ethnic minority workers grew from 800 in 1959 to 1,700 in 1983; most became skilled workers. According to interview materials, the two decades from the beginning of the Kashgar Cotton Mill to the early 1980's coincided exactly with the years of growth, development and sharpening of skills of the first generation of Uyghur workers. From the skilled workers of various departments, two elite groups gradually developed, one with specialized technical skills and the other with ideological and political (managerial) expertise. A female workshop worker named Z recalled that after she entered the factory in 1976, she spent three months learning the basics and then was assigned to a group in the post-spinning workshop. The group had a total of one hundred and thirty people, divided into eight groups. Of the group members, nearly seventy – about 50% – were ethnic minorities. By the 1990s, the number of Han workers gradually declined, leading to an imbalance between the ethnic groups. A survey from 2013 shows that 90% of the workers were Uyghurs; some teams only had one or two Han workers, and some did not have any. This made maintaining the Han/Uyghur apprenticeship relationship difficult. Because of the imbalance between Uyghur and Han workers, the apprenticeship system lacked the conditions for sustainable operations, and because of the change in ownership status of the mill, the apprenticeship space of exchange between Uyghurs and Han was broken.

According to the author's research, we see that: first, the number of workers in 1959, in the construction phase, was 1,522 and by 1999 it had reached 6,766. In 2003, after the layoffs that accompanied restructuring, the workforce numbered 2,227. Second, the proportion of Han workers and ethnic minority workers was roughly equal in the mill's early years. This balanced ethnic makeup constituted a sound population foundation for interaction between ethnic groups. After 1966, however, the proportion of Han workers declined and on the eve of bankruptcy in 1999 Han employees made up only 39.65% of the workforce. Likewise, the ratio of male to female workers was more balanced in the 1960s than it was the 1990s, by which time women were in the majority.

TABLE 5.1 Changes in the number of workers by ethnic group and gender in the Kashgar Cotton Mill

Year	Number of Workers	Ethnic Han Workers	Ethnic Minority Workers	Male	Female
1959	1,522	722 (47.44%)	800 (52.56%)	-	-
1966	2,995	2,106 (70.32%)	889 (29.68%)	1,501 (50.12%)	1,494 (49.88%)
1983	4,319	2,570 (59.51%)	1,749 (40.49%)	2,108 (48.81%)	2,211 (51.19%)
1996	6,321	2,529 (40.01%)	3,792 (59.99%)	2,245 (35.52%)	4,076 (64.48%)
1997	4,458	1,591 (35.69%)	2,867 (64.31%)	-	-
1999	6,766	2,683 (39.65%)	4,083 (60.35%)	-	-
2000	4,181	-	-	-	-
2002	2,257	-	-	-	-
2003	2,227	-	-	-	-

SOURCES: DATA FOR 1959 TO 1999 IS FROM THE *HISTORY OF THE 41 YEARS OF KASHGAR TEXTILE MILL*, NOVEMBER 23, 1999 (INTERNAL INFORMATION); DATA FOR 2000 IS FROM *INTRODUCTION TO XINJIANG KASHLUXIN TEXTILE CO., LTD.*, MAY 10, 2000 (INTERNAL INFORMATION); DATA FOR 2002 TO 2003 IS FROM *INTRODUCTION TO THE NEW COTTON GROUP KASHGAR TEXTILE CO., LTD.*, JUNE 15, 2004 (INTERNAL INFORMATION).

4   Fragmentation of Living Space

Residential housing allocation policies resulted in changes in living space. Labor production needs had been the basis of the development of the Kashgar Cotton Mill community, and the professional (production) area and the daily life (residential) area were close together. This meant that in the course of many years of production, residents from different ethnic groups, generations, and regions came into regular contact and had a chance to interact.

The arrangement of the living space has also been affected by the nature of ownership rights. As a state-owned enterprise, the mill's production and residential areas were separated by a single lane. The mill was a tightknit community of acquaintances. Taking one apartment building as an example, between the 1980s and 1990s, residents of bungalow zone No. 302 comprised nine families. They were workers of various job titles and of three ethnic groups – Han, Uyghur and Hui (回族) – from seven departments including the transport fleet, the control laboratory, the preparation workshop, the dining hall, the post-production department, the standby workshop, and the hygiene section. The mill residents included Han, Uyghur, Hui, Uzbek (乌孜别克族), Xibe (锡伯族), Zhuang (壮族) and Manchu (满族) workers. In the 1980s, the Kashgar Cotton Mill residential area was divided into twelve zones and included a building for single employees; the gender ratio was 48.8% men and 51.2% women (Li et al., 1984).

From its founding to the beginning of the 21st century, the textile mill built a wide variety of housing, from single-person dormitories, to "cleaver-shaped cottages," "cave dwellings," bungalows, and small two-story buildings. The residential area grew from one to seventy-one buildings. Having apartments in all types of buildings allocated to people of various ethnic groups helped maintain harmonious ethnic interactions. For example, the residential area established an ethnic minority dining management committee as well as an ethnic minority kindergarten. When ethnic festivals came around, the committee would supply goods so that the ethnic minority workers could celebrate. Ethnic minority workers took their Han comrades into consideration too, and when apartments in a new four-story building were ready for allocation, they took the initiative to propose that older Han workers who had large families and had worked in the factory for many years receive apartments (Dong and Yan 1982).

During the state-owned period, housing issues at the mill were discussed, negotiated and resolved internally in the mill's housing department. In the transitional period, however, a number of housing conflicts came to the surface. For example, Ms. C posted an angry message online complaining that the mill's laid-off workers who were eligible for subsidized housing had been ignored, while many people from other work units had been offered housing by the mill. What was interesting was the response of the Kashgar District State-Owned Assets Supervision and Administration Commission (SASAC):

> Dear Ms. C, Prior to March 2009, there were still 419 former mill worker families (including retired and redundant workers) living in unsafe bungalows built in the 1960s and 1970s in what is now the Huayuan Community (the old Kashgar Cotton Mill residential area). The authorities, following national instructions, have put all their efforts into solving the toughest issues in society, caring for the people and improving peoples' living conditions. In April 2009, the government funded the building of 1,254 new social housing units, and after resolving the housing issues of those 419 households, used all the remaining units for other redundant employees of Kashgar Cotton Mill.

From August 2009, authorized by the Kashgar Municipal Government and the Kashgar SASAC, the restructured Kashgar Cotton Mill started to verify the preliminary qualification of applicants for the affordable housing and received down payments. In accordance with the higher authorities and the arrangements of the relevant departments, the restructured Kashgar Cotton Mill proceeded as follows. First, the 419 households whose homes were to be demolished were given priority in resettlement, according to Kashgar guaranteed housing agreements that they all had signed. Second, when building the guaranteed housing in Huayuan Community, the Kashgar Municipal Government planned to resettle workers from other factories whose homes were set for demolition, after the 419 households were resettled. The problem was that they ended up with too many workers to house. At the highest point, the Kashgar Cotton Mill had more than 10,000 workers, including 8,000 working and those already retired. With the restructuring and reorganization, there are a large number of workers who have been laid-off, have resigned, or have been removed from the employment roll. More workers applied than could be accommodated. After the 419 households were resettled, there remained 835 units. All were used to house former Kashgar Cotton Mill workers. There were not enough new units for everyone. Third, essential conditions were put in place for applying for guaranteed housing in accordance with a document issued by Kashgar Municipal Government: applicants must have an average household income of less than 660 yuan, currently have an average housing area per capita of less than 13 square meters, and have Kashgar *hukou*. Special requirements were in place for those who already had their own houses, who were strictly prohibited from buying a guaranteed housing unit. Fourth, priority for purchasing the 835 remaining units was given to families in which the couple were both laid-off Kashgar Cotton Mill workers, families in which one party of the couple was laid-off while the other party was unemployed, families in which one party of the couple was retired while the other party was unemployed, and families with disabled workers. Fifth, in the process of allocating affordable housing, those with disabilities and those above the age of 50 were given preference. Sixth, later applicants, even if they were qualified, were not accommodated. For this reason, in 2010 the Kashgar District Party Committee and administrative authorities tried their best to locate a tract of land appropriate for construction and this year [2011] witnessed the development of units for 300 more households, due for completion in the first half of 2012. Seventh, the families that have moved into the guaranteed housing units will have their guaranteed housing units taken away from them if they are found to be unqualified for guaranteed housing in the process of granting property rights titles.[3]

The root of the above housing dispute was very simple: laid-off workers at the Kashgar Cotton Mill were not given the guaranteed housing units because they already had economy housing, and non-mill workers were being allocated the guaranteed housing instead. Kashgar Cotton Mill workers had become a social group over years of working together, and their identity was further developed into a boundary of interest between themselves and others. After two such official replies, the facts became clearer. Four hundred and nineteen of the 1,254 housing units built by the mill were offered to households whose former homes had been demolished, and the remaining 835 were given to those deemed to be in difficulties. The "reply" mentioned reasons for these difficulties: First, there were too many applicants for the small number of guaranteed housing units. The mill had 10,000 people in total. Second, per capita income and per capita floor area were the priority criteria; redundant, unemployed or retired status came second; and being disabled or over 50 years old came third. In general, these criteria were justified, as they were in line with the situation as well as the spirit of the Kashgar government directive. The problem was with the sixth point, "early applicants who meet the criteria will have their applications processed but later applicants will not." The reply avoided two questions: First, with regard to the small but unspecified number of homeless laid-off workers from other factories who were allocated homes in the former cotton mill residential community: why was this not included in the plan and explained? Second, were people given prior notice of the "first in line" policy and other requirements?

Resolving these housing disputes in the private enterprise era became a problem that embroiled the former Kashgar Cotton Mill workers and the Kashgar regional SASAC. The residential area of the mill was renamed the Huayuan Community, spelling the end of the state-owned enterprise era. How were homes allocated during the state-owned era? One worker told the author: First, according to years of service; second, according to performance (for example, being a model worker, or working overtime or getting an award in a production contest); third, whether an employee was single or married. After consultation among the mill Party committee, the workshop leadership, housing personnel, and worker representatives, each household would be assigned points and a

---

3 Interview on Xinguang Xingfeng, Uyghur government communication channel, 21 June 2012.

list would be issued. As the mill workers had lived together for years and were very familiar with each other's situation, conflicts of interest did not exist. On the contrary, they focused on hard work and efficiency. Seniority and work performance were the main basis for assessment, eliminating potential conflicts of interest. In fact, as mentioned above, there were cases in which Uyghur workers accommodated the housing needs of senior Han workers.

Enterprise restructuring led to a profound dislocation between management and staff groups. When the mill became a private enterprise, it only needed to focus on production, so issues of livelihood were passed on to the Kashgar Municipal Government and the relevant Kashgar regional departments to deal with. For example, with the guaranteed housing dispute, Kashgar District SASAC had to explain the problem and appease the residents. On the one hand, this increased the workload of the Kashgar regional authorities, as the 71-building community was the largest residential community in the area. On the other hand, changes in living and working arrangements created difficulties for former mill worker-residents, who could not find a responsible management body in case of a problem. Without transparency of information, administrative efficiency failed and the constant frustrations of workers were not conducive to production or social stability.

In fact, when neighbors lived together, learned each other's languages, and gained mutual understanding and respect for each other's customs, it was easy for people to get along and become good friends for life. We came across examples of Uyghur and Han colleagues who socialized with each other, including choosing names for each other and visiting at festival time. When issues and tasks in everyday life, such as dealing with sewage or transporting coal, were carried out without regard for ethnicity, it reveals the depth of the 30-year-friendships formed in the cotton mill, and shows that the best way of understanding another culture is respect and learning. S, an old Han worker, told the author:

> I started learning Uyghur when I was about 40. I sat in a class for Han people that cost me 50 yuan. At the time, I thought Uyghur was very important, and after studying it, I realized in talking to Uyghur people that many of them had a high level of culture and were very reasonable and fair. Actually, as a child in Kashgar, I had a Uyghur babysitter. At the time [1954], many Han people often employed Uyghurs to care for their children. Salaries were not high, [around] 28 yuan, and the fee for childcare was 5 yuan. All the salaries were low, so Han and Uyghur people did not feel discrimination. My home at the time was in a courtyard, and

the Uyghur neighbors all spoke Chinese, and offered us food when they cooked, boiled lamb and so forth, all really tasty. A boy named Abdul lived upstairs, and there weren't any problems, no conflicts; everyone got along fine. His parents were also old workers at the cotton mill, and if there was any little issue, we would just talk about it directly. For example, if their grandchildren were naughty, throwing things downstairs when they were on vacation, I just talked to them. I asked them to talk to their kids and grandkids. The atmosphere was very good, we didn't have any problems at all.

If the interaction space in production tended to be about individual promotion, then the interaction space in the residential area was more about group dynamics. The most important day of the year for ordinary people was the New Year holiday, which for Han people was Spring Festival and for Uyghurs were the Eid al-Adha and Eid al-Fitr festivals. Before the Kashgar Cotton Mill went bankrupt, every Spring Festival, workers received meat and vegetables from the general services section, and the union put on a fireworks display and a variety of cultural activities to create a festive atmosphere. For the Eid al-Adha and Eid al-Fitr festivals, each workshop organized activities, greeted each other and organized open-air movie screenings. Every March, on "Learn from Lei Feng day," teams of Han and Uyghur workers were organized. Getting together on the mill's basketball court, they helped families solve practical issues, such as repairing bicycles, motorcycles and household appliances. In addition, May is ethnic unity month in the Xinjiang Uyghur Autonomous Region, and every year the mill would carry out relevant cultural activities. Whether it was commending the work of outstanding individual workers and model workshop collectives, or summarizing the work of the mill's committee for ethnic unity, or expressing commitments to ethnic unity, what was important was that the factory attached as much importance to leading and promoting ethnic unity and political study in the enterprise as it did to promoting production quality. In addition, state-owned enterprise workers, whether ethnic minority or Han, all recognized the importance of developing a cultural space in production and living. This was universally accepted and it shaped the group identity of "Kashgar Cotton Mill people" (喀纺人).

The Kashgar Cotton Mill changed shape as the company was restructured. In the state-owned era, interaction spaces included the canteens, the bathhouses, the company vehicle fleet, the hospital, and the schools. The breakdown between production and residential spaces occurred when the residential area was renamed and management and ownership changed hands. The residential side of the cotton mill became the Huayuan Community and its management was handed over to the Huayuan Community Real Estate Management Company. While we were conducting field research, the canteens, the bathhouses, and the vehicle fleet were closed, and the hospital became a branch of the Kashgar District No. 2 People's Hospital. The kindergarten was contracted by a private Uyghur entrepreneur to create a "bilingual kindergarten," and all the students were Uyghurs. The Kashgar Cotton Mill school branch was turned over to the Kashgar Board of Education to manage, and was renamed the Kashgar No. 19 Middle School. After the cotton mill was privatized, the open-air cinema was dismantled, and the movie ticket sellers and snack sellers lost their jobs. The company canteens, with their cheap and delicious food, were shut, and with them an important space for workers to eat together and interact. A few old workers still played chess, poker or billiards in their leisure time in the retirement services office. The lighted basketball court was shabby and neglected. In the center of the residential area, the water in the rockery and the pool lay stagnant. From time to time, residents of the mill complained that no one cleaned up the garbage or repaired the aging pipes. The split between the residential area and the production space not only broke people's enjoyment of life but also broke their spirit.

A Uyghur teacher named D, a *minkaohan* (民考汉) who had gone to Han schools, lived in the residential area of the cotton mill.[4] After the mill went bankrupt, she managed to buy a commercial apartment and moved out. She was not happy with the conditions in the residential area. After the change in ownership, it seemed as though the residential and production areas were two completely different entities. If former workers wanted to visit the mill, they had to ask for permission from a company manager. The company neither cared for nor had any contact with the older workers in the residential area. Although there had been no geographical change in the two areas' spaces and they remained across the street from each other, operationally, the two had completely split up.

D said that because she had gone to Han schools, she felt stuck in the middle, with Han people not being close and Uyghurs not welcoming her either. Her eight-year-old child would play on the porch, across from three or four Han families. If her child wanted to play on a skateboard, the kids across the way would get in the way and the parents would not say anything. If she went

---

4 A *minkaohan* is an ethnic minority student who opts to study in Chinese, who takes the regular National College Entrance Examination, and attends a regular institute of higher learning which offers courses in Chinese. – Ed.

outside to say anything, she would be told she wasn't supporting ethnic unity. She felt really hurt, and longed to return to the former relationships shared by people in the mill residential area. When her child bumped into and knocked down a Han student, she added, a Han teacher reacted by asking the Uyghur child to find his teacher. D thought this could have easily been handled with a simple apology. But by this time it had become a very sensitive issue. Many residents of the cotton factory residential compound were now from outside and they hardly knew each other. It was not like before, when parents knew each other and children knew each other, and they would become good friends. She indicated that she would really like to return to those times. She had happy memories of her childhood, but was not so sure about today's children. Since the company's restructuring, a society of familiar acquaintances has become one of familiar strangers. Moreover, although the newly recruited Uyghur mill workers all live in the company dormitories located in the factory area just across the road from the residential area, there are no relations – individual or public – that reach across the divide.

In the state-owned enterprise period, apprenticeship relationships naturally crossed over from production to living quarters. In the private company era, however, the apprenticeship relationship exists only at work and is cut off from daily life. A cotton mill worker named Z told the author that when she became a *tudi* in 1989 her wage was only 30 *yuan*, and that it increased to 45 *yuan* once she was skilled. After that, she started to work with the machines. Her Han *shifu* was very strict at work and was not one for New Year's visits. She felt she had helped her *shifu* do her work, operating her machines. Now, in the private enterprise, she had not been allocated a *tudi*. There were now many more Uyghur workers than Han workers in the workshop, and the canteen was divided – Uyghur workers sat on their side and Han workers sat on their side, with little contact. She spoke Chinese, as she was unable to speak Uyghur. At work, the two groups did not help one another. She felt that people were very selfish these days, just to earn a bit extra. Uyghurs did not help Uyghurs either, and the attitude in the workshop was that you just did your own work, and let others do theirs. Who had time for more? At home, there were children, so you just spoke to the managers and took a half hour "break." Now the workshops had standby workers. People didn't visit each other at the New Year. Now, people just cared about making money and there was not much interaction. She said:

> Now there is almost no interaction with Uyghurs, that is, in our workshop (pointing to her workspace), if Uyghurs are next to each other, then

they will occasionally say something during a ten hour shift. You have to keep walking for ten hours, you have no time to talk. If the Uyghurs cook something delicious, they don't invite us to share, and likewise we don't invite them. We might say hello when we run into each other after work, but if a Uyghur goes to a Han household, what can you give him to eat? Uyghurs are very picky about food and usually don't eat Han food. In the past, colleagues were friends, but none of that is left now. You work as colleagues and hardly know each other after work. Now people are like that. Even among Han people, it's the same way. They might say hello to each other, but no more. Maybe it's because of the money that they have become like that. There are no contradictions, but if there is something that could cause an issue, it is allocating workstations. If you get a good station, you can earn more money than you can if you get a poor station. It is the managers who do the allocation. Some managers are Han, and some are Uyghur.

In this case study we can see that today the production and living interaction spaces inhabited by female workers of Uyghur and Han ethnicity have been split apart and there is little room for social interaction. First, the change in ownership has altered concepts of labor. Before, the idea was that work was undertaken for public benefit; today, with private ownership, it is for individual profit. Second, in the current apprenticeship system, the new generation of workers understands knowledge transmission as being purely technical in nature, and they are indifferent to interpersonal emotional space. Third, the division of production and living spaces mean that the new generation of Uyghur workers does not live in the same courtyards as Han workers, and the original link between working and living together has been broken. Fourth, personal interests are now put first. Old production and social systems have broken down and new systems have not been developed, narrowing the space for interpersonal interactions.

The social interaction space that was created by the apprenticeship system meant that in the 1960s and 1970s *shifu* and *tudi* often ate at each other's homes, and *tudis* were treated like sons and daughters by their *shifus*. In the 1980s, mentoring was not just about working or eating together but also about helping each other in production and even in resolving family issues. After 2000, however, *shifus* no longer took their *tudis* home to eat, and *tudis* would not bring dinner for their *shifus*. In the 1970s, *tudis* had respect for their *shifus*, and they did small things to show their respect.[5] They had deep feelings for their

---

5   For example, when a *shifu* was weaving, a *tudi* would hold the cotton yarn. When taking a break to eat, a *tudi* would get the *shifu* some water. In the residential areas, if the *shifu* was

shifus, expressed in regular visits. Some retired workers felt that by the 1980s, this kind of relation had already weakened, and the new cohorts of *tudis* were lazy or unused to hard work. Only at important festivals, would *tudis* make a call to greet or pay a visit to their *shifu*. By the 1990s, the relationship between *shifu* and *tudi* was further estranged, with just a hello or a visit at the New Year sufficing. Nowadays, *tudis* still greet their *shifus* when they meet, but the relationship does not carry as much respect as before. At the New Year, *tudis* are no longer obliged to visit their *shifus*; many explain that the distance is too great, or that visits are not necessary.

5   Reflection and Discussion

The cause of ethnic unity and progress is an important element of socialism with Chinese characteristics. Consistently promoting this cause is the most important and honorable work that ethnic unity departments should shoulder. To carry on in this endeavor today is one of the most important measures of the success of the Party and the country in its scientific development mission. As the western border areas are mostly populated by minority groups, multi-ethnic social interactions are a basic feature of life in these areas, and ethnic relations constitute the foundation of the structure of social relations. To better understand the mechanisms of inter-ethnic interaction, we need to carry out more research into society and social relations. Ethnic relations are the base of stability in the border areas, and are essential to the construction of a harmonious society. This is critical to ensuring people's livelihoods and security in the border areas. Work relating to ethnic minorities increasingly requires the promotion of multi-ethnic exchange, communication and integration in order to deepen understanding, promote unity and achieve common prosperity (Gong 2012).

After the July 5 incident in Ürümqi in 2009, people began to reevaluate the situation in Xinjiang. Some raised doubts about the ability of the government to guarantee security in Xinjiang, and some thought major adjustments to ethnic policies were needed. There were different opinions, particularly with regard to how to develop Xinjiang's economy, how to resolve the issues that led to social upheaval, and how to safeguard ethnic unity. Historical experience has shown that speed is not necessarily in the best interest of economic

---

busy cooking, the *tudi* might occasionally look after the children. The *tudi* would be like a member of the family. Exchanging such meaningful gestures was a positive way of interacting. There was no obligation to do so, but it made daily life and work between *shifu* and *tudi* a little bit smoother.

development. Though we take livelihood issues as Xinjiang's biggest challenge now, we should also note that Xinjiang's problems include questions of cultural sensibilities and social order. Xinjiang's ecological environment is fragile and minority groups have not yet been initiated into the large-scale industrial revolution taking place, and therefore need time to adapt to concepts of modernization, modern forms of production, and modern ways of living. How different cultural groups experience spatial issues of production in a period of economic transition is critically important in describing and understanding the state of ethnic relations in Xinjiang.

The Kashgar Cotton Mill is a mainly Uyghur and Han multi-ethnic factory community and its salient feature has been work-life interconnectedness. As production and livelihood fed off each other, the Han–Uyghur interaction space developed cross-cultural characteristics. The skilled workers in the Kashgar Cotton Mill were not like those described by Michael Burawoy (1979; 1985); they were not dependent on hegemony or coercion-based monopolistic labor processes, nor on voluntary servitude, and they were certainly not, in the labor process, producing consent through "the game of making out." These workers had their own interests to satisfy. First, identity transformation: The mill cultivated the very first cohort of Uyghur industrial workers and of the first 800 workers, 300 were sent to Qingdao, 200 to Zhengzhou and 100 to Ürümqi and other places for training and study, laying the foundation for the mill's ethnic labor force and the backbone of its expertise. That is the historical background of the creation of a Han–Uyghur interaction space in production.

Second, promotion opportunities: In the fifty-five-year production history of the Kashgar Cotton Mill, the promotion opportunities for its workers were vastly different during the period it was a state-owned enterprise compared to after it became a private company. As a state-owned enterprise, the mill allowed and encouraged workers to become managers, but as a private enterprise, the owners, who had spent money to buy the mill, could not be expected to give management positions over to producers. In the original production structure, production workers, especially Uyghurs, could aspire to management positions. But after enterprise restructuring, skilled workers could not even get close to the high-level management space. Of course, the private owners would not want to surrender their own economic and social status, but even so, it is notable that workers' basic skill development in inner China was also eliminated. This move was not conducive to creating good spatial interactions between Uyghur and Han workers, and it has had a negative influence on Uyghur-Han social relations.

Labor processes are key to Marx's concept of capitalist surplus value production. How the labor process is organized so that labor power is transformed into labor is at the heart of the study of labor processes in Marxism. In describing changes in the production and living relationships of Han and Uyghur workers during the period of social transformation in Xinjiang, the author returns to viewing workers as agents and looks closely at internal and external factors of the labor process, including the influence of ethnicity, property relations, the apprenticeship system, and interaction spaces on factory politics and ethnic relations. In particular, with respect to Uyghur and Han groups, we see that in relationships connected to production and living, cultural spaces were developed and then ruptured. Structural changes and practical processes were closely linked. It can be said that the quality of labor relations in the mill has mirrored Uyghur-Han relations in Xinjiang. We see that during changing periods, spatial cohesion and separation reflect changing ethnic relations. By developing an ethnic perspective and using spatial theory, this study increases our understanding of economic and social changes during the transitional period, particularly with regard to inter-ethnic interaction, and provides important theoretical and practical insights.

References

Bao Erhan 包尔汉. 1984. 新疆五十年 [*50 Years of Xinjiang*]. Beijing: Literary and Historical Document Press.

Burawoy, Michael. 1979. *Manufacturing Consent: Changes in the Labor Process under Monopoly Capitalism*. Chicago: The University of Chicago Press.

Burawoy, Michael. 1985. *The Politics of Production: Factory Regimes Under Capitalism and Socialism*. London: Verso.

Dong Jiansheng 董建生 and Yan Meiran 严美然. 1982. 喀什棉纺织厂坚持进行民族政策教育 各族职工和睦相处齐心协力搞生产 ["Kashgar Cotton Mill Adheres to the Nationalities Policy in Education; All Ethnicities Work and Live Together for the Sake of Production"]. 新疆日报 (*Xinjiang Daily*), February 9, 1982.

Durkheim, Emile. 1999. 宗教生活的基本形式 [*The Elementary Forms of the Religious Life*]. Translated by Qu Dong 渠东 and Ji Zhe 汲喆. Shanghai: Shanghai People's Publishing House.

Fei Xiaotong 费孝通. 1989. 中华民族的多元一体格局 ["The Pluralistic Pattern of Chinese Ethnicities"]. 北京大学学报 (哲学社会科学版) [*Journal of Peking University (Philosophy & Social Sciences)*], 4: 3–21.

Foucault, Michel. 1999. 必须保卫社会 [*Society Must Be Defended*]. Translated by Qian Han 钱翰. Shanghai: Shanghai People's Publishing House.

Goffman, Erving. 1959. *The Presentation of Self in Everyday Life*. New York: Doubleday.

Gong Xuezeng 龚学增. 2012. 正确理解和把握党中央提出的 "各民族交往交流交融" ["The Correct Understanding and Grasp of the Chinese Communist Party's Statement on 'Interethnic Interaction, Communication, and Integration'"]. 中国民族报 [*China Ethnic News*], May 4, 2012.

Gong Yikuang 龚一匡. 1994. 喀什市场 ["Kashgar Market"]. In 中国人民政治协商会议喀什市委员会文史资料委员会编 [Chinese People's Political Consultative Committee Kashgar Cultural and History Materials Committee] 喀什市文史资料 (第 9 辑) [*Kashgar cultural and historical materials* (Vol. 9)], Kashgar: Kashgar Daily Printing Factory.

Gordon, Milton M. 1964. *Assimilation in American Life: The Role of Race, Religion, and National Origins*. Oxford: Oxford University Press.

He Mingjie 何明洁. 2009. 劳动与姐妹分化: "和记" 生产政体个案研究 ["Labor and Sisterhood Division: Case Study of 'Heji' Production Policy"]. 社会学研究 [*Sociological Studies*], 2: 149–176.

Huang Dayuan 黄达远. 2011. 乌鲁木齐城市社会空间演化及其当代启示 ["Evolution and Contemporary Enlightenment in Ürümqi's Urban Social Space"]. 西北民族研究 [*Northwest Ethnic Studies*], 3: 70–77.

Jarring, Gunnar. 1999. 重返喀什噶尔 [*Return to Kashgar*]. Translated by Cui Yanhu 崔延虎 and Guo Yingjie 郭颖杰. Ürümqi: Xinjiang People's Publishing House.

Lefebvre, Henri. 2008. 空间与政治 [*Space and Politics*]. Translated by Li Chun 李春. Shanghai: Shanghai People's Publishing House.

Li Ze 李泽 et al., ed. 1984. 喀什棉纺织厂调查资料集 (二) 资料统计集 [*A Collection of Survey Materials from Kashgar Cotton Mill (2) Material Compilation*]. Ürümqi: Ethnic Research Institute, Xinjiang Academy of Social Sciences.

Lin Aiyun 林蔼云. 2006. 漂泊的家: 晋江 – 香港移民研究 ["Diasporic Home: Jinjiang-Hong Kong Migration Research"]. 社会学研究 [*Sociological Studies*], 2: 134–161.

Liu Ming 刘明. 2013a. 新疆社会转型中维吾尔族劳工生产交往探研: 以喀什棉纺织厂为例 ["Research into Uyghur Labor Production Interactions in a Transitioning Xinjiang Society: The Example of Kashgar Cotton Mill"]. In 社会转型与新生代农民工 [*Social Transformation and a New Generation of Migrant Workers*], edited by Shen Yuan 沈原. Beijing: Social Science Academic Press.

Liu Ming 刘明. 2013b. 新疆民族学人类学理论与实践 [*Anthropological Theory and Practice of the Study of Xinjiang Ethnicities*]. Ürümqi: Xinjiang People's Publishing House.

Liu Ming 刘明 and Cui Yanhu 崔延虎. 2006. 工厂社区的多民族交际研究: 以喀什棉纺织厂师徒交往为例 ["Research into Communication Between Workers of All Ethnicities in Factory Social Quarters: Kashgar Cotton Mill's Apprenticeship System"]. 新疆师范大学学报 (哲学社会科学版) [*Journal of Xinjiang Normal University (Philosophy and Social Sciences)*], 3: 60–64.

Liu Yongqian 刘永谦, ed. 1984. 喀什棉纺织厂调查资料集(一)个案资料集 [*A Collection of Survey Materials from Kashgar Cotton Mill (1) Material Compilation*]. Ürümqi: Ethnic Research Institute, Xinjiang Academy of Social Sciences.

Long Xifeng 龙锡丰. 1987. 喀什棉纺织厂连续三年向苏联出口印花布 ["Kashgar Cotton Mill Exports Patterned Cotton Cloth to the USSR for Three Years in a Row"]. In 喀什年鉴 [*Kashgar Yearbook*]. Ürümqi: Xinjiang People's Publishing House.

Ma Rong 马戎. 2000. 新疆喀什地区的民族人口分布 ["Kashgar's Population Distribution by Ethnicity"]. 西北民族研究 [*Northwest Ethnic Studies*], 2: 1–9.

Marx, Karl and Friedrich Engels. 1995. 马克思恩格斯全集 [*The Collected Works of Marx and Engels*] (Vol. 30). Beijing: People's Publishing House.

Miao Jianxing 苗剑新. 1985. 喀什棉纺织厂婚姻家庭问题调查 ["A Survey of Marriage and Family Issues at Kashgar Cotton Mill"]. 新疆大学学报 [*Journal of Xinjiang University*], 2: 1–10.

Pan Zequan 潘泽泉. 2008. 农民工融入城市的困境: 共有的空间何以可能 ["Issues in the Integration of Migrant Rural Workers into the Cities: The Possibilities of Public Space"]. 中州学刊 [*Academic Journal of Zhongzhou*], 3: 109–113.

Ren Yan 任焰 and Pun Ngai 潘毅. 2006. 宿舍劳动体制: 劳动控制与抗争的另类空间 ["Dormitory Labor System: An Alternative Space for Labor Control and Protest"]. 开放时代 [*Open Times*], 3: 124–134.

Shen Yuan 沈原 and Wen Xiang 闻翔. 2012. 转型社会学视角下的劳工研究: 问题, 理论与方法 ["Labor Research from the Perspective of Social Transition Studies: Theory and Methods"]. In 面向社会转型的民族志 [*Ethnography of Social Transition*], edited by Guo Yuhua 郭于华, Beijing: Social Sciences Academic Press.

Simmel, George. 1997. "The Sociology of Space". In *Simmel on Culture*, edited by D. Frisby, David and Mike Featherstone. London: SAGE Publications, Ltd.

Wang Hua 王华. 2011. 空间的底边与底边的空间: 对南京安德门民工就业市场的研究 ["The Lowest Side of the Space and the Space at the Lowest Side: Nanjing's Andemen Migrant Employment Market"]. 江苏行政学院学报 [*Journal of Jiangsu Administration Institute*], 5: 70–75.

Weber, Max. 2010. 新教伦理与资本主义精神 [*The Protestant Ethic and the Spirit of Capitalism*]. Translated by Zheng Zhiyong 郑志勇. Nanchang: Jiangxi People's Publishing House.

Zeng Heping 曾和平. 1988. 喀什棉纺织厂族际交往调查研究 ["Survey Research into Inter-Ethnic Communication at the Kashgar Cotton Mill"]. 新疆大学学报 [*Journal of Xinjiang University*], 4: 30–36.

Zhou Xiao 周潇. 2007. 关系霸权: 对建筑工地劳动过程的一项田野研究 [*Owning the Relationship: Field Research into the Process of Construction Site Labor*]. 清华大学硕士学位论文 [Unpublished master's thesis, Tsinghua University, Beijing, China].

CHAPTER 6

Corporate Social Responsibility in the Global Toy Industry's Supply Chain: an Empirical Study of Walmart Supplier Factories in China

Yu Xiaomin (余晓敏)
Translated by Shayan Momin

Abstract

Since the 1990s, Walmart, the world's largest retailer, has faced growing public criticism for using sweatshop labor in its supply chains. In 1992, when corporate social responsibility practices centering on adoption and implementation of codes of conduct regarding labor standards were gaining steam, Walmart also adopted its own codes of conduct, "Standards for Suppliers," requiring its overseas suppliers to comply with certain minimum labor standards. Based on empirical studies at three of Walmart's toy supplier factories located in Shenzhen, this paper examines the dynamics and effectiveness of Walmart codes on workplace labor standards.

Keywords

anti-sweatshop movement – corporate social responsibility – global supply chains – labor standards – toy industry – Walmart

1   Introduction[1]

In the 1990s, facing pressure from the anti-sweatshop movement, many world-famous brand operators and retailers began to formulate their own "corporate codes of conduct" to assume social responsibility in addressing labor issues within global supply chains. These codes required suppliers to improve working conditions and respect basic worker rights and interests. Various monitoring mechanisms were developed in order to ensure the proper implementation of

---

[1] This article originally appeared in *Open Times* 2008, no. 5, pp. 77–87.

the codes, including "internal monitoring," "external monitoring," and "multi-party surveillance" (Yu 2006). The world's toy industry has become a leader in the corporate social responsibility (CSR) movement. As the world's largest toy retailer, Walmart developed a list of labor standards for its suppliers 1992.

Known as the "world's factory," China is the world's largest toy producer and exporter. With over 8,000 toy factories and 3.5 million employees, 75% of the global toy industry's output is located in China.[2] Toy production in China is mostly located in the southeastern region. In 2005, 95% of domestic toy production was located in five provinces and one municipality: Guangdong, Jiangsu, Zhejiang, Shandong, Fujian, and Shanghai.[3] For many years, China's competitive advantage in toy production came from cheap land, labor, resources and materials. At the same time, however, labor practices in China's export processing sector became a subject of international concern. Since the 1990s, China's toy export industry not only saw the rise of corporate social responsibility, but it became the "world's laboratory" in experimenting with various codes of conduct and monitoring mechanisms.

How is corporate social responsibility, led by retailers, implemented within supply chains in China? In implementing codes of conduct, what kinds of real improvements in labor conditions in China's export industries can be observed? These questions have become a common research subject in many different disciplines (Pun 2005a; Tan and Liu 2003; Yu 2007; Egels-Zandén 2007; Frenkel 2001; Pun 2005b; Sum and Pun 2005; Yu 2008). In examining the results of implementing codes of conduct, many researchers emphasize local Chinese institutional factors such as the effects of legal and corporate culture (Frenkel 2001) and the motivations of suppliers and management strategies (Pun 2005). Few studies, however, have investigated the impacts of global supply chains, the particulars of globalized industry, and business strategies of international brands as they relate to the implementation and effectiveness of corporate codes of conduct.

This paper attempts to fill this gap in the research. Focusing on the corporate social responsibility movement in the global toy industry, this paper uses Walmart's toy supply chain in China as a representative case and investigates the effects of the unique characteristics of the toy industry's global supply chain and Walmart's "Everyday Low Prices" business strategy on the labor situation in suppliers' factories and on the implementation of corporate codes

---

2 "Toy markets uncertain of year's profits," *Global News Wire – Asia Africa Intelligence Wire*, December 23, 2005.
3 "Bigger and better: The continued growth of China's toy industry," *Playthings*, October 1, 2006.

of conduct. At the same time, the author examines Walmart's fundamental mechanism for implementing their code of conduct, which consists of a self-monitoring, "punishment-oriented" model. Finally, through a comparative study of the implementation of codes of conduct in three of Walmart's toy factories in Shenzhen, this article discusses the effects of Walmart's conduct code on three aspects of labor conditions: working times within supplier factories, wages, and workers' living conditions. Empirical materials for this study include in-depth interviews with nineteen workers in the three factories.[4] At the same time, the author has analyzed secondary materials, such as corporate annual reports, industrial organization reports, and online resources from Lexis Nexis and Chinainfobank, in order to gain a comprehensive understanding of the global toy industry, Walmart's supply chain and the CSR movement.

2   The International Toy Industry's "Walmartization" and Labor Standards

2.1   *The Unique Characteristics of the Structure of the Global Toy Supply Chain*

Over the last forty years, the global toy industry has rapidly expanded. Annual sales currently reach up to US$60 billion. For many years, the global toy market has been dominated by several large American manufacturers. Starting in the 1950s, these manufacturers began to move low value-adding production to Asian countries or regions with low wages (Japan, Taiwan, Hong Kong, and China) in order to cut costs. The original toy manufacturers then gradually became "brand operators," specializing in research and development, design, marketing, and other high value-adding links in the supply chain. At the same time, toy production and consumption continued to separate – most consumers were located in North America, Western Europe and other developed countries, while production took place in developing countries in Asia.

Today, the most important structural feature of the global toy industry's supply chain is monopolization by large corporations. This trend can be traced back to the 1980s. For example, of the main toy companies operating in 1976, eleven went out of business by 1995, and twelve were acquired by the two largest toy companies operating today, Mattel and Hasbro (Clark 2007). There are also monopolies at the retail terminal segment of the supply chain. Over the

---

4   Thanks to Jenny Wai-ling Chan for major contributions during our research and for providing many useful suggestions for analyzing the data.

last twenty years, the share of the toy retail market held by smaller department stores has been gradually shrinking. Discount stores, such as Walmart, Kmart and Target, and chain toy stores, such as Toys R Us, are continuously expanding.

2.2   The Walmartization of the International Toy Industry

In 2000, Walmart surpassed Toys R Us to become the world's largest toy retailer. For example, in the US, the world's largest toy consumer, Walmart's market share has increased year after year, reaching US$21.9 billion in 2005, amounting to 30.8% of the total market share. Walmart's overwhelming market position has had a huge impact on the global toy industry's competitive landscape and business models. In order to survive, companies in other parts of the global supply chain have had to adapt to Walmart's "large volume, low prices, low costs" business model. As Walmart has the largest share of the global toy market, its "everyday low prices" business strategy has intensified price competition within the market, eliminating retailers without competitive advantages in price. In 2003, Walmart launched the most brutal "price war" in the history of the American toy industry, reducing average market prices and forcing the closure of hundreds of toy retailers (Clark 2007).

Walmart's strategy depends on a management model that constantly decreases costs within the supply chain. Walmart currently has more than a thousand suppliers worldwide, with most of its purchases taking place in China. Since Walmart opened its global sourcing center in Shenzhen in 2003, China's exports to the company have increased further, reaching US$18 billion in 2004. But Walmart's massive sales and purchases are a double-edged sword for suppliers – larger orders for Walmart mean smaller margins for suppliers. At the same time, toy retailers continue to introduce "private label" products in an attempt to achieve higher profits by effectively controlling pricing and production costs. Comparatively speaking, Walmart's private label product suppliers must actively adjust to Walmart's low-cost strategy.

2.3   The "Race to the Bottom" of Labor Standards

When brand retailers and operators at the top of the supply chain adhere to Walmart's low-pricing strategy and compete to lower their production costs, workers at the bottom of the supply chain suffer. The proportion of "labor cost" to "retail price" is decreasing year by year. In 2001, the Hong Kong Christian Industrial Committee began researching labor costs embedded in toys from Mattel, Hasbro, McDonald's, and Disney. Their report showed that for fifty types of toys, labor costs (as a proportion of retail price) ranged from 0.4% at the lowest to 6% at the highest (Hong Kong Christian Industrial Committee 2001a).

Price wars and top-down-driven cost reduction in the supply chain led to an overall decline in labor standards within the toy industry. Countless news reports and international nongovernmental organization (NGO) reports exposed all kinds of labor problems within the toy industry – injuries, fires, occupational illnesses, excessive overtime, child labor, forced labor, and low wages.[5] In 1993, more than 200 people were killed and over 500 were injured in two major toy factory fires in Thailand (Kader toy factory) and Shenzhen (Chili factory). These major industrial accidents caused occupational health and safety within the global toy industry to become a focal point of public criticism. In the 1990s, civic organizations in developed countries, including NGOs, student groups, unions, and religious groups, launched a global "anti-sweatshop movement," demanding that brand retailers and operators take responsibility for labor issues within their supply chains. The ensuing flood of negative press and pressure from civil society had a significant impact on companies' marketing and brand images as well as a negative effect on the stock market. In response, major retailers and brand operators in the global toy industry developed company codes of conduct, announced commitments to social responsibility, and demanded that suppliers within the larger global supply chain adhere to codes of conduct to improve working conditions and respect basic rights and interests of workers in their factories.

3 The International Toy Industry's Corporate Social Responsibility Movement

In the 1990s, the global toy industry's developing corporate social responsibility movement revolved around the formulation and implementation of a series of corporate codes of conduct. In 1992, Walmart developed "standards for suppliers;" in 1993, Hasbro formulated a "global code of business ethics;" in 1995, the International Council of Toy Industries (ICTI) passed their "business practices code of conduct;" in 1997, Mattel developed their "global manufacturing standards;" in the same year, Toys R Us, the largest toy retailer in the United States, developed a "supplier code of conduct." By comparing the specific

---

5 See "Inside Santa's sweatshops Chinese workers slave in firetraps to make our toys," *The Toronto Star*, December 17, 1995; "Santa Finds a Bargain in China: Low-Paid Workers Make Toys by the Millions," *The Washington Post*, December 24, 1995; "Chinese workers make Christmas toys for UK at 10p an hour," *The Independent*, December 24, 1995; "Furby's dirty secret: Chinese workers toil in dingy factories to churn out the cuddly toy," *The Ottawa Citizen*, December 11, 1998; Asia Monitor Resource Center, 2000; and Hong Kong Christian Industrial Committee, 2000, 2001a, and 2001b.

content of each company's code of conduct, we find that most codes follow the principle of "legal minimalism," requiring suppliers to respect the lawful rights and interests of workers – labor conditions, working time, remuneration, etc. (see Table 6.1) – in accordance with the legal requirements of the country or region where they are invested. With regard to the content of the codes, their biggest problem lies in their failure to touch on the inadequate rights and protections of workers. Taking the problem of wages as an example, in many

TABLE 6.1 Comparison of "codes of conduct" and implementation/monitoring mechanisms for major global brand operators and retailers

	Hasbro	Mattel	Toys R Us	Walmart	ICTI
1. Contents of the codes of conduct					
– No forced labor	✓	✓	✓	✓	✓
– No child labor	✓ Workers are 16 years old and up	✓	✓	✓	✓
– Wages	✓ Legally mandated minimum wage or local industry wage	✓ Legally mandated minimum wage or local industry wage	✓ Legally mandated minimum wage or local industry wage	✓ Legally mandated minimum wage or local industry wage	✓ Legally mandated minimum wage or local industry wage
– Worktime	✓ Adhere to local laws	✓ Adhere to local laws	✓ Adhere to local laws	✓ No more than 14 hours a day, no more than 6 days/72 hours a week	✓ Adhere to local laws

TABLE 6.1 Comparison of "codes of conduct" and implementation/monitoring (cont.)

	Hasbro	Mattel	Toys R Us	Walmart	ICTI
– No bullying	✓	✓	✓	✓	x
– Health and safety	✓	✓	✓	✓	✓
– Free association	✓	✓	✓	✓	✓
2. Monitoring	Internal monitoring (first party, second party)	Internal monitoring (first party); Independent monitoring	Internal monitoring (first party); External monitoring (SA8000)	Internal monitoring (first party, second party)	External monitoring (CARE process)

SOURCES: HASBRO, INC., 1993; INTERNATIONAL COUNCIL OF TOY INDUSTRIES, 1995; MATTEL, INC. 1997; TOYS R US INC. 2002; WALMART, 2005.

developing nations, the legally mandated minimum wage is set too low to meet the basic standards of workers. In some countries, even though the statutory minimum standards are relatively high, the rights and interests of workers are difficult to guarantee because of problems with legal enforcement.

Unlike national legislation, company codes of conduct lack enforcement mechanisms. As seen in Table 6.1, the primary enforcement mechanisms of the codes of conduct for international toy companies are internal monitoring, external supervision and independent supervision. Most of the large brand operators and retailers (such as Hasbro, Walmart, and Toys R Us) rely primarily on internal supervision, which includes first-party supervision (implemented by company employees) and second-party supervision (implemented by supervisory organizations hired by the company or other for-profit organizations). But the credibility, transparency, and effectiveness of internal monitoring have long been questioned. Critics point out that internal monitoring is usually carried out with prior notice given to inspection sites. Factories under inspection often falsify written records pertaining to wages, overtime, labor contracts, and social insurance. Workers also receive instructions about how to correctly answer questions they might receive from internal monitors. As a result, internal monitors often fail to understand the reality of working conditions within factories.[6] At the same time, internal monitoring reports are not open to the public and therefore lack necessary transparency.

In response to criticisms of internal monitoring, some toy brands began experimenting with external monitoring – namely, inspections from certified third-party monitoring agencies. For example, Toys R Us uses the SA8000 certification system promoted by the American organization Social Accountability International for supplier certification. Currently, the most influential monitoring system is the CARE program, which was created by the International Council of Toy Industries (ICTI) in 2004. In the CARE program, a certified and professionally trained auditing firm uses ICTI's "business code of conduct" to conduct factory inspections. By the beginning of 2007, 1,022 toy factories had joined the CARE program, with 533 receiving certification.[7] However, because external monitoring relies on for-profit auditing companies for factory certification, its credibility and independence is still under question.

Continuing public criticisms of both internal and external monitoring mechanisms led to the emergence of "independent monitoring" mechanisms. There is still no uniform definition for independent monitoring, but broadly speaking, independent monitoring may be conducted by various supervisory agencies that are not directly paid by companies or factories, such as NGOs, trade unions, and private monitoring companies (O'Rourke 2003). A more rigid definition includes only monitoring activities conducted by non-profit organizations (Esbenshade 2004). Mattel is the only toy company to use independent monitoring systems. The company set up a non-profit monitoring organization in Baruch College's Zicklin School of Business (part of the CUNY system). The Mattel Independent Monitoring Committee (MIMCO), which consists of scholars and experts, is part of this monitoring organization. MIMCO serves to monitor the implementation of Mattel's global manufacturing standards in supplier factories and to report directly to the public. However, due to the lack of participation on the part of workers and other interested parties, NGOs have criticized Mattel's supervisory agency, believing that the agency should increase worker influence and participation (Asia Monitor Resource Center 2000; Hong Kong Christian Industrial Committee 2001a).

So far, we have found that in the past ten years, the exacerbation of labor issues caused by the structural features of the global toy industry as well as the "Walmartization" of business practices has aroused the concern of different

---

6 For detailed discussions, see Hong Kong Christian Industrial Committee (2001b); China Labor Watch and National Labor Committee (2005); Students and Scholars Against Corporate Misbehavior (2006); The National Labor Committee (2005); The National Labor Committee and China Labor Watch (2006).
7 http://www.icti-care.org.

stakeholders all over the world. The anti-sweatshop movement and widespread criticism have given rise to the promotion and development of corporate social responsibility within the global toy industry, most clearly represented in a variety of company codes of conduct and their implementation mechanisms. But how are codes of conduct that are developed by toy companies implemented within the Chinese supply chain? For workers and enterprises, what is the practical effect of the implementation of these codes? In the following section, we will search for answers to these questions through an empirical study of three of Walmart's supplier factories.

4   Empirical Research on Walmart's Codes of Conduct and Their Implementation

4.1   *Factory Profiles and Labor Problems*

Our research focused on three factories we call TX, XTX, and ZX. The specific characteristics of these factories are presented in Table 6.2. Most of them are Hong Kong invested enterprises, but they each have unique characteristics with regards to the time of establishment, scale of investment, number of workers, types of products, and value of output. Accordingly, the general situation of the toy industry can be represented through these three factories.

TABLE 6.2   Overview of three toy supplier factories

	TX	XTX	ZX
Location	Shenzhen, Longgang District, Buji township	Shenzhen, Bao'an District, Xixiang township	Shenzhen, Bao'an District, Songgang township
Year of establishment	1992	1995	1995
Type of company	Hong Kong invested	Hong Kong invested	Foreign invested
Registered capital	4 million HKD	5.7 million HKD	88 million HKD
Product	Toys and gifts (plush, plastic, and electric toys)	Toys and gifts (plastic and electric)	Toys and gifts (electric)
Main clients	Walmart, JC Penny, Kay Bee, K-Mart	Walmart and others	Walmart and others
Annual exports	400 million RMB	unknown	unknown
Number of workers	5000–6000	~1000	1000–2000

Global toy sales are extremely seasonal. For example, about 45% of toy sales occur in the six weeks before Christmas. The seasonal nature of sales requires manufacturers to use certain employment systems in order to maintain flexibility in number of workers and hours of work. Of the three factories in our study, over 80% of workers were migrants from Hunan, Hubei, Sichuan, Jiangxi, and Henan. Most were females between the ages of eighteen and thirty, and most did not have formal contracts for a fixed number of years. This allowed factories flexibility in adjusting the number of workers and working hours in accordance with changes in order quantities. For example, in these three factories, the total number of workers and working hours during the busy season (from April to November) were double those of the low season (December to March).

With regards to labor conditions, all three factories had many well-publicized problems. In our study, we found that the main labor problems included excessive overtime, illegal nonpayment of overtime hours, and occupational health and safety hazards. The problems in the factories were not only closely related to the autocratic management style of many enterprises based in Hong Kong and Taiwan, but they were also rooted in China's specific labor structure during the market transition period. Under this system, the mechanisms underpinning labor laws, social security, minimum wage guarantees, and trade unions have deficiencies that prevent them from being able to protect the legitimate rights and interests of migrant workers in foreign-funded enterprises. Even though the [1994] Labor Law has strict regulations with regard to workers' rights and interests, local governments often either lack the power to supervise the implementation of Labor Law provisions or are unwilling to enforce them for the sake of developing the local economy. Second, social security protections for migrant workers are extremely limited. In August 2006, the National Bureau of Statistics surveyed 29,425 migrant workers as part of a study on the quality of migrant worker living conditions. The report, titled "Urban Migrant Workers' Labor, Employment, and Social Security Status,"[8] showed that the proportion of migrants without insurance, including life insurance, health insurance, unemployment insurance, and work injury insurance totaled 73.37%, 73.77%, 84.65%, and 67.46% respectively.[9] In the three factories in our survey, we found that only a small number of workers in TX factory purchased work injury insurance. No workers in XTX or ZX factories bought any form of social insurance. Third, the minimum wage system cannot meet the basic demands and needs of workers. The Ministry of Labor formulated the "Minimum Wage Regulations for Enterprises" (企业

---

8 城市农民工劳动就业和社会保障状况.
9 http://www.syntao.com/Page_Show.asp?Page_ID=3297.

最低工资规定) in 1993, establishing China's minimum wage system. In 2004, the Ministry of Labor and Social Security provided a revised set of "Minimum Wage Regulations" (最低工资规定). Currently, all provinces, autonomous regions and municipalities have established minimum wage guarantee systems. However, as the minimum wage standards have become localized, local governments have acted to curb wage inflation in order to maintain competitive advantages in cheap labor. This has led to low minimum wages that fail to meet the standards established by labor laws and that do not guarantee the livelihood of workers. For example, the minimum wage in the Bao'an (宝安) and Longgang (龙岗) districts of Shenzhen municipality in 1999 was 419 yuan. By 2005, it rose to only 580, making it difficult for workers to fulfill basic needs such as housing, clothing, food, travel, and medical needs. Finally, the union's role in representing and protecting migrant workers is also extremely limited. As in many other foreign-invested enterprises, there is no trade union in the three factories surveyed in our study, so it is difficult for workers to express themselves and maintain their own interests through formal mechanisms.

In recent years, the CSR movement has continued to develop within the global toy industry, leading to the emergence of a variety of new codes of conduct and implementation mechanisms. If these codes can be effectively implemented at the factory level, then there may be hope for improving labor conditions in the toy manufacturing industry. The next section will take Walmart's code of conduct as an example to explore how codes of conduct are implemented within the supply chain.

4.2   Implementation of Walmart's Code of Conduct

In 1992, Walmart formulated its "standards for suppliers," banning companies from using child labor and forced labor. They also required suppliers to provide safe working conditions, reasonable hours, fair pay, and to comply with local laws and legislation. In the 1990s, Walmart created a "factory inspections" system and hired Hong Kong's Pacific Resources Export, Ltd. (PREL) to carry out inspections to monitor the implementation of the "standards for suppliers" in various factories. In 2002, Walmart terminated its contract with PREL and began global procurement. Factory inspections were then done by in-house personnel or audit firms and certification bodies directly employed by Walmart (Walmart Stores, Inc. 2004).

Generally speaking, Walmart's implementation schemes have two characteristics. The first is "self-policing" – Walmart has complete control over the formulation and implementation of the monitoring mechanisms as well as the publication of monitoring reports, and other stakeholders do not participate or have substantial influence. For many years, critics have demanded, to no avail, that Walmart create credible and transparent "independent monitoring" systems. Second, Walmart's code implementation is embedded within a "buyer-oriented commodity chain," in which there is an unequal power relationship between brand operators and retailers and their suppliers. This relationship features a type of "punishment-oriented" implementation mechanism. The cost of improving labor conditions is passed onto Walmart's suppliers. Factories found to be in serious violation of the code will no longer supply Walmart. For example, in 2004, 108 of Walmart's 5,300 overseas suppliers were removed from the supply chain because of the use of child labor or other serious offenses.[10]

The three factories in our survey had different experiences with Walmart's factory inspections. As one of Walmart's main toy suppliers in China, TX Factory had undergone many inspections in the last few years. XTX and ZX, on the other hand, were rarely monitored. Through interviews with workers at TX, we found that Walmart conducted three or four factory inspections a year, mainly during the busy season. Workers were often asked about working hours, wages, and their willingness to work overtime. However, for a number of reasons, workers believe that it was difficult for client companies to know the reality of their working conditions through factory inspections. Factories received advance notice of inspections and managers would tell workers how to answer questions. Workers were also warned that "if they gave wrong answers, the factory would lose Walmart as a client, and they would be out of a job." Therefore, workers were afraid to tell the truth. At the same time, in order to pass inspections, there were many "false appearances" in the factory. For example, in order to give the appearance that workers did not work more than 72 hours a week during the busy season, the factory required workers clock out at 8 PM. After clocking out, however, they were required to go back to work until midnight, and there was no record of their overtime hours.

4.3   *The Effects of Inspection on Working Hours*

By comparing information collected in three factories, we found that Walmart's factory inspections did help shorten working time. As seen in Table 6.3, weekly working hours during the busy season at TX – the only factory with frequent inspections – were under 72 hours. At XTX and ZX Factories, the number of weekly working hours reached as high as 108 and 96 hours, respectively. Additionally, workers at TX had one day off per week, while workers at XTX and ZX worked seven days a week during the busy season with only one day off per month.

---

10   "Walmart Approach to Ethics Goes Global: Firms Seen Adding Execs to Hedge Liability," *Arkansas Democrat-Gazette*, March 7, 2006.

TABLE 6.3 Factory comparisons

TX Factory (undergoes Walmart factory inspections)

Worktime	Scheduled working days	Monday to Saturday: 7:30–11:30 AM (4 hrs.) 1:30–5:30 PM (4 hrs.) 6:30–9:30 PM (3 hrs. overtime) Sundays off
	Workday	11 hours
	Workweek	66 hours
	Workweek plus overtime	72 hours (3 overtime hours × 6 days × 4 weeks)
Wages	Structure	Basic wage (local minimum wage, 480 yuan in 2004, 580 in 2005) + overtime pay + subsidy bonus – food and boarding fees (180–190 yuan)
	Average monthly pay	600–700 yuan in the busy season, 300–400 in low season
Dorm conditions		50 yuan deducted from every worker's monthly pay. 12 people to a room, new dorms have toilets and showers, but old dorms have common showers and bathrooms in poor conditions
Cafeteria conditions		130–140 yuan deducted every month for food, but the food quality is poor

XTX Factory (not inspected regularly):

Worktime	Scheduled working days	Monday to Saturday: 8:00–12:00 AM (4 hrs.) 1:30–5:30 PM (4 hrs.) 6:30–9:30/10:30 PM (3–4 hours of overtime) Sundays off in off season, 11–12 hours overtime in busy season
	Workday	11–12 hours
	Workweek	66–72 hours (off season), 77–84 hours (busy season)
	Workweek plus overtime	72–96 hours (off season), 83–108 hours (busy season)
Wages	Monthly wages plus overtime	Basic wage (local minimum wage, 480 yuan in 2004, 580 in 2005) + overtime pay + subsidy bonus – food and boarding fees (180–190 yuan)

TABLE 6.3 Factory comparisons (cont.)

XTX Factory (not inspected regularly):

	Average monthly pay	600–700 yuan in the busy season, 300–400 in low season
Dorm conditions		50 yuan deducted from every worker's monthly pay. 12 people to a room, new dorms have toilets and showers, but old dorms have common showers and bathrooms in poor conditions
Cafeteria conditions		130–140 yuan deducted every month for food, but the food quality is poor

ZX Factory (not inspected regularly)

Worktime	Scheduled working days	Monday to Saturday: 8:00–12:00 AM (4 hrs.) 1:30–5:30 PM (4 hrs.) 6:30–9:30/10:30 PM (3–4 hours of overtime) Sundays off
	Workdays	11–12 hours
	Workweek (off season)	66–72 hours
	Workweek (busy season)	72–96 hours
Wages		Wages are based on piece rates
	Average monthly pay	1100–1200 yuan in the busy season, 300–400 in low season
Dorm conditions		Free dorms. 8–9 people to a dorm, dorms have toilets and showers
Cafeteria conditions		Free

4.4   Effects of Inspections on Wages

As Table 6.3 illustrates, however, Walmart's factory inspections had basically no effect on raising wages. Of the three factories, the one with the highest wages was ZX, which also had the fewest number of factory inspections. Walmart's code of conduct stipulates that wages should "be either the legally set minimum wage or the average local wage, whichever is higher" (Walmart Stores, Inc. 2005). During our research, documents provided by TX factory showed that it paid workers: (1) a basic salary, which was set at minimum wage standards for Longgang district in Shenzhen (in 2004, minimum wage was 480 yuan a month; in 2005 it was 580 yuan a month) and (2) legally-set overtime pay (which is 1.5× during the work week, 2× on weekends, and 3× on legal holidays). Why didn't factory inspections result in higher wages for workers at TX Factory? According to workers, payroll records provided by the factory during inspections did not reflect reality. As one worker said, "Wages are supposed to include both the basic salary and overtime pay. In 2004, minimum wage was 480 yuan a month. Overtime was 4.3 yuan per hour, and every hour on Saturdays was 5.74 yuan. If you count like this, our monthly salaries should be over 1,000 yuan, but we only got between 600 and 700 yuan. Every month they take 180 out in 'living expenses' and housing fees. In the low season we walk away with just over 300 yuan a month. That's not enough to live on." However, in ZX, workers had more overtime and their wages were based on piece rates, so their monthly wages were as high as 1100–1200 yuan.

4.5 *Effects of Inspections on Worker Living Conditions*

Similarly, as seen in Table 6.3, Walmart inspections did little to improve working conditions with respect to food and shelter. TX factory offered very little in the way of living conditions in comparison to ZX, which did not have many inspections. According to a worker at TX, "The factory takes 180 yuan a month from us in living expenses and dormitory fees. There are 12 people in each dorm. They are divided into new and old dorms; new dorms are a bit better. They have private bathrooms and shower rooms. Every time monitors come for inspections, they go to the new dorms. The old dorm has one common bathroom and shower per floor. In the summers, you have to line up for three hours before you can shower and wait 20 minutes to go to the bathroom." TX workers were even more disappointed in the food in the cafeteria. "The food in the factory is awful. We have to leave once a week to either go to the home of someone from our hometown or to a friend's just to eat something decent and make up for the poor nutritional value of the food served in the cafeterias."

5   Conclusion

Within the context of the global toy industry's CSR movement, this article analyzes the implementation of Walmart's code of conduct in its supply chain to understand the effects of these codes and their implementation mechanisms on improving labor conditions. Through a comparative study of three different factories, we find that Walmart's "factory inspections" have done little to improve working conditions. Although factories did reduce overtime hours, they did not increase wages or improve working conditions. In recent years, eyewitness testimonies found in media and NGO reports confirm that our conclusions have a certain universality.[11]

What factors have contributed to the ineffectiveness of CSR "codes of conduct" as a tool to improve workers' lives? First, as with most codes of conduct formulated by international companies, Walmart's "standards for suppliers" reflects a type of "legal minimalism," which emphasizes the importance of strict implementation of national legislation. Taking wages as an example, Walmart's decision to pay "basic salary + overtime" had basically no benefit to workers in TX factory. This was mainly because in many parts of China minimum wages are set quite low and legally-set overtime fees lack effective enforcement mechanisms. Second, Walmart currently uses "self-monitoring" and "punishment-oriented" code implementation mechanisms, both of which are limited in their ability to improve labor conditions. These mechanisms restrict the participation and influence of other stakeholders (such as workers or their representative institutions) and therefore lack legitimacy, credibility and effectiveness. Additionally, due to a lack of reasonable cost sharing, these mechanisms severely restrict supplier factories' active participation in the industry's CSR movement to improve workers' conditions and seek creative solutions to sustainable development, and instead end up leading to forgeries and falsifications during factory inspections that turn the codes of conduct into mere formalities.

Looking to the prospects for corporate social responsibility to improve labor conditions in China's export industries, we hope to see a fairer, more democratic and more effective implementation model for company codes of conduct. First, a code of conduct enforced by "self-monitoring" can only be effective in continuously improving labor conditions in an environment with strong national legislation and enforcement. Second, effective implementation means enterprises must seriously discuss cost sharing with suppliers. Operators and retailers making high profits at the top of the supply chain must work with suppliers to share the economic costs associated with improving labor conditions or provide resources to help factories improve production processes and output capacity in order to offset higher costs. Finally, because workers are the most important stakeholders within the corporate social

---

[11] See "The Hidden Downside of Santa's Little Helpers," *The Irish Times*, December 21, 2002; "Sweatshop Hell for China's Toy Makers Worse than Ever," *The Independent*, December 24, 2002; "Season of Discontent: Santa's Chinese Elves Plumb out of Goodwill," *Ottawa Citizen*, December 23, 2004; See Asia Monitor Resource Center (2000); China Labor Watch (2005); China Labor Watch and National Labor Committee (2005); Hong Kong Christian Industrial Committee (2000, 2001a, 2001b); Students and Scholars Against Corporate Misbehavior (2006); The National Labor Committee (2005); The National Labor Committee and China Labor Watch (2006).

responsibility movement, it is extremely important to increase the participation of workers and their representative organizations (unions and NGOs) in the formulation and implementation processes for codes of conduct. This can help increase the credibility and effectiveness of codes of conduct in the eyes of workers. In summary, based on empirical research, we advocate for a corporate social responsibility that represents a conceptual fusion of "legislation, business ethics and worker empowerment" based on the common participation of the state, enterprise, and employees.

References

Asia Monitor Resource Center. 2000. "Monitoring Mattel: Codes of Conduct, Workers and Toys in Southern China." http://www.somo.nl/monitoring/reports/monitoring-mattel.PDF.

China Labor Watch and National Labor Committee. 2005. "Walmart Sweatshop Toys Made in China: 'Always Low Prices' Means Rolling Back Respect for Human Rights." http://www.chinalaborwatch.org/upload/WalmartLungcheongReport.pdf.

Clark, Eric. 2007. *The Real Toy Story Inside the Ruthless Battle for America's Youngest Consumers*. New York: Free Press.

Egels-Zandén, Niklas. 2007. "Suppliers' Compliance with MNCs' Codes of Conduct: Behind the Scenes at Chinese Toy Suppliers." *Journal of Business Ethics*, 40 (1): 45–62.

Frenkel, Stephen. 2001. "Globalization, Athletic Footwear Commodity Chains and Employment Relations in China." *Organization Studies*, 22 (4): 531–62.

Hasbro, Inc. 1993. "Global Business Ethics Principles." http://www.hasbro.com/default.cfm?page=ci_csr&sec=ethics.

Hong Kong Christian Industrial Committee. 2000. "McDonald's Toys: Do They Manufacture Fun or More Exploitation?" http://www.cic.org.hk/download/McDonald%20Toys%20(1).doc.

Hong Kong Christian Industrial Committee. 2001a. "How Hasbro, McDonald's, Mattel, and Disney Manufacture their Toys." http://www.cic.org.hk/download/CIC%20Toy%20Report%20Web%20eng.pdf.

Hong Kong Christian Industrial Committee. 2001b, "BOM!! Beware of Mickey-Disney Sweatshops In South China." http://www.cic.org.hk/download/whole%20report 2.doc.

International Council of Toy Industries. 1995. "Code of Business Practices." http://www.toy-icti.org/info/codeofbusinesspractices.html.

Mattel, Inc. 1997. "Global Manufacturing Principles." http://www.mattel.com/about_us/Corp_Responsibility/GMPoverview.pdf.

Pun Ngai 潘毅. 2005a. "全球化工厂体制与 '道德理念重构' – 跨国公司生产守则与中国劳动关系" ["Global Production and 'Reconstruction of Moral Concept': Code of

Conduct for Transnational Corporations and China's Labor Relations"]. 开放时代 [*Open Times*], 2: 108–124.
Pun, Ngai 潘毅. 2005b. "Global Production, Company Codes of conduct, and Labor Conditions in China: A Case Study of Two Factories." *The China Journal*, 54: 101–113.
Students and Scholars Against Corporate Misbehavior. 2006. "A Second Attempt at Looking for Mickey Mouse's Conscience: A Survey of the Working Conditions of Disney's Supplier Factories in China." http://www.sacom.org.hk/html/uploads/ Disney%20Research%20Report%202006%20_ENG_.pdf.
Sum, Ngai-Ling and Pun Ngai. 2005. "Globalization and Paradoxes of Ethical Transnational Production: Code of Conduct in a Chinese Workplace." *Competition & Change*, 9 (2): 181–200.
The National Labor Committee. 2005. "Blood and Exhaustion: Behind Bargain Toys Made in China for Walmart and Dollar General." http://www.nlcnet.org/reports .php?id=110.
The National Labor Committee and China Labor Watch. 2006. "The Sweatshop Behind the Bratz." http://www.nlcnet.org/article.php?id=197.
Tan Shen 谭深 and Liu Kaiming 刘开明, eds. 2003. 跨国公司的社会责任与中国社会 [*Corporate Social Responsibility of Transnationals and Chinese Society*]. Beijing: Social Sciences Academic Press.
Toys 'R' Us, Inc. 2002. "Toys 'R' Us Annual Report 2002." http://www5.toysrus.com/ investor/ar2002/page21.html.
Walmart Stores, Inc. 2004. "Factory Certification Report: March 2003–February 2004." http://walmartstores.com/Files/FactoryCertificationReport2003.pdf.
Walmart Stores, Inc. 2005. "Standards for Supplier: Supplier's Responsibility." http:// walmartstores.com/Files/SupplierStandards.pdf.
Yu Xiaomin 余晓敏. 2006. 经济全球化背景下的劳工运动: 现象、问题与理论 ["Labor Movement under Economic Globalization: Issues, questions and Theories"]. 社会学研究 [*Sociological Studies*], 3: 188–218.
Yu Xiaomin 余晓敏. 2007. 跨国公司行为守则与中国外资企业劳工标准: 一项 '跨国-国家-地方' 分析框架下的实证研究 ["Transnational Corporations' Code of Conduct and Labor Standards in China's Foreign-Invested Enterprises: A Transnational-National-Local Empirical Study"]. 社会学研究 [*Sociological Studies*], 5: 111–132.
Yu Xiaomin 余晓敏. 2008. "Impacts of Corporate Code of Conduct on Labor Standards: A Case Study of Reebok's Athletic Footwear Supplier Factory in China." *Journal of Business Ethics*, 81 (3): 513–529.

CHAPTER 7

Direct Labor Union Elections: Lessons from Guangdong

Wen Xiaoyi (闻效仪)
Translated by Matthew A. Hale

Abstract

The 2012 direct union elections in Guangdong Province have received widespread attention from the public and are widely regarded as the direction of reform for China's unions. Behind this reform lies not only bottom-up pressure of the workers' movement, but also top-down demands for social development, as well as the outcomes of Guangdong's industrial transformation policies. Although Guangdong's model of direct union elections has been successful in some enterprises, especially with regard to collective bargaining and the work style of union officials, the further adoption of direct union elections has continued to encounter many obstacles, including the power of capital, the level of maturity of the workers themselves, the local government's way of thinking, and the attitudes of higher level unions. These obstacles have impeded the further development and improvement of direct union elections.

Keywords

direct union elections – strikes – Guangdong – labor relations

1   Introduction[1]

In May 2012, widespread public attention focused on the news that direct union elections would take place in 163 enterprises in Shenzhen Municipality, Guangdong Province. In China, the topic of union elections has been rather

---

[1] This article originally appeared in *Open Times* 2014, no. 5, pp. 54–65. Research for this article was supported by the "Research on Multifaceted Participation and Mechanisms in Labor Relations" (12CSH046) program of the National Social Sciences Fund (PRC).

obscure. The reason Shenzhen's unions were targeted in this way was a result the promotion of the union at the Ricoh Company (理光公司) by Wang Yang (汪洋), then secretary of Guangdong's Provincial Committee of the Chinese Communist Party (CCP). Due to its achievement in direct elections, Ricoh's union was able to both protect workers' rights and help the enterprise decrease labor conflicts and labor turnover. This mechanism for stabilizing labor relations was roundly praised by Wang Yang, who encouraged workers to directly elect their union leaders, saying "only the good fortune that is achieved through struggle feels like real good fortune." He called for the promotion of the Ricoh experience throughout Guangdong Province (Min 2012). Wang Yang made this speech at a time when China was still reeling from the Foxconn (富士康) suicides and the Honda (本田) strike in Nanhai (南海). His call inspired popular hope in union reform, since it was widely believed that the root of industrial contradictions lay in unions' failure to represent workers. Many people thus regarded this direct election in Shenzhen as the way forward for China's union reform.

Actually, this was not the first time an enterprise-level union had held direct elections in China. As early as 1984, "sea elections" (海选) [i.e. direct nomination and election of enterprise union chairpersons by all members] took place in the unions of county-level industrial state-owned enterprises (SOEs) in Lishu County, Jilin Province.[2] Later, direct union elections at the enterprise level took place in the provinces of Zhejiang, Fujian, Shandong, and Guangdong (Chan 2005). Among these, relatively large-scale elections took place in Yuhang District (余杭区), Zhejiang. There, in 1999, a pilot direct election for union chair took place at an automobile transport company. As the pilot was successful, more such elections were then promoted throughout Yuhang District. The electoral procedure at the time was no different from that used today: first, employees who were union members chose representatives, then those representatives directly nominated candidates, and, after the candidates gave campaign speeches, the representatives cast votes to elect

---

[2] In these pilot elections for union chairpersons in county-run SOE factories, the county-level federation of trade unions requested that "higher levels of the union and higher level party committees should not set the tone or nominate the candidates, but should instead hand the right to elect union chairpersons over to the masses of union members," with the county federation of trade unions carrying out direct management of the basic-level union chairpersons. This sort of "sea election" model obtained the support of the ACFTU. From July 27 to 29, 1999, the ACFTU convened a Conference on the Theory and Practice of the Lishu Union Work Experience in Siping, Jilin, which called for the promotion of the Lishu experience far and wide. Secretary Li Yonghai of the ACFTU said that the direct election of union chairpersons in Lishu displayed persistent democratic spirit (Zhuang 1998).

leaders for the union (chair, deputy chair and committee members). That year such direct union elections were carried out in nearly half of the enterprises in Yuhang District.

It could be said that over the past three decades, experimentation with direct union elections has taken place continuously throughout China. Overall, however, such elections are still few and far between. On the one hand, with the advance of industrialization, labor-capital relations have become more tense, labor disputes and disturbances that have bypassed the union have become more frequent, and the scale of workers' spontaneous rights-defense is growing. On the other hand, direct union elections have not only remained stuck at the level of local governance, they also often take two steps back for every step forward: enthusiasm for direct union elections has depended on local Party, government, and union officials, and when those individuals leave their posts, the union may revert to its earlier condition. At present, we have not seen any institutionalization of direct union elections beyond a single locale, and the activities in that locale fall far behind the development of basic-level democracy in village self-government [village committee elections] and urban neighborhood resident self-government [neighborhood committee elections].

In contrast, the push for direct union elections in Guangdong exhibited some new features. For one thing, it was the first time that the highest ranks of local Party and government officials affirmed and called for direct union elections, as opposed to adhering to the negative or passive role that local governments have played in the past with regard to labor laws and workers' right to organize (Gallagher 2005). Moreover, the putting into practice of direct union elections in Guangdong maintained a certain temporal continuity. Starting in 1986, the Shekou Industrial District (蛇口工业区) in Shenzhen took the lead in launching a pilot project for direct union elections that was promoted more widely in 1988. An important aspect of the "Shekou union model," which was highly praised by Wei Jianxing (尉健行), former head of the All-China Federation of Trade Unions (ACFTU), was its work method of "six rates" (六率), one of which was "ensuring the rate of democratic direct elections."[3] Shekou's experience

---

3   Drawing on the experience of the directly-elected management committees of the Shekou Industrial District, in 1986 the Shekou union launched a pilot project for democratic direct elections in basic-level unions. In early 1987, the Shekou union chose ten relatively large and representative enterprises to serve as pilot sites for the democratic direct election of union committee members in enterprise-level unions. In June of 1988, after receiving feedback from various sides, the Shekou union formulated the "Provisional Guidelines for Union Committee Elections in Shekou Industrial District, Shenzhen" (深圳蛇口工业区工会委员会选举暂行办法). Beginning in 1989, these guidelines were widely promoted throughout the district.

with direct union elections reflected the ACFTU's "Basic Framework for Union Reform" (工会改革的基本设想) drafted in 1988. Clause Forty-Three of Article Seven of the "Basic Framework" encouraged "gradual implementation of the direct election of leaders by union members among basic-level union committees with the necessary conditions." Since then, direct union elections have continuously taken root and germinated in the soil of Guangdong. In 2003, Kong Xianghong (孔祥鸿), deputy chair of the Guangdong Provincial Federation of Trade Unions (GDFTU), found that one third of basic-level union organizations in Guangdong had been created through democratic elections (Wu 2003).[4] Then in 2012, the province launched a new campaign for direct union elections. In 2014, the GDFTU announced a plan to achieve democratic union elections throughout all enterprises in the province within five years.

Why did Guangdong continuously serve as the soil for direct union elections? And why did this practice of direct union elections nevertheless fail to achieve a high level of institutionalization? What was the background for this campaign promoting direct union elections? What is the relationship between direct union elections and labor relations stability and political stability? What are the experiences and lessons of direct union elections? This article attempts to answer these questions by analyzing the work of basic-level union elections recently carried out in Guangdong.

2 The Impetus for Direct Union Elections in Guangdong

Although academics have long regarded direct union elections as a goal of union reform in China (Chen 2004; Wang 2004), there have been differing views about which social force would be capable of pushing this reform forward. Some have argued that workers' activism is the main impetus for union reform – suggesting that unions will reform themselves in order to prevent the emergence of a radical workers' movement (Clark and Pringle 2009). Others contend that direct union elections face multiple obstacles in China's existing political environment, and so, given both the union's own bureaucratism and the specific considerations of CCP-union relations with regard to political principles, the main motive force for implementing such elections could only come with the transformation of the political environment (Howell 2008).

---

4 In another report in the *Southern Metropolis Daily* (南方都市报), the GDFTU calculated that direct elections for union chairpersons had been carried out in about five thousand enterprises throughout the province, accounting for two percent of Guangdong's basic-level union committees. Although various estimates are inconsistent, it is clear that more direct union elections have taken place in Guangdong than in other provinces, and that the province is more willing to promote such elections on a large scale (Yi 2014).

In Guangdong's campaign for direct union elections, two kinds of forces have operated together. As the province with the biggest economy in China, Guangdong has the largest workforce with the most intense pressure in labor relations. At the same time, Guangdong has a unique economic and political climate, having always played a pioneering role in China's political life. Because of this special status, the Central Government has often located pilot projects for reform in Guangdong, and provincial leaders have felt a strong impetus to seek out new paths of reform, so all types of reforms in Guangdong have tended to bear nationwide significance. Of course, Guangdong prefers to continue pushing forward with reforms through the forces of the market and society rather than through relying on the short-term mobilization by the state (Zheng 2012).

One major force pushing for direct union elections in Guangdong has been workers' ever more militant activism that has put increasing pressure on the state's governance. This force comprises several sources of pressure including, first of all, the rapid maturation of the new generation of rural migrant workers (农民工) in their twenties. Although their wages are much higher than the legally designated minimum wage, these workers are less tolerant than their parents' generation of unfair treatment and are more willing and eager to improve their situation. They are less content with the status quo and they demand more rights. Due to the increased level of organization imparted by their ability to use cell phones and the internet, they are more willing and able to organize labor strikes (Pun and Lu 2010).

A second source of pressure has come from the "generalized sense of alienation" expressed by workers with regard to the government. A nationwide survey of migrant workers found that the new generation has a much lower level of trust in the government than their parents (Fu 2013). This low level of trust has made it more difficult for the government to deal with strikes. During strikes, it is increasingly common to find discourse about collusion between capital and the state, and workers are less receptive to lobbying efforts by local government officials. They refuse government efforts to mediate conflicts, sometimes even attacking the officials sent in for that purpose. In such a context, any rash action that the local government carries out can lead to an even larger-scale riot. Ironically, when union personnel are sent in to deal with a strike and then face a crowd of workers, in order to win their trust the union personnel often have to shout slogans such as, "We're the union, not government officials! We stand on your side one hundred percent!"[5]

---

5 In general, the union and the Department of Labor Administration are the main agencies that deal with strikes. Since the demands of increasing numbers of workers surpass existing legal standards, unions have begun to play a guiding role in dealing with strikes.

A third source of pressure has come from the vigorous development of labor nongovernmental organizations (NGOs). Among the hundreds of labor NGOs flourishing in the Pearl River Delta (PRD), some have helped workers communicate experiences of collective action (Xu and Chan 2012). What has worried the government most is that a few labor NGOs have begun to actually intervene in strikes. Through the internet and informants (眼线), NGOs are able to quickly come into contact with militant strikers and help them organize other workers, provide training and carry out negotiations with the employers. Some NGOs have gone even further and have begun to cultivate labor leaders among the workers (Chen 2012). In southern China, a united force of workers is beginning to emerge, with labor NGOs helping scattered migrant workers get organized, and these activities are receiving a great deal of support from transnational networks (Huang 2011). One local union official even used the word "competition" to describe the unions' relationship with labor NGOs.[6]

The second major force pressing for direct union elections in Guangdong has been the state's top-down push for "social development" (社会建设). After the Seventeenth CCP National Congress [in 2007], "social development" became a new political discourse in China. In contrast with *economic* development, *social* development focuses more on people's livelihoods and happiness. The state's Twelfth Five-Year Plan promises to double the income of urban and rural residents by 2020, to raise the minimum wage by at least thirteen percent each year, and to strongly promote "collective consultation" (集体协商) about wages at enterprises, with wages decided together by employers and workers. At the same time, there has been an upsurge of labor legislation in China, with the "Labor Contract Law"[7] of 2008, the "Labor Dispute Arbitration Law"[8] of 2008, the "Employment Promotion Law"[9] of 2008 and the "Social Insurance Law"[10] of 2010, each, one after the other, granting workers various kinds of social protections.

In addition to emphasizing livelihood, "social development" also calls for "social self-governance" (社会自治), including the fostering and development of "social" [non-state and non-profit] organizations. The state hopes to turn social organizations into another avenue for the organization of popular demands, not only increasing the ability of disadvantaged individuals to articulate their interests, but also incorporating their disorderly indignation

---

6   Interview with a Guangzhou union official, August 21, 2012.
7   劳动合同法.
8   劳动争议调解仲裁法.
9   就业促进法.
10 社会保险法.

into institutionalized channels of expression (Cai 2012). In the past, social organizations have always been a rather sensitive issue, involving questions of political stability related to citizens' right to assemble within the sphere of society. The government thus established a "two-tiered management system" for social organizations, with two "mothers-in-law" [i.e., authorities] assigned to each organization – a "unit for directing [the organization's] affairs" (业务主管单位) and an agency where the organization is registered – which together limited and controlled the development of social organizations. When the Central Government chose Guangdong as a pilot site for the reform of the social organization management system, it reformed the system for registering such organizations, changing the system's task from "directing affairs" (业务主管) to "guiding affairs" (业务指导), and it supported the expansion and development of social organizations and helped local governments transform their functions.

There has been some debate, however, regarding whether labor NGOs that had been limited or suppressed in the past should now receive support and development. The debate has centered on the question of whether these NGOs might evolve into "second unions." In order to circumvent this debate, Guangdong has implemented two important measures. One is the establishment of a Federation of Employee Service Organizations (职工服务类社会组织联合) under each level of the union in order to bring together all kinds of labor NGOs. Although this is a mechanism of control, it also grants legal status to the NGOs. The second measure is the transformation of enterprise-level unions, using democratic elections among workers to turn them into organizations of worker self-governance within enterprises.

Ricoh (Shenzhen) is a Japanese-invested manufacturing enterprise with five thousand employees. When its union was established in 2007, the workers did not approve of the candidate for chairperson nominated by the company, so that person lost in the election. Instead they chose a worker representative who was not among the candidates and elected that person as a union committee member, and that person was then elected by the committee members as chairperson. Neither the company nor higher levels of the union intervened, so a union formed entirely through workers' democracy came into being. Later, collective consultation through bargaining achieved continuous increases in the workers' wages, bringing steady improvements in the workers' welfare, and the enterprise thus overcame its plight of high labor turnover and constant labor disputes. Ricoh's employment turnover rate fell to under four percent, in contrast with an average of twenty percent for the industry. Direct union elections thus achieved an extended period of industrial harmony between labor and capital. In April 2012, Wang Yang met with the Ricoh union, praising it and concluding that the union had stabilized labor relations at the enterprise, improving workers' ability to govern themselves, and that this was entirely due to the fact that the union had been formed through a democratic election. This not only restored the union to its original purpose but also resonated with Guangdong's campaign to reform social organizations.

Wang Yang called for promoting the Ricoh experience throughout the province. Shortly thereafter, the GDFTU held an on-site meeting in Shenzhen about the development of enterprise-level unions, calling on the entire province to further push forward the work of democratic elections for union chairs at the enterprise level, and to implement the "Work Guidelines for the Democratic Election of Enterprise-Level Union Chairs".[11] Other places such as Foshan (佛山) had already issued regulations including the "Foshan Guidelines for Implementing the Democratic Election of Basic-Level Union Chairs."[12] At the same time, Guangdong attempted to speed up the legislative process for the "Guangdong Provincial Regulations Regarding the Democratic Management of Enterprises"[13] and the "Shenzhen Special Economic Zone Regulations Regarding Collective Consultation",[14] which both dealt with deepening direct union elections and further promoting collective consultation (Xu and Chan 2012).

The third force pushing for direct union elections in Guangdong came from the province's policy of industrial restructuring. Hitherto, Guangdong's economic model had been a typical export-oriented one. This model could take advantage of the immense scale of China's population to replace expensive machinery with labor power, continually lowering costs, reaping profits and achieving economic takeoff (Lin and Ren 2007). The development of export-oriented industrialization was based on a workforce that was inexpensive, disciplined and inexperienced, and the PRD was the place in China with the largest concentration of enterprises characterized by the "three supplies, one compensation" (三来一补) model [the supply of materials, models and parts by foreign capital supplemented by support from local entities]. However, the costs of this economic model for Guangdong have been too high. For one thing, the costs of economic development have outweighed its benefits, burning through scarce resources on a large scale and destroying the environment. Moreover, emphasis on low-end industry has led to a low-end population

---

11　企业工会主席民主选举工作实施办法.
12　佛山市基层工会民主选举工会主席试行办法.
13　广东省企业民主管理条例.
14　深圳特区集体协商条例.

structure, giving rise to all kinds of social problems and contradictions, making it more difficult for the government to govern (Liang 2008).

In response, Guangdong has promoted industrial restructuring, transferring the PRD's traditional low-end manufacturing to the northern, eastern and western parts of the province, drastically decreasing the concentration of labor-intensive industry in the PRD, and instead attracting advanced manufacturing and high-end service industries to the region. Actually, Guangdong's recent labor shortage and the constant upward pressure on wages have also been major factors behind this industrial restructuring. Investors in industries such as electronics and apparel have turned their eyes toward the Philippines, Vietnam, Pakistan and Sri Lanka, while Guangdong has attempted to attract more investment in heavy industry and high-tech. Moreover, in order to facilitate this transition, labor policy has been required to make adjustments to increase workers' stability and responsibility, thereby promoting an increase of labor productivity in order to attract investment and make Guangdong more competitive. This required changing the labor policy centered on a high pressure environment [for workers] to a more cooperative one, uniting workers, enterprises and the structures controlling those industries in order to fully achieve the stimulation of workers' initiative on the economic front (Deyo 1991). This is the background behind the promotion of direct union elections.

3   The Conditions and Procedures of Direct Union Elections

Even the most active reformists in the ACFTU do not believe that all enterprises are appropriate for direct union elections. They worry that if such elections are implemented at inappropriate enterprises, it will lead to a loss of control with regard to labor relations. In general, there are roughly three types of situations in which enterprises are not appropriate for direct elections. The first type consists of enterprises where labor relations are relatively tense. It is easy for such enterprises to elect militant union chairs, since "agitators" are more likely to be protected by workers, but such a situation is not beneficial for the stability of labor relations. The second type consists of those with antagonistic relations among workers based on their place of birth. In a *Southern Metropolis Daily* (南方都市报) report on direct union elections at an enterprise producing gas stoves, there were roughly equal numbers of employees from Sichuan and Hunan, so the union chair election became a competition between workers from these two provinces. No matter which province won the election, it would be hard for work to be carried out (Wu 2003). The third type consists of newly-invested enterprises, where the workers do not know each other well, so elections are impossible. As early as 1991, when Shenzhen's Investment Promotion Bureau (招商局) was asking enterprises in the Shekou Industrial District to implement direct union elections, it also stipulated four conditions deemed inappropriate for direct union elections: (a) the establishment of the first union committee, (b) labor turnover rates over forty percent, (c) the clear formation of place-based factions among employees, and (d) serious artificial interference in democratic direct elections. The GDFTU also listed these conditions among its work guidelines for union reorganization.

These limitations on direct union elections clearly reflect the ACFTU's contradictory and evasive strategy. In an enterprise where labor relations are tense, it is far preferable to elect a union chair who is loved by the workers than to have a vacuum in which workers' spontaneous action could take place. The deeper reason behind this concern is that higher levels of the union are extremely worried about losing control over the lower levels (Howell 2008). Of course, some local union officials know that if direct elections fail to mobilize the workers, such elections would be little more than a mere formality. For example, the municipal-level union leadership in Shenzhen has recommended the implementation of direct elections in enterprises with tense labor relations, especially those where strikes had recently taken place. This is mainly due to the influence of events at Yantian International Container Terminals (盐田国际). After a strike in 2007, direct enterprise-level union elections were conducted and most of the workers elected as committee members were indeed people who had been active in the strike (Wang 2011). Surprisingly, however, the Yantian union was not hard to control and even became closer to superior unions. In the 2012 election, moreover, those workers who had been militant in 2007 were not re-elected, and the new committee members were all more moderate worker representatives. It thus appears that enterprises where strikes have taken place can be appropriate soil for the growth of direct union elections. The implementation of direct elections in such enterprises can absorb and utilize the organizational consciousness and abilities that the workers developed through strike action, while also electing elite leaders from among the workers. As for the issue of control, in the words of one local union official, "It's obviously easier to control one person than it is to control a group."[15]

The limitations on direct union elections concern not only the type of enterprise but also specific procedures. The "Trade Union Law" requires that "union committee members at all levels be determined through democratic elections by assemblies of union members or their representatives." To this end, in 1992 and 2008 the ACFTU promulgated its "Provisional Regulations on Basic-Level

---

[15] Interview with a Shenzhen union official, July 29, 2013.

Union Elections"[16] and the "Guidelines for the Selection of Enterprise Union Chairs",[17] respectively. Within the framework of democratic centralism, these regulations focus on two points: the nomination of candidates and the implementation of elections. Although the regulations propose that candidates be determined through discussion among the collective of employees, they also emphasize that the candidates must be approved by the enterprise-level CCP organization and higher levels of the union, who should "make adjustments when candidates fail to meet the conditions for the position." This requirement displays the centralized organizational character of the union, which emphasizes top-down control. That being the case, when it comes to actual practice, the nomination of candidates is more centralized than democratic, with centralism coming before democracy: namely, the organizations first nominate candidates and then the assembly of union members rubber-stamps them. Although these two ACFTU documents contain provisions such as the rule that "there should be more candidates than positions for enterprise-level union chairs," the lack of a popular basis for the selection of candidates in the first place reduces the elections to a mere formality.

Moreover, the regulations for electoral procedures also seem excessively ambiguous: "The chairpersons of enterprise-level unions may be determined through direct election by all union members or their representatives, or by the enterprise-level union committee members, and these elections may take place at the same time as the election of enterprise-level union committee members or separately." Academics tend to use the concepts of "direct" and "indirect" to classify different types of elections, with "indirect" referring to the election of the union chair by the union committee members, and "direct" referring to the election of the union chair by all union members or their representatives. In general, direct elections have a better popular basis and a stronger degree of democracy (Wu 2008). The ACFTU has not stated a clear position about this in writing; instead it has attributed the reasons elections take different forms in different places to a variety of factors caused by differences among enterprises and locales. However, one deputy chair of the ACFTU who was responsible for the development of basic-level organizations, did state that direct elections would be more democratic: "So-called 'direct elections' refers to the direct election of basic-level union chairs and deputy chairs by an assembly of all members of the basic-level union, or by an assembly of their representatives. This differs from another type of democratic election

---

16 工会基层组织选举工作暂行条例.
17 企业工会主席产生办法.

where the union committee members elect the chair and deputy chair during a plenary meeting" (Wang 2003).

The procedures for democratic union elections in Guangdong strengthen democracy in three respects. The first is the "democratic selection of union member representatives." Enterprise workers usually select union member representatives according to a certain ratio per department or workshop (the ratio usually being defined by the number of frontline production workers). If this procedure is conducted without interference, the assembly of union member representatives is fully representative of the body of workers at the enterprise.

The second respect in which the Guangdong model strengthens democracy is "the democratic selection of union committee members." In this environment, the nomination of candidates is completely open-ended and may include self-nomination, mutual-nomination (workers can nominate each other), organizational nomination (nomination by higher levels of the union or by the enterprise-level union [leaders]), or enterprise recommendation, after which the union member representatives vote to confirm the candidates. This point is important. In the past, candidates for union committee member positions were "nominated by the incumbent union committee, a higher-level union, or the group preparing to establish [a new] union, according to the will of the majority of union members." This procedure was completely directed by the enterprise organization or by officials of the higher-level union, with the popular will playing merely a supplementary role for consultation. In contrast, while the new Guangdong model of having union member representatives vote to confirm the slate of candidates for union committee member positions still grants union officials of the superior organizations the power to examine the slate, at least this centralized mechanism is founded on a democratic basis and does not replace or negate the popular will.

The final respect in which the Guangdong model strengthens democracy is "the democratic selection of union chairs." This is a form of completely direct elections. After the union committee has nominated candidates for the positions of chair and deputy chair, the assembly of union member representatives then votes from among these candidates. Union chairs may also be selected through a vote by the union committee, but letting the assembly of union member representatives make its decision further strengthens the bottom-up mechanism for selecting chairpersons.

Of course, the direct election of union chairs has also undergone a reversal: their election by the assembly of union member representatives means that control from higher levels becomes more difficult. In the direct union election at Ohm (欧姆), after the union committee members were elected, it was unpredictable who among them would then be elected as chair. If the method of indirect election were adopted – with the committee members electing the chair – higher levels of the union could still influence the election by putting pressure on the committee members. If direct election were adopted, however, such pressure from higher levels would have very little effect. In the event, Zhao Shaobo (赵绍波) was unexpectedly elected as chair, while neither of the two candidates for deputy chair obtained a majority of the votes, so Ohm's union ended up without a deputy chair (Zhang 2012). This led to a rift between the popular will of the committee members and that of the worker representatives, resulting in Zhao's inability to lead the union committee. Due to resistance from committee members, the union's work could not be carried out normally, and this sowed the seeds for the eventual move to recall the chair from his post.[18] Although Zhao's election was unexpected, he still proved extremely compliant with higher levels of the union, displaying no antagonism. This led the higher level officials to again recognize that it is more important to elect a chair who is loved by the workers than it is to control him. Thus, the direct election of union chairs involves a certain flexibility. If it is the first time that a union is being established in a given enterprise, there is an inclination to adopt indirect elections in order to facilitate solidarity among the union leadership. When it is time for an established union to change its leaders, there is an inclination to adopt direct elections in order to strengthen the union's democratic character.

4 Experiences and Lessons of the Guangdong Model

First, from the perspective of the effects of implementation, direct elections at Japanese-invested enterprises have been relatively successful. These enterprises are more supportive of such elections. As an example, the Ricoh experience came from a Japanese-invested enterprise. In comparison with other enterprises, Japanese-invested enterprises are more seriously affected by industrial conflicts. First, most Japanese-invested enterprises are Chinese factories with their own brands whose just-in-time production and zero-inventory supply chains require a great deal of stability, so any stoppage of production will have devastating effects. Second, due to their position at the higher end of the manufacturing sector, workers at Japanese-invested enterprises are more highly skilled, with lower rates of turnover, higher levels of seniority, heavier

---

18 Interviews with the Ohm union chairperson and several enterprise union committee members, January 13, 2013.

familial burdens, and a greater number of grievances. Third, due to the "glass ceiling" effect on management in Japanese-invested enterprises, many middle managers have no hope of obtaining promotions, so grievances are constantly accumulating. Fourth and most importantly, industrial conflicts are always mixed together with complex nationalist sentiments, and labor relations in such enterprises are frequently influenced by relations between China and Japan. Thus, Japanese-invested enterprises tend to regard direct union elections as an autonomous form of organization by Chinese workers. Although they require the enterprise to sacrifice a portion of its profit, that can be counterbalanced by industrial peace and predictable order in production. One remarkable phenomenon is that, during a series of anti-Japanese protest marches, workers in Japanese-invested enterprises that had carried out direct union elections were more orderly and behaved in a less militant fashion in the marches. Moreover, after implementing direct union elections, such enterprises can convert workers' grievances into motives for improving their own techniques of management. This can be combined with the culture of "quality control circles," in which Japanese-invested enterprises emphasize constant improvements, in order to further promote the development of the enterprise.

The second lesson of the Guangdong model is that, in enterprises that have carried out direct union elections, collective consultation between labor and capital has taken on an entirely new appearance. In the past, the process of collective consultation usually consisted of no more than a ritual in which a company representative and a representative of the company-controlled enterprise-level union signed and stamped a standardized contract provided by the local union. It was not a process of true bargaining, with widespread worker participation, in which labor and capital could face off with one another (Wen 2013). With the implementation of direct elections, however, unions finally have a certain degree of independence and representativeness in collective consultation. This form of collective consultation usually has a few main characteristics. First, in order to ensure that the workers' position is represented during collective consultation, the enterprise union will organize bottom-up elections for consultation representatives, both to strengthen the union's own democratic character and to strengthen the union's bargaining power through workers' broad-based involvement, forming pressure mechanisms for the bargaining process. Second, the consultation process is full of various proposals, contestations and adjournments. Both parties argue strongly, each according to their own reasoning, displaying a rarely seen process of bargaining, so these consultations require many rounds of back-and-forth before a contract can be signed. Thirdly, the results of most consultations achieve a significant increase in workers' wages, especially in comparison with the local minimum wage, initiating a linkage between wages and enterprise performance. The results of collective consultation vastly advance the union's legitimacy, not only strengthening its basis in the popular will, but also giving the factory's workers a basic understanding of and personal feelings about the union.

Of course, it is unrealistic to invest excessively high hopes in collective consultation based on the implementation of direct union elections, for its mechanisms are completely different from those of collective bargaining in the West. The deeper reason for this is that, first, even if the union is created through democratic election by the workers, it is still responsive to multiple stakeholders. While helping the workers fight for their interests, it must also constantly keep in mind what the enterprise is able to bear. This is not only a political requirement of higher levels of the union, but also the practical situation of the enterprise-level union's own part-time administrative staff – a double pressure coming from the enterprise-level union's bottom-up democratic elections on the one side, and top-down management authority on the other. This is true to the point that, in the collective bargaining process of many enterprises, once the union's consultation representatives enter the bargaining room, they discover that their opponents on the other side of the table are their own superiors. Furthermore, there is a serious lag in the institutional development of access to information related to collective consultation. Unions' sources of information used in collective consultation are generally limited to the CPI (consumer price index) and the average increase of wages in the industry. They are unable to access data about the enterprise's actual economic situation, so the consultation representatives rely mainly on their personal feelings when they negotiate. This form of collective consultation has thus failed to achieve wage increases above the standard of the labor market, aiming merely to fasten increases to that standard, actually making it more sensitive and closely reflective of increases in the standard market wage. Even that, however, is already a major accomplishment compared to the norm for labor relations in China.

Moreover, the implementation of democratic union elections has significantly changed the work style that predominated in the past. As soon as unions become an institutionalized channel for workers' collective grievances, all sorts of demands rise to the surface, so unions face increasing pressure and become busier than ever before. On the one hand, these directly-elected union officials must face the pressure to represent the workers in fighting for their interests against their employers, while on the other, they must also expend more effort to appease and pacify the workers' feelings of discontent. At any time they can be reproached by the workers, to the point that many of the union officials I have interviewed complain that union work is too stressful, that they have suffered personal attacks, and that they do not have enough time to do their full-time work. Not only this, but in order to develop, the unions must also be extremely careful, especially regarding the use of union funds. The Ricoh union's annual budget is over two million yuan, but its administrative expenses are only seven thousand. Even the bonuses that higher levels of the union grant to the enterprise-level union chair are all spent on union activities. This is clearly a change that only democratic union development could bring, as the union has finally come under the democratic supervision of the workers' watchful eyes. Although, in general, directly-elected unions still play the role of an "adhesive" with regard to labor relations, their progress lies in the fact that enterprise-level unions have achieved workers' democracy for the first time, so at first they need to show concern for workers' grievances, take root among the workers, and obtain their trust.

Although direct union elections have brought many changes, it is still unclear how they will develop in the future. They still face many structural obstacles, such as the power of capital, the workers' own level of maturity, the local government's way of thinking, and the attitude of higher levels of the union. All these obstacles inhibit the further development and perfection of direct union elections.

First, the question of whether enterprise-level unions can carry out direct elections is still overly dependent upon the attitude of the company. This has yet to break free from the political principles and logic of labor relations in China. In many enterprises where direct union elections have taken place at the request of higher levels of the union, company management has used multiple ways to influence or control the election process and outcome, and the resulting unions are nothing more than "old wine in new bottles." In one factory, where the previous union chair was a relative of the employer, after the boss agreed to the implementation of direct union elections, the new chair elected by the workers turned out to be the same person. Higher levels of the union have expressed powerlessness in the face of such outcomes, saying there is nothing substantial that they can do. Even in those Japanese-invested enterprises where first steps have been taken, unions still have to face the power of capital. At present these enterprise-level unions are all worried that the effectiveness of collective consultation is decreasing and the pace of wage growth is slowing. When enterprise managers realize that they have given away too much to the workers and prepare to take it back, the unions find that they have not established any way to prevent this. Enterprise-level unions would absolutely not launch or lead a strike, as this is a political taboo that, if violated, would lead to the complete negation of direct union elections. This has become a paradox where direct elections are fostering workers' collective power, yet unions cannot lead or support workers' collective action. The only role unions can play, therefore, is still that of an advisor; they do not constitute a force. Once an employer makes a decision, the union can only try to lobby the company and appease the workers. One union official interviewed quipped that, as far as employers are concerned, direct union elections are nothing more than a tiger without teeth.[19]

Second, direct union elections also face the test of workers' maturity. For young migrant workers who are constantly on the move and not familiar with the ways of the world and are not yet accustomed to possessing democratic rights, voting is a meaningless thing, and their decision about who to vote for is not based on in-depth or rational understanding of the candidates. Since they have been at the workplace for only a short time and will probably not stay for long into the future, unions seem to bear little relation to their lives. This reflects a ubiquitous phenomenon: enterprises throughout the PRD still face high rates of worker turnover. At the same time, when it comes to even those few workers who harbor hopes for the union, their understanding of unions is often excessively utilitarian: they regard unions as merely a means to increase wages, and they lack a basic sense of organization. They often discover that when enterprise-level unions launch activities, many workers join the union, but as soon as the activity is over, those workers withdraw from the union simply to avoid paying the five yuan in monthly dues.[20] This kind of attitude does a major disservice to the unions, preventing them from developing an effective organizational foundation. Without a base of loyal and stable members, unions cannot establish an effective management system, and enterprise-level unions that are weak to begin with become even weaker.

Finally, the government's conventional thinking is also a factor in the promotion of direct union elections. There is probably no statistical relationship between strikes and direct union elections, nor is there sufficient evidence to demonstrate that the mere procedural implementation of direct elections for union chairs can completely prevent strikes from taking place. However, if a strike takes place at an enterprise that has implemented direct union elections, local government officials then adopt a negative attitude toward direct elections. After the union chair at Ohm was recalled, the various district and subdistrict government agencies were nearly unified in criticizing the Shenzhen Municipal Government for its policy of promoting direct union

---

19   Interview with a directly elected chairperson of an enterprise union in Guangzhou, August 22, 2012.
20   Interview with a directly elected chairperson of an enterprise union in Shenzhen, July 28, 2013.

elections. They worried that such elections would stir up rights consciousness among the workers and lead to an increase in instability. This sort of criticism reflects the fact that local governments are more interested in colluding with capital and prioritizing the maintenance of local economic development than in defending workers' interests. In order to promote economic development, local governments are often more willing to provide enterprises with a cheap and docile workforce than to risk any adverse effects of direct union elections on the enterprises or local economic development. As a result, with regard to the policy of direct elections, higher levels of the union are fated to receive public support but private opposition from local governments. At the same time, conflicting incentives for different levels of the administrative bureaucracy insure that social development remains stuck at the superstructural level. As one subdistrict government official bluntly put it, "The municipal government has plenty of money, but we don't."[21]

Besides the structural obstacles described above, higher levels of the union still have an ambiguous attitude toward direct union elections. This reflects their continued worries about losing control over basic-level union organizations, about labor NGOs using union elections for their own ends, and so on. The work of implementing direct union elections is thus constrained by a tense and sensitive environment. In addition, the actual situation is not optimistic, as an increasing numbers of enterprises in which union leaders have been directly elected suffer from "dependence on strikes." Workers have already lost patience with negotiating wages through collective consultation, as they have seen that strike actions have achieved major wage increases. In one Shenzhen enterprise where direct union elections have taken place for many years, the wage increases obtained through five years of collective consultation amounted to only fifty-eight percent, whereas, in contrast, a strike in 2013 immediately won an increase of thirty to forty percent. Since 2008, many rounds of collective consultation over wages have taken place at the Honda plant in Nanhai, yet strikes have continued to take place.[22] Due to the lack of any real supporting mechanisms, directly-elected unions are still not effective enough at helping workers to fight for their interests. And it is precisely because research on direct union elections has remained mired in debates about political sensitivity that the elections have failed to develop at a deeper

---

21 Interview with an official of a subdistrict union in Shenzhen, January 14, 2013.
22 After the 2010 strike at the Honda plant in Nanhai, Kong Xianghong (Deputy Chair of the GDFTU) personally served as the head of the Nanhai Honda Industrial Relations Consultation Team, leading a union team to guide collective wage bargaining at the enterprise each year. Nevertheless, the workers still used multiple strikes to win wage increases. The term "dependence on strikes" comes from the difficulties of labor relations at Nanhai Honda.

level. Deeper development would necessarily touch on questions about the right to strike, the right to collective bargaining, etc., which would again pose a challenge to sensitive political nerves.

5   Conclusion

Over the past three decades in general, unions have proven effective at protecting and promoting workers' interests, but they have been unable to play the role of organizing workers. In the latter respect, the biggest obstacles have been the power of capital and the dominant position of the Party-state. Unions can only use their connections within the establishment to seek the passing of labor laws, but attempting to resolve labor issues through legal methods is basically just a case-by-case solution that ignores the bigger problem rather than empowering workers to become capable of effectively defending their rights from being trampled upon (Chen 2003). The adjustment of labor relations on an individual basis is incapable of resolving industrial disputes or maintaining the stability of labor relations, as the experience of Guangdong makes especially clear. The rise of the new generation of migrant workers has expanded the scope of demands, such that the minimum wage and labor laws are no longer able to satisfy all kinds of "demands beyond the law." The labor shortage that has spread throughout the PRD is increasing workers' bargaining power to demand improvements in their working conditions alongside wage increases, and endless strikes and protest activities display the workers' mood of discontent. Meanwhile, due to the failure of unions to provide rapid and concrete responses to workers' demands, Guangdong's labor NGOs have sprung up like mushrooms after rain, continuously taking up positions in the labor market and using labor disputes as opportunities to intervene and thus expand their own organizational foundations.

Under such pressures, the dilemmas faced by unions have undergone a change in Guangdong as the local Party-state departments have begun to encourage unions to "hand power over to the workers" and try to constitute a force that can restrain capital (Wang 2013). This marks a turn toward collectivization in Guangdong's labor relations, and the most important measure has been the promotion of direct elections in enterprise-level unions. Two complementary forces and paths are pushing this process forward: government-directed top-down institutional reform and spontaneous worker-led bottom-up pressure (Chang 2013). Looking at the experience of Guangdong, however, the former's integration of the latter still seems far from adequate, and in this regard there are three main structural obstacles. The first derives from the manipulation of unions by enterprise management, as opposed to direction by the government;

the unions do not yet have substantial independence (Clark et al. 2004). The second derives from different incentives guiding distinct levels of local government, with lower levels more concerned about maintaining close ties with enterprise owners, leading to inconsistencies in the implementation of policies. The third obstacle derives from incorrect understandings of "stability." Within the establishment, stability is understood as the absence of industrial conflicts or strikes, and the main reason that direct union elections were able to obtain support was the hope that they might eliminate industrial conflicts. Such an instrumentalist understanding loses sight of these elections' true significance for the government, which is the ability to institutionalize industrial conflicts. As soon as this ability becomes established at an enterprise, industrial conflicts can be resolved institutionally within the enterprise, so their destructive impact on society becomes smaller and smaller, along with the costs to the government itself, eventually leading to the "depoliticization" of strikes (Zhao 2012). Apparently, however, most Party-state officials lack this sort of understanding.

These obstacles have limited direct union elections to procedural formality, preventing further development, especially with regard to discussion and experimentation involving the right to strike and the right to collective bargaining. Although we do not deny the possibility that some form of democratic unions might emerge within the present legal framework, it is still too early to achieve effective and institutionalized enterprise-level unionism. This points to two interrelated phenomena concerning labor relations in Guangdong. First, the development of direct union elections is still not a right that allows workers to play the leading role; it is entirely decided by the enterprise itself whether and how a union election may take place. This is why direct union elections are relatively common among Japanese-invested enterprises, and why such elections have continuously existed in Guangdong. Second, the main method workers adopt to fight for their rights in the PRD region is still the strike.

References

Cai He 蔡禾. 2012. 利益诉求与社会管理 ["Interest Demand and Social Management"]. 广东社会科学 [*Social Sciences in Guangdong*], 1: 209–216.

Chan, Anita. 2009. "Challenges and possibilities for democratic grassroots union elections in China: a case study of two factory-level elections and their aftermath." *Labor Studies Journal*, 3: 293–317.

Chang Kai 常凯. 2013. 劳动关系的集体化转型与政府劳工政策的完善 ["The Collectivization Transformation of Labor Relations and the Improvement of Government Labor Policies"]. 中国社会科学 [*Social Sciences in China*], 6: 91–108.

Chen, Feng. 2003. "Between the state and labour: the conflict of Chinese Trade Unions' double identity in market reform," *The China Quarterly*, 176: 1006–1028.

Chen, Shengyong 陈剩勇 and Zhang Ming 张明. 2005. 中国地方工会改革与基层工会直选 ["Reform of Local Labor Unions in China and Direct Election of Labor Unions at the Grassroots Level"]. 学术界 [*Academic Forum*], 6: 37–48.

Chen, Weiguang 陈伟光. 2012. 忧与思 – 三十年工会工作感悟 [*Concern and Meditation: Reflecting on Thirty Years' Labor Union Work*]. Beijing: China Social Sciences Press.

Clarke, Simon and Tim Pringle. 2009. "Can Party-Led trade Unions Represent Their Members?" *Post-Communist Economies*, 21 (1): 85–101.

Clarke, Simon et al. 2004. "Collective Consultation and Industrial Relations in China." *British Journal of Industrial Relations*, 42 (2): 235–254.

Deyo, Frederick C. 1989. *Beneath the Miracle: Labor Subordination in the New Asian Industrialism*. Berkeley and Los Angeles: University of California Press.

Fu Ping 符平. 2013. 中国农民工的信任结构: 基本现状与影响因素 ["The Trust Structure of Chinese Peasant-Workers: Basic Facts and Influencing Factors"]. 华中师范大学学报 – 人文社会科学版 [*Journal of Huazhong Normal University: Social Science Edition*], 2: 33–39.

Gallagher, Mary Elizabeth. 2007. *Contagious Capitalism: Globalization and the Politics of Labor in China*. Princeton: Princeton University Press.

Huang Yan 黄岩. 2011. 全球化与中国劳动政治的转型 [*Globalization and the Transformation of Chinese Labor Politics*]. Shanghai: Shanghai People's Press.

Howell, Jude A. 2008. "All-China Federation of Trade Unions beyond Reform? The Slow March of Direct Elections." *The China Quarterly*, 196: 845–863.

Liang Guiquan 梁桂全. 2008. 生于忧患死于安乐 – 一论解放思想 ["Prosperity Originating from Hardships, while Destruction from Hedonism: Debate on Opening Mind"]. 南方日报 [*Southern Daily*], February 18.

Lin Yifu 林毅夫 and Ren Ruo'en 任若恩. 2007. 东亚经济增长模式相关争论的再探讨 ["Probe into the Debate about the Economic Growth Model in East Asia"]. 经济研究 [*Economic Research Journal*], 8: 4–12.

Min, Jie 闵杰. 2012. 民选工会的 "理光经验" ["The 'Ricoh Experience' of Direct Labor Union Election"]. 中国新闻周刊 [*China News Weekly*], 20.

Pun Ngai and Lu Huilin. 2010. "Unfinished proletarianization: self, anger and class action of the second generation of peasant-workers in reform China." *Modern China*, 36 (5): 493–519.

Wang Jiaoping 王娇萍. 2003. 直选: 在规范中平稳推进 – 全总副主席苏立清就基层工会直选答记者问 ["Direct Election Advancing Steadily with Rules: Responses to Reporters' Questions from Su Shuqing, Chairman of All-China Trade Union Federation"]. 工人日报 [*Workers Daily*], July 25.

Wang Jinhong 王金红. 2005. 工会改革与中国基层民主的新发展 – 非公有制企业工会直选的案例分析 ["Labor Union Reform and the New Development of Grassroots Democracy in China: A Case Study of the Direct Election of Labor Unions in

Non-Public Enterprises"]. 华南师范大学学报 – 社会科学版 [*Journal of South China Normal University: Social Science Edition*], 5: 35–42.

Wang Tongxin 王同信. 2011. 规则的力量 ["The Power of Rules"]. 中国职工教育 [*China Staff Education*], 9: 17–18.

Wang Tongxin 王同信. 2013. 把权力交给工人 ["Giving Power to Workers"]. 中国工人 [*Chinese Workers*], 5: 4–13.

Wen Xiaoyi 闻效仪. 2013. 集体合同工作中的行政模式以及工会困境 ["Administrative Mode in Collective Contract Work and the Dilemma of Labor Unions"]. 中国党政干部论坛 [*Chinese Cadres Tribune*], 5: 11–14.

Wu Hui 吴辉. 2003. 直选不是作秀: 广东省 1/3 企业基层工会直接选举产生 ["The Direct Election is Not Just for Show: Labor Unions are Directly Elected in One Third of Guangdong Enterprises"]. 南方都市报 [*Southern Metropolis Daily*], July 9.

Wu Yaping 吴亚平. 2008. 关于基层工会主席直选的几个问题 ["Several Questions about Direct Election of Labor Union Chairmen at Grassroots Level"]. 工会理论研究 [*Labor Union Studies*], 2: 21–24.

Xu Shaoying 许少英 and Chen Jingci 陈敬慈. 2011. 工会改革的动力与矛盾: 以本田工人罢工为例 ["The Motivation and Paradox of Labor Union Reform: A Case Study of Workers' Strike in Honda"], in 中国劳动者维权问题研究 [*Chinese Trade Union and Labor Law: A Critical Review and Reflection*], edited by Zhao Minghua 赵明华 et al., Beijing: Social Sciences Academic Press.

Yi Xiaoxia 伊晓霞. 2014. 5 年内全省企业工会普遍民主选举产生 ["Labor Unions to be Democratically Elected in Enterprises in all the Province in 5 Years"]. 南方都市报 [*Southern Metropolis Daily*], July 3.

Zhao Dingxin 赵鼎新. 2012. 民主的限制 [*The Limitations of Democracy*]. Beijing: CITIC Press.

Zhang Wei 张伟. 2012. 欧姆工会主席直选背后 ["Behind the Direct Election of Labor Union Chairperson in Ohm"]. 南方日报 [*Southern Daily*], June 5.

Zheng Yongnian 郑永年. 2012. 广东改革与中国的未来 ["Reform in Guangdong and the Future of China"]. 凤凰周刊 [*Phoenix Weekly*], 2.

Zhuang, Huining 庄会宁. 1998. 从职工直选工会主席做起 – 吉林省梨树县工会改革追踪 ["Starting from the Direct Election of the Labor Union Chairperson: The Reform of Labor Union in Lishu County"]. 瞭望 [*Outlook*], 35: 20–21.

CHAPTER 8

Patterns of Collective Resistance among the New Generation of Chinese Migrant Workers: from the Politics of Production to the Politics of Life

Wang Jianhua (汪建华) and Meng Quan (孟泉)
Translated by Matthew A. Hale

Abstract

In *The Politics of Production,* Michael Burawoy emphasized how different production regimes shape the political and ideological aspects of workers' resistance. However, the present study's analysis of collective struggles by the new generation of Chinese migrant workers shows that, aside from the regulatory role of production regimes themselves, the unique life experiences and social traits of China's new workers influence how different production regimes are experienced. Moreover, through the combination of different production regimes, workers' experiences and traits also engender unique forms of life, bonds of solidarity, and methods of mobilization. This article emphasizes the political significance of life. The social relations and experiences forged through production and life give rise to three patterns of struggle among China's new workers: (a) offensive struggles to advance their interests based on relationships among coworkers and classmates, (b) atomized struggles to both defend and advance their interests, and (c) riots. Each pattern of struggle demarcates a unique challenge in China, "the world's workshop."

Keywords

new generation migrant workers – patterns of collective struggle – production regimes – politics of life

1   Inter-Generational Change and the Transformation of Industrial Relations in the World's Workshop[1]

For workers born in the 1980s, the environment in which they grew up and the process of their socialization were worlds apart from those of their parents. Post-reform China's continuous economic development and the implementation of family planning policies increased the resources that children of this generation could obtain from their families. They thus generally acquired less experience with farming and received higher levels of education. In recent years, the gradual popularization of the internet and especially the emergence of the mobile internet have vastly expanded the scope of this generation's information access, social interaction and field of vision. As they have entered the world's workshop, their social traits, including consumption habits, ability to use information technology, social networks, identities, and developmental expectations, have in turn differed vastly from those of the previous generation. This has been illustrated by multiple reports and academic studies (Wang 2001; Guo et al. 2011; Pun et al. 2011; Tsinghua University Sociology Department Research Group 2012; Pun and Lu 2010; Gallagher 2011).

The miracle of the world's workshop has been largely based on a developmental model of "low labor costs," which was not an issue for the previous generation of rural migrant workers (农民工). Considering the poverty and surplus potential labor-power in rural China during the early Reform period, leaving the countryside to supplement the household economy seemed like an effective path for upward mobility. In an authoritarian context, the old generation of migrant workers – especially women of that generation – often appeared to be submissive. In the face of various injustices such as the non-payment of wages, inadequate compensation for work-related injuries, and affronts to personal dignity, their resistance tended to be moderate and defensive (Lee 1995, 1999, 2007; Pun 2005).

This model of development is clearly being challenged by the younger generation of workers, however, as demonstrated over the past few years by strike waves, riots, and the suicide wave at Foxconn. Such challenges are primarily expressed in affective experience and demands for development. The new generation of migrant workers is no longer a migrant group that produces without consuming or works without developing, but the system of using migrant workers that centered on intimidation and division is hardly able to provide adequate space for workers' long-term development in the cities. Between

---

[1] This article originally appeared in *Open Times* 2013, no. 1, pp. 165–177.

cities in which they cannot stay and villages to which they cannot return, this new generation is stuck with no way forward and no way back. At the same time, the improved environment in which they grew up has made them more resistant to alienating labor processes, authoritarian management, dysfunctional community life and discriminatory second-class citizenship. The lack of opportunities for development and prevalence of miserable work experiences have been regarded as an important basis leading to their more frequent and dramatic acts of rebellion (Pun 2009; Guo 2011; Tsinghua University Sociology Department Research Group 2012; Pun and Lu 2010).

The other challenge emanates from the enhancement of their capacity for action that has benefitted from the improvement of their education and their mastering of information technology (Gallagher 2011). Our research also demonstrates the empowering influence of the internet on young workers' resistance. The internet is a medium through which workers can coordinate internal actions, mobilize external support and accumulate experiences of struggle (Wang 2011).

Some sociologists have also observed clear differences in the patterns of resistance by the new generation of migrant workers. From this perspective, the recent wave of struggles can be partly explained by generational changes in the composition of the workforce in the world's workshop. However, differences between the patterns of resistance associated with Honda and Foxconn, respectively, derive instead from differences between those companies' factory regimes. Compared with Foxconn, the residential arrangements and social networks at Honda saved the workers there from the fate of total atomization, providing the potential for collective solidarity (Guo et al. 2011).

The perspective of intergenerational change sees only the impact of workers' past experiences on factory life experiences and the ability to mobilize resistance, while neglecting workers' efforts to build their own lives in the city and how those efforts shape patterns of resistance. The theoretical tradition associated with the politics of production tends to emphasize the factory regime's independent regulatory influence on contentious politics, ignoring workers' social characteristics and social lives. Our analysis, in contrast, attempts to combine workers' intergenerational characteristics with the factory regime in which they are located. The patterns of workers' resistance are shaped not only by the factory regime's top-down regulation,[2] but also by the workers' own life experiences, modes of interaction, ability to take action and affective

---

2 In *The Politics of Production*, Burawoy (1979) maintains that workers' external social characteristics are unimportant.

experience. When both the old and the new generations of workers entered the world's workshop, not only did they bring with them their own ways of life and social networks, they also created, expanded or remolded their social networks under various factory regimes. The bonds of solidarity formed through their everyday lives and the ability to use information technology that they acquired facilitated various patterns of mobilization. However, the enormous gap between the life experiences of these two generations of workers led each to experience alienation and exploitation in unique ways. In the course of struggle, each generation made demands corresponding to the combination of their own experiences and the situation of their particular workplaces. Workers' lives thus involved both political effects (bonds of solidarity, patterns of mobilization) and ideological effects (experiences, demands), hence the term "politics of life." The politics of life are constrained by the broader systemic arrangements of state institutions and capitalism, but they can challenge those arrangements through workers' collective action (Wang 2012).[3]

This article aims to abstract patterns of migrant workers' resistance from three typical cases and to analyze the underlying mechanisms for their formation. Adopting a "politics of life" analytical perspective, this study attempts to make sense of the new generation of migrant workers' experiences of growing up, consumption patterns, housing arrangements, social networks and ways of using information technology, with a focus on how these affect their patterns of collective resistance. Regimes of production certainly play an important regulatory role, but their effects can be understood only in combination with the social characteristics of young workers. The three cases in this study – Honda's plant in Nanhai (南海), Ohm in Shenzhen (深圳) and Foxconn in Taiyuan (太原) – have all been widely reported in the news media, so the companies'

---

3 In "Life and Contentious Politics among New Workers," Wang (2012) analyzes three political aspects of the lives of new workers, namely: (a) the foundation of state institutions and the capitalist system, (b) political and ideological influences, and (c) further influences on state institutions and the capitalist system. He then analyzes the relationship between ways of life and patterns of resistance. Under different production regimes, old and new generations of workers have experienced different ways of life and corresponding demands and bonds of solidarity have emerged through collective struggles, as outlined in this chart:

	Authoritarian Regime	**Semi-Authoritarian Regime**
Old Generation	Atomized defensive resistance	Defensive resistance based on relationships among coworkers and locality
New Generation	Atomized defensive and offensive resistance/riots	Offensive resistance based on relationships among coworkers and classmates

real names are used. The authors have conducted multiple studies of collective struggles in suppliers of products to transnational corporations in the Pearl River Delta since 2011, supplementing these with a study of Foxconn in Taiyuan based on Foxconn typicality. Since these cases have attracted widespread attention from news media and academia, there have been many reports and studies about them. Since today's workers' struggles increasingly utilize the internet in order to interact with the outside world, the authors have also done their best to collect secondary sources that the workers have left online. These sources can supplement and confirm sources from our own field research (mainly interviews, and our month-long ethnographic study of Honda).

In the following three sections, the authors use empirical data to analyze these three cases with regard to regimes of production, ways and experiences of life, and the development of collective struggles, so as to abstract patterns of workers' resistance from each case and reveal each pattern's foundation in the workers' lived experiences. The authors categorize Nanhai Honda, Shenzhen Ohm, and Taiyuan Foxconn as, respectively, semi-authoritarian, authoritarian, and semi-militarized regimes.[4] All three factories depend on the "split household" mode of labor force reproduction, which makes it difficult for young workers to see hope for further development there.[5] The factories differ, however, with regard to their management models: Honda is able to place a degree of value on workers' feelings and to respond, in limited ways, to their opinions within the channels provided by the management of production. Foxconn, on the other hand, completely excludes workers from participation in management, stringently disciplines them in production and even, at times, insults them. Ohm lies between these two regimes, neither responding to workers' opinions nor using excessively harsh management methods.

The new generation of migrant workers at Honda and Ohm undertook peaceful and rational strike actions in response to their experiences of injustice, whereas the workers at Taiyuan Foxconn vented their feelings through rioting in response to their sense of total oppression and desperation. The Honda workers used their informal social networks and internet skills to effectively achieve their demands. By contrast, the workers at Ohm and Foxconn had difficulty controlling the direction of their collective actions due to their lack of communication and coordination. The modes of action by these three

---

4 In "Contemporary Migrant Workers' Struggles and the Transformation of China's Labor Relations," Guo Yuhua et al. (2011) categorize Foxconn and Honda respectively as "semi-militarized authoritarian" and "conventionally authoritarian" regimes. Here we use slightly different categories.
5 The authors refer to the situation in which some members of rural families migrate to work in cities, while other members continue to live in the countryside. – Ed.

groups of workers also demonstrated three typical patterns of collective resistance by the new generation of migrant workers: offensive struggles to advance their interests based on relationships among coworkers and classmates, atomized struggles to both defend and advance their interests, and riots. Each of these patterns directly challenged the existing regimes of production that are based on migrant labor.

2   Offensive Struggles Based on Relationships among Coworkers and Classmates

This type of struggle usually occurs in enterprises with investment from European, American or Japanese capital that are managed according to the "human resource pattern of management."[6] This type of enterprise pays more attention to workers' feelings, listens to workers' opinions when these do not affect production operations, and regularly organizes leisure activities for employees. This cultivates a certain degree of loyalty among young workers and decreases their turnover rate to some extent. Young workers are often recruited from vocational high schools or colleges where they have become accustomed to urban life and have developed the ability to interact freely with their classmates and coworkers in a variety of ways. Their bonds of solidarity usually form through such everyday interaction. Due to the lack of mechanisms for the expression of interests and collective bargaining, however, the issue of improving workers' conditions and wages is not addressed, and that is what leads to the accumulation of young workers' grievances and the eruption of collective resistance.

Nanhai Honda is such an enterprise. Owned exclusively by Honda and located in the city of Foshan's Auto Parts Industrial Park, Nanhai Honda began operating at capacity in 2007, mainly producing auto parts such as transmissions, transmission shafts and crankshafts. By the time the strike took place in 2010, the plant had over 2,000 employees, most of whom were males recruited from vocational high schools and colleges.

2.1   *The Production Regime*
For a long time the biggest problem for workers at Nanhai Honda had been low wages, with entry-level workers receiving only about 1,200 yuan per month

---

6   Anita Chan identified two categories of labor relations in foreign-invested companies – a "Western" (including Japanese) pattern of "human resource management" and an "Asian" pattern of "authoritarian management."

before the strike. This was related to the lack of overtime. Basic-level workers (普工) normally worked only 40 hours a week, so their work was more relaxed than an average manufacturing job in the China. In departments where the work was more strenuous, the managers also attempted to organize leisure activities in the hope of boosting workers' morale.

Upon being hired, workers usually went through a week of training. The company also encouraged workers to participate somewhat in the management of production, for example, by asking workers to submit proposals for improvements (although most of the time the company did not care about workers' opinions). The union did not represent workers, but it did regularly help the company organize leisure activities such as New Year's galas, travel opportunities, and birthday parties. Workers were relatively free in their housing options, with the company providing transportation to and from rental complexes after completion of the training period.

2.2 Experiences and Way of Life

Although the low wages forced many workers to quit their jobs, a lot of the older workers chose to stay. Most workers had been hired in groups from vocational schools, and through the processes of training and living together, they had expanded the scope of their interactions with each other. The modes of interaction that had begun among classmates at school continued developing through their lives together at the factory. During their free time, workers frequently took part in various activities together (usually with members of the same shop floor team), such as going out to eat supper after work, celebrating birthdays, singing karaoke, roller-skating and playing cards (often involving gambling). Through the combination of these independent activities and those organized by the company, employees came to know each other fairly well. This was especially true for workers in the transmission assembly department, both because their work on the assembly line required a great deal of cooperation and because the department frequently organized leisure activities. Such relationships were also strengthened through the internet, with each department having its own QQ (instant messaging) group. During the strike, workers quickly set up special "super groups" for employees throughout the factory to communicate across departmental lines.

Workers universally complained about the company's wage rates. They had paid attention to inflation and the company's profitability over the past few years. In three years, the company had adjusted wages by only a few dozen yuan per month, and the workers found this extremely unreasonable. The way of life to which they had grown accustomed, which required money for leisure activities, made the workers especially sensitive to inflation, with many often living beyond their means. A few workers also noticed the union's inactivity, so the demand to reorganize the union gradually rose to prominence in the course of the strike. Other than wages and union reorganization, the workers had few major grievances.

2.3 Collective Resistance

Before 2010 the Nanhai Honda workers actually had organized many smaller-scale strikes and petitions. Three had occurred in the transmission assembly department alone. Through these collective actions, the workers had begun to forge and express a perspective of solidarity. The 2010 strike began on May 17 when several workers who were preparing to quit their jobs attempted to fight for the rights of their coworkers. This effort was sparked the previous month when the government raised the minimum wage, but the company failed to increase its wages accordingly (the few annual wage adjustments in the past had been small to begin with), instead merely adding small bonuses to the basic wage. After some workers met a few times to make plans, early in the morning on Monday the 17th, they pressed the emergency stoppage buttons on two assembly lines.[7] As the managers acquiesced, the workers rushed out of their workshops and marched to other production departments, though only a few colleagues from the axle processing department joined the group of strikers. At the same time, the strikers made rapid use of internet tools such as QQ groups and forums. When the head of the union came to persuade them (做工作) to end the strike, the workers ignored him and instead kept making phone calls asking, "Where are the journalists?" The management promised to respond to their demands within a week, and the second shift of two production lines went back to work. Members of the first shift later criticized members of the second shift sharply for this, saying this decision could have undermined their efforts. This may be a reason why the second shift eventually took on a more effective leading role when the entire factory went on strike. Colleagues from other departments also began communicating with the assembly department, saying that if the strike were to resume, they would definitely join it.

That Friday evening, some workers heard that the company was recruiting replacement workers and planned to fire the strikers. Hearing this, the workers quickly went into action and resumed the strike. This was fueled by the company's attitude in its previous negotiation with the workers' delegates. Many

---

7 Workers recognized the pivotal status of the assembly department. As long as the assembly department refused to work, other departments could not continue production because they produced components for this department.

workers felt insulted by the company's meager offer of a 55 yuan raise. As soon as the strike was resumed, it immediately swept the entire factory. In addition to demonstrating on-site and talking to journalists, workers were especially active on QQ groups and internet forums. The company fired two workers who had taken a lead in the strike, but this only added fuel to the flames of the other workers' anger. Such repeated confrontations with the company helped nurture the workers' self-confidence. When Japanese Honda representatives showed up with cameras, the strikers responded by donning masks and using their own phones to take pictures of the representatives. When the company's lawyers said the workers were breaking the law, the workers looked at legal documents online and determined that this was not true. The workers not only conveyed information about the strike to the outside world via the internet, they also obtained support in this way. For example, the call to reorganize the union derived from a few workers looking up the "Trade Union Law of the People's Republic of China".[8] The upswing of the workers' mood went hand in hand with the development of their demands. Considering both the impact of the strike, which forced many assembly plants in China to stop production and thus caused severe economic losses, and the company's profitability (as mentioned by the general manager at the previous annual meeting), the workers proposed a raise of at least 800 yuan per month, rejecting the company's offer of a 355 yuan raise.

Events took another turn on May 31. The company had been controlling the strikers' actions to a certain degree by separating the workers into different departments and workshops. Some of the workers decided to resist this separation by leaving the workshops, which led them to come into conflict with township union officials, whom some workers said were actually police in disguise, who were stationed outside. When workers who remained inside heard that their colleagues were being beaten, they rushed outside to support them. Some of these workers, who had previously maintained a civil and rational attitude throughout the strike, suddenly grabbed tools from the assembly line and brought them outside to brandish as weapons, at which point the township union officials panicked and fled. The next morning, nearly all the workers from all three shifts came to the factory,[9] ready for a battle. The workers published an open letter online chastising the behavior of the township union officials and asking for support from all sectors of society. It was

---

8 中华人民共和国工会法.
9 Basic-level workers at this plant were divided into three shifts: early, middle and late. In order to maintain the quality of production, the assembly department had only two shifts.

not until a member of the People's Congress (who was the general manager of the Guangzhou Automobile Group Co., Ltd.) came to mediate that both parties (Nanhai Honda and the workers' delegates) came back to the bargaining table. The workers also invited a famous scholar of labor relations to participate in the negotiations. Finally, the company agreed to raise wages by 500 yuan a month. Later, the union was also reorganized and a system of collective bargaining was implemented.

The strike at Nanhai Honda sparked a strike wave throughout China, especially in the auto industry, with major strikes breaking out continuously. Many enterprises took the initiative of granting wage raises to decrease the risk of a strike.

2.4   Life and Contentious Politics

The workers' everyday consumption and leisure activities not only fostered the formation of bonds of solidarity, they also exacerbated the tension between the workers and the enterprise. Their interaction and communication online facilitated their internal communication and their procurement of support from external sources. Supportive information was shared among the workers in this way, which further helped foster solidarity. Their economic and institutional demands were internally generated, which doubtless benefitted from the sources of information they could access at any moment. As the strike continued, the workers used online platforms to discuss and refine their demands.

Workers' habits of consumption, ways of interaction, and use of information technology mostly took shape during their years in vocational high school or college. Although the education at such schools might not necessarily teach them many skills (Su 2011; Pun, et al. 2011), it can help them develop an entire set of urban ways of life. Therefore, the formation of social networks among classmates and colleagues throughout the factory, the widespread use of the internet in the mobilization process, and the articulation of economic interests and institutional demands were all closely related to the workers' life experiences at school. Considering the gradual spread of secondary education throughout China, its influence on the contentious politics of the new generation of migrant workers will probably became more universal as well. From the perspective of its social foundation, the pattern of resistance carried out by the workers of Nanhai Honda is probably not unusual; at least the authors have observed similar patterns of solidarity and demands emerging in struggles at other auto parts plants. However, other cases show that without the specific soil provided by a semi-authoritarian regime, it is hard for workers to form large-scale social networks and coordination, and the role of the internet in mobilization is more limited.

3 Atomized Struggles to Both Defend and Advance Workers' Interests

The Ohm factory in Bantian (坂田), Shenzhen mainly functions as a supplier for several Japanese electronics companies. Original equipment manufacturers (OEMs) such as Ohm are extremely common in the Pearl River Delta, so there is stiff competition among them. If an OEM cannot obtain the best orders, its profit margin remains low, and basic wages are often close to the local minimum wage. To varying degrees, illegal practices are also common in such factories, such as with regard to the payment of social insurance, the calculation of overtime, and restrictions on employees' ability to take time off from work. The work is also so strenuous that it is hard for the younger generation of workers to bear. Employee turnover is thus extremely high in such enterprises. Management, however, is no longer characterized by the old "intimidation" model of authoritarian factories. According to the authors' interviews and ethnographic observation of such medium- and small-scale OEMs, it seemed rather uncommon for managers to adopt extreme disciplinary measures such as personally insulting or beating employees. Once workers become accustomed to the environment, it is normal for them to bargain with their managers regarding the allotment of responsibilities and positions in the production process.

The Ohm factory was established in 1996. For several years the company developed smoothly; employees' income was higher than those at other enterprises in the area and many of the workers recruited at that time had a secondary school education. After 2010, however, the company's business declined because it failed to upgrade, and the workers' income in turn began to fall. With the exception of the managers, few longer-term employees remained. At the time of the strike in 2012, the company had about 850 employees, mainly women, with their age averaging about 20. Most of the supervisors had at least a senior high school education, while most of the basic-level workers had only completed junior high school.

3.1 The Production Regime

At the time of the strike, the company had just raised wages in accordance with the minimum wage, so the basic-level workers did not have any major wage grievances, but the supervisors' and other managers' salaries were not increased accordingly, and that was what sparked the strike. In addition, the employees as a whole had two main grievances that were raised by the managers: the food subsidy had not been increased in over ten years, and employees were charged for housing rather than having it provided for free, as had been promised.

Since most of the positions required standing while working and required working night shifts, many of the younger workers had difficulty adapting to the job. Due to this and the low wages, the employee turnover rate had grown rather high over the previous few years. The company's management was not particularly strict, but it did not provide any opportunities for employee participation and the union was purely a formality. As for housing, employees could choose whether to live in company dormitories or rent their own apartments. The company dormitories had four or five people sharing a room, and offered some basic leisure facilities such as televisions and fitness equipment. The industrial district surrounding the dormitories had lots of snack bars and places to go for fun.

3.2 *Experiences and Way of Life*

It is precisely the relatively high standard of living of the new generation that makes it hard for them to adapt to the simple, repetitive, strenuous work of the world's workshop. Such experiences create high rates of employee turnover, which in turn obstructs the development of relationships among basic-level employees and the establishment of bonds of solidarity. Although there was no lack of facilities for eating, drinking and hanging out together nearby, the workers could not develop the sort of broad-based ties with each other seen at Nanhai Honda. Instead, the workers' main way of spending time was to surf the internet on their phones, chat on QQ and read e-books. The middle and lower layers of management, on the other hand, had worked at Ohm longer and thus had the opportunity to become more familiar with one another. Although their interests and institutional demands were rather vague at the beginning, through the process of struggle, some of the workers began to sense their importance.

3.3 *Collective Resistance*

The main factor leading to the strike was the failure to increase managers' salaries accordingly when basic-level workers received a raise corresponding to the rise of the local minimum wage. After three failed attempts on the part of shift leaders, acting as employee representatives, to negotiate with the company, on March 29, 2012, middle and lower managers launched a strike. Since the other employees had just received a raise, they did not have any serious grievances, but because the managers wanted to organize a strike, the other workers felt it would be inappropriate to go in to work.

The strike was obviously planned in advance. The evening before the strike, employees announced it in advance to the media via Weibo [microblogging website]. When the strike began, all the participants had in their hands a copy of "A Summary of Our Demands" (《问题诉求总结》), which centered on reforming the union, raising managers' salaries, increasing all employees' living subsidies by 200 yuan,[10] getting rid of the 30 yuan charge for living in company dormitories, and paying into employees' social insurance accounts according to the law. The workers unfurled a banner reading "Defend Our Rights" (维权) and staged a sit-in at the factory compound. Officials from the local branch of the labor bureau, the company senior management and the union all came and tried to persuade the workers to go back to work, but this was met with jeers from the crowd. The workers clocked in and had lunch in an orderly fashion, as if everything were normal. They continuously sent updates about the strike to the outside world via Weibo, and they published "An Open Letter to Society from the Workers of Ohm".[11] There was also a certain amount of interaction among the workers via Weibo, although most of them had not met each other previously.

The next day, the district-level Bureau of Human Resources and Social Insurance arranged for 48 delegates from the employees to negotiate with the company, but the company's attitude was inflexible to the point that the delegates refused to continue the negotiations. On the third day, however, things started to change. The company ordered the employees to return to work, saying it would hire replacements if they did not, and it removed the machine for clocking in, instead having workers sign a form when they came into work. The company also attempted to divide the managers from the workers, promising the managers it would increase their salaries while telling the workers that the managers had already agreed to return to work. Many of the management staff indeed began to waver, and workers began to suspect that their shift leaders had been bought off. The divisions were already quite obvious. The company seized this occasion to announce a four-day holiday for Grave Sweeping Day (清明). As events developed, many workers expressed more interest in fighting for more rights and unwillingness to be used by management, so some workers called for the strike to be continued to the end. The first day after the holiday, although some workers wanted to continue the strike, the overall momentum had evaporated, so they had no choice but to return helplessly to work.

---

10   Workers reported that this subsidy had been calculated sixteen years earlier and they said it had fallen far behind inflation over the intervening period.
11   欧姆工人致社会公开信.

On April 6, the employees were even forced to sign a pledge that they would not go on strike again.[12]

In the end, the company agreed only to raise managers' salaries and to end workers' 30 yuan monthly charge for using the dormitories – the latter being merely a symbolic concession. Later, however, the company was chosen as a pilot site for Shenzhen's reform of basic-level unions, and direct union elections were carried out.

3.4   *Life and Contentious Politics*

Like the workers at Nanhai Honda, the young people at Ohm had begun to form demands based on their collective interests and the local institutional situation, and they had become savvy at using media to try to obtain support from the outside world. Their shift from using internet forums to Weibo demonstrates the evolution of their means of resistance and the accumulation of experience. However, the Ohm case reminds us to pay attention to the weakness of the Honda pattern of solidarity. The "split household" system of labor force reproduction and the universality of strenuous work at OEMs forced the younger generation of workers to constantly move from one job to another, "like duckweed," although such movement does not bring about an improvement of their situation or a better pairing of their abilities with appropriate positions at work. In each of these two patterns of resistance, moreover, we can observe differences internal to the new generation of migrant workers. The Ohm workers, with their lower level of education, had less extensive social networks among classmates than did the Honda workers. The interaction among coworkers was less close, and they had fewer group activities, with most of their free time spent in smaller groups of old friends or alone on their cell phones. The slow and passive development of their demands could perhaps be partly attributed to their different expectations about career development. Considering the ubiquity of such authoritarian factory regimes and the high mobility of the new generation of migrant workers, atomized collective resistance may continue to be the dominant pattern of solidarity among new workers for the next few years, although their demands may constantly develop.

---

12   This study focuses on basic-level workers. In the Ohm strike, although there was coordination among the managers, the basic-level workers were not unified. When they were betrayed by the managers, the workers were unable to respond in a unified manner, so we categorize their struggle as "atomized."

4   Riots

In contrast with middle and small-scale OEMs such as Ohm, there is another, larger-scale type of "OEM empire" that obtains orders from more enterprises due to the use of strict Taylorist management. Economies of scale further increase such enterprises' competitive advantages and the need for strict management. However, the harsh management and immense scale of such factories lay the foundation for even more dramatic conflicts.

Foxconn is the most typical representative. Since the company is headquartered in Taiwan, the adoption of militarized management seems to have another layer of necessity. Foxconn has registered over 30 companies in China's mainland, with over a million employees. Taiyuan Foxconn was founded in 2003. Divided into four factory compounds, the complex mainly produces 3C magnesium-aluminum alloy parts, precision molds, and electronics products. It has about 80,000 employees, most under the age of 30, with more men than women, and with most basic-level workers having a junior secondary school education. At the time of the riot, there was a rush to produce the iPhone 5, so workers had been transferred from Shandong, Henan, Guangdong and Hubei provinces to augment the workforce in Taiyuan.

4.1   *The Production Regime*

The average workday at Taiyuan Foxconn was about 10 hours, with overtime on Saturday. In addition, breaks were unusually short, so young workers found it hard to become accustomed to the work there. Employees reported that the production tasks were also very strenuous, and if they did not complete them fast enough, they had to take time out of their breaks to complete them.

After a spate of suicides, the company improved its management somewhat, for example, by gradually organizing all kinds of collective leisure activities for the employees, such as matchmaking, performances, and birthday parties, and by adding some leisure facilities to the factory compounds (considering the immense numbers of workers, these resources were extremely limited). In production management, however, the brutal style of management was difficult to change. According to employees' analyses, the pressure to meet output quotas, the tendency to select authoritarian-type personnel, and the cultivation of authoritarian personalities further strengthened the semi-militarized management culture. Most obvious was the management style of the security guards, who frequently scolded and beat employees.

Wages were somewhat higher at Foxconn than at other factories in Taiyuan, but after wages increased, a lot of benefits disappeared. With regard to housing, if a worker chose to rent his or her own place, it was then difficult to move back into Foxconn's dormitories. Each dorm room was normally shared by eight people. Residents were often disturbed by bedbugs, the risk of losing things, and bad relations among roommates.

4.2 Experiences and Way of Life

Although the pay at Foxconn was not low, it was not high enough to prevent many employees from resigning. The high rate of turnover impeded the establishment of stable relationships and bonds of solidarity, and it also played a negative role in workers' social lives. The situation of living concentrated in dormitories further worsened workers' social lives and relationships. In such living conditions, it was difficult for workers to use their limited resources and space to spend money on leisure activities and relieve the pressures of work, to say nothing of creating their own networks of colleagues as the Honda workers did. The brutal style of management and alienating labor processes only exacerbated the workers' misery.

Such living conditions also gave rise to the formation of another demographic group: "idle youngsters" (混混). According to workers, since these young people were unwilling to work in factories, many just hung out around Foxconn and some ended up joining gangs. Once they ran out of money or wanted to "pick up girls," they temporarily went to work in the factory, but their lazy behavior annoyed not only the managers but even some of the other workers. In response to managerial discipline, however, they immediately responded with acts of revenge outside the factory. In the riot at Taiyuan Foxconn, it was precisely these "idle youngsters" who played the role of agitators.

4.3 Collective Resistance

The incident began one evening when employees who had been temporarily transferred from Henan and Shandong got into a fight after getting drunk, and a security guard hit one of the workers from Henan (or maybe one of the workers from Shandong, according to conflicting accounts). After the worker called over a few of his fellow Henanese, the guard called for reinforcements, and the workers in turn called even more fellow Henanese to come over. This occurred just as a shift was ending and workers were clocking out. Still more workers from Henan and Shandong joined the fight, and the guards ran away. Angry workers then began to chase the guards, attacking them and smashing up their guard stations. This attacking and smashing took place in two rounds. The first round started around 12:30 a.m. and progressed from the D-block dormitories through the commercial street and two gates on the southern side of the factory complex. During that round, the main result was the smashing of guard stations, with little damage occurring on the commercial street. Most workers just gathered around and watched – just over a hundred people participated actively. It was not until after the armed police (武警) took action that many other workers joined the group causing destruction of property. However, after the factory gates were smashed, some "idle youngsters" snuck in and took part in the destruction and looting. On the way back to the dorms, at about one o'clock, the armed police intervened, forcing workers from the athletic field, causing many injuries; among the injured were many workers who had not participated in the riot.

The angry workers did not dare to attack the police. Instead, they waited until one or two in the morning to begin a second round of rioting. This time, bakeries, internet cafes, cell phone stores and many public facilities on the shopping street were smashed up and police vehicles were overturned. Two phone stores were looted, but other stores were protected by their employees. Participants explained, "We were mainly motivated by anger; we're not bandits." At first, the workers who initiated the riot urged people to attack only security guards and their stations, but later things got out of control. The police were hesitant to take action during the course of the riot. Later, after more police arrived, they began to use batons to drive the workers back into their dorms.

As the workers were marching, they shouted slogans, such as, "Down with Japan!" "Boycott Japanese goods!" "Reclaim the Diaoyu Islands!" and even "Bring out the murderers!" It was said that one of the security guards and several workers died, and that several dozen people were injured.

After the police had dispersed the crowd, another conflict emerged in the dormitory area. As multiple squads of armed police approached, the workers called for reinforcements, mustering over ten thousand workers at the peak. They pulled out some nearby firehoses and sprayed them directly at the police. From inside higher levels of the dorm buildings, workers threw things. They attacked the police "as if they were Japanese devils." At that time, the police did not dare assault anyone, and the two sides arrived at a stalemate. The police did not take action until after five o'clock in the morning, when they dispersed the crowd and arrested people. Only then did the conflict come to an end. For the next few days, police stationed themselves at Foxconn. The company announced a day of vacation for everyone to calm the situation down.

Two weeks later, in Zhengzhou's Foxconn complex, large-scale physical confrontations and strikes broke out.

4.4 *Life and Contentious Politics*

The lack of social life and destruction of interpersonal networks among Foxconn workers in Taiyuan led to atomization in collective resistance and generated tensions with the factory. Under conditions of semi-militarized management, strenuous labor, and total repression, the Foxconn workers released their anger through collective violence. The "idle youngsters" inside and outside of Foxconn were a group that is especially worth noting. To a certain extent, precisely because the young generation of migrants had not become accustomed to authoritarian factory life, some ended up living as parasites on the factory environment or chose to join "dark forces." Therefore, it is worth further research to investigate the conditions in which young migrants are likely to join criminal organizations and gang politics are likely to influence labor politics.

The Taiyuan Foxconn incident was the first large-scale act of violent resistance by the new generation of workers, and it led to confrontation between workers and violent organs of the state. In the past, almost all collective actions by new workers attempted to confine their actions within the limits of the law and fight for their rights in a peaceful and rational manner. However, the alienation derived from the labor process, production management discipline, the destruction of interpersonal networks, and the lack of social life all led to anxiety among workers in the world's workshop. In the face of broader structural conditions, for instance, the "split household" system of labor force reproduction, the discriminatory system of household registration (户籍), the lack of mechanisms for the expression of interests, and the low profitability of OEMs, workers saw no possibility of improving their situation. It was in the midst of this all-encompassing anxiety and desperation that the workers chose to participate in the riot. Judging by the videos and photos uploaded by Foxconn workers, the riot was characterized by a universally festive atmosphere.

5 Conclusion and Discussion

Each of these three patterns of collective resistance has its own basis in the participants' social lives. Their experiences and demands in specific factory regimes are not unrelated to their past experiences with farm work and education. The interaction of their ways of life with different types of production regimes led to the emergence of different bonds of solidarity and forms of mobilization.

Through their everyday lives in the community, past experiences in school, and relatively stable work, the Honda workers had developed wide social networks, a broad field of vision, pluralistic knowledge and a mature ability to use new media. All of these factors contributed to solidarity among workers and facilitated their mobilization. Their social networks, knowledge and field of vision also helped them to rationally assess the company's existing wage structure and mechanisms for meeting workers' interests. In the end, by adopting a method of orderly, sustained collective withdrawal of their labor, the Honda workers forced the company to address their demands.

The workers at Taiyuan Foxconn lacked the sort of social lives and networks enjoyed by their fellow workers at Honda. The labor processes and management culture they experienced were also completely different from those at Honda. As far as they were concerned, there was neither space for wage bargaining nor opportunity for career development. When they encountered a spark, they chose to vent their anger through rioting.

The workers at Ohm also lacked stable social networks among coworkers, but they did not experience the overwhelming anxiety caused by the lack of social life and all-encompassing discipline experienced by Foxconn workers. Sometimes their collective resentment was spurred by agitation by other groups (see Table 8.1). Of course, it is possible that this type of resistance will become increasingly autonomous as young workers grow older, gain experience, and as secondary school education becomes more universal.

We must not fail to mention the systemic origins of the politics of workers' lives and struggles. The developing global capitalist system both pursues the cheapest labor power and attempts to open up the widest markets for consumption. Between their paltry wages and the ubiquitous wave of consumerism, the new generation of migrant workers experiences a structural tension that cannot be mitigated. Their leisure activities thus contain foundations for solidarity and resources for mobilization. In all three patterns, it is easy to detect the influence of the internet, but this raises the question: isn't widespread use of cell phones and computers by workers a result of consumerism? The networks, knowledge and perspectives formed through workers' consumption have reshaped their experiences and demands in the factories. Systemic arrangements have thus simultaneously provided sources of structural tensions, solidarity and mobilization, which have in turn reshaped workers' demands and experiences.

These three patterns of resistance by the new generation of migrant workers have, in various ways, challenged the existing production regime based on migrant labor, to some degree foretelling the direction of industrial relations in China. The Honda struggle demonstrates that workers can form informal bonds of solidarity, despite the lack of formal organizations. Their demands, moreover, demonstrate workers' desire for the reasonable sharing of profits and the need to establish regular mechanisms for bargaining.

However, this is possible only in industries with a high rate of profit (a possibility constrained by the state's attitude toward workers' collective actions, the relationship between capital and the local government, and the distribution of profits along industrial value chains). In industries with a high level of competition, such as the electronics industry to which both Ohm and Foxconn belong, workers' space for bargaining is extremely limited. Under conditions where there is no hope of improving their basic conditions, it is unlikely that workers in authoritarian enterprises can limit their resistance to peaceful, rational and legal forms. As soon as mass struggles of industrial workers become violent and disorderly, this constitutes a major challenge to the maintenance of peaceful industrial relations and the socioeconomic order that previously appeared to be stable. The universal usage of the internet in all types of struggles means that the direction of workers' collective resistance is becoming even harder to predict.

TABLE 8.1   Comparison between three patterns of resistance

	Offensive struggles based on relationships among coworkers and classmates	Atomized struggles to defend rights or advance interests	Riots
Typical Cases	*Nanhai Honda*	*Shenzhen Ohm*	*Taiyuan Foxconn*
Regime of production	Semi-authoritarian	Authoritarian	Quasi-militarized authoritarian

Experiences in production and life

Alienation from the labor process	Normal	Strong	Strong
Harsh production management	Weak	Normal	Strong
Lack of social life	Weak	Normal	Strong
Lack of career development opportunities	Strong	Strong	Strong

Solidarity bonds and mobilization models

Labor turnover	Normal	High	High
Informal networks of interpersonal relationships	Strong	Weak	Weak

TABLE 8.1 Comparison between three patterns of resistance (*cont.*)

	Offensive struggles based on relationships among coworkers and classmates	Atomized struggles to defend rights or advance interests	Riots
Internal communication on the internet	Strong	Weak	Weak
External communication on the internet	Strong	Strong	Normal

References

Burawoy, Michael. 1979. *Manufacturing Consent*. Chicago: The University of Chicago Press.

Burawoy, Michael. 1985. *The Politics of Production: Factory Regimes under Capitalism and Socialism*. London: Verso.

Cai He 蔡禾. 2010. 从 "底线型" 利益到 "增长型" 利益 – 农民工利益诉求的转变与劳资关系秩序 ["From 'Defending' Interests to 'Advancing' Interests: Changes in the Demands of Migrant Workers and the Labor-Capital Relations System"]. 开放时代 [*Open Times*], 9: 37–45.

Chan, Anita. 1995. "The Emerging Patterns of Industrial Relations in China and the Rise of Two New Labor Movements." *China Information*, 9 (4): 36–59.

Gallagher, Mary. 2011. "Changes in the World's Workshop: The Demographic, Social, and Political Factors Behinds China's Movement." Paper submitted to the Symposium of Analysis on the Development of Chinese Labor Relations held by Research Center of Labor Issues in Beijing Normal University, Beijing.

Guo Yuhua 郭于华 et al. 2011. 当代农民工的抗争与中国劳资关系转型 ["Contemporary Migrant Workers' Struggles and the Transformation of China's Labor Relations"]. 二十一世纪 [*21st Century*], 124: 5–14.

Lee, Ching Kwan. 1995. "Engendering the Worlds of Labor: Women Workers, Labor Markets, and Production Politics in the South China Economic Miracle." *American Sociological Review*, 60 (3): 378–397.

Lee, Ching Kwan. 1999. "The Politics of Working-class Transitions in China." Conference paper presented at the International Symposium of Globalization and Labor Issues held by Research Center of Contemporary China in Tsinghua University, Beijing.

Lee, Ching Kwan. 2007. *Against the Law: Labor Protests in China's Rustbelt and Sunbelt*. Berkeley, CA: University of California Press.

Pun, Ngai. 2005. *Made in China: Women Factory Workers in a Global Workplace*. Durham & Hong Kong: Duke University Press and Hong Kong University Press.

Pun, Ngai and Lu Huilin. 2010. "Unfinished Proletarianization: Self, Anger and Class Action among the Second Generation of Peasant-Workers in Present-Day China." *Modern China*, 5: 493–519.

Pun Ngai 潘毅 et al. 2011. 富士康辉煌背后的连环跳 [Chain of Suicides behind Foxconn's Splendor]. Hong Kong: Commercial Press.

Su, Yihui. 2011. "Student Workers in the Foxconn Empire: The Commodification of Education and Labor in China." *Journal of Workplace Rights*, 15 (3): 341–362.

Tsinghua University Sociology Department Research Group 清华社会学系课题组. 2012. 困境与行动 – 新生代农民工与 "农民工生产体制" 的碰撞 ["Dilemma and Actions: The Clash between the New Generation of Migrant Workers and the 'Migrant-Worker Production Regime'"], in 清华社会学评论 [*Tsinghua Sociology Review*] vol. 6, edited by Shen Yuan 沈原, Beijing: Social Sciences Academic Press.

Wang Chunguang 王春光. 2001. 新生代农村流动人口的社会认同与城乡融合的关系 ["The Relationship between Social Identity and Urban Integration of the New Generation of Migrant Workers"]. 社会学研究 [*Sociological Studies*], 3: 63–76.

Wang Jianhua 汪建华. 2011. 互联网动员与代工厂工人集体抗争 ["Internet Mobilization and Collective Protest of Workers in Supplier Factories"]. 开放时代 [*Open Times*], 11: 114–128.

Wang Jianhua 汪建华. 2012. 新工人的生活与抗争政治 – 基于珠三角集体抗争案例的分析 ["New Workers' Politics of Livelihood and Contention: A Case Study on Collective Protest in Pearl River Delta"]. 清华社会学评论 [*Tsinghua Sociological Review*], 6: 190–214, edited by Shen Yuan 沈原, Beijing: Social Sciences Academic Press.

Index

All-China Federation of Trade Unions
(ACFTU)   52–54, 58, 64, 68–69, 115,
134–135
   Migrant workers and   68–69, 71–72, 82,
134–135, 148, 159, 161
   Staff and workers congresses and   34–45
(passim)
   Role in strikes and protests   171–178
(passim)
   Elections   143–162 (passim)
Anshan Iron and Steel Constitution   76
Apprenticeship   11, 14, 104–106, 109, 117–119
   See also Education and training

Bonuses and incentives   12, 18, 22–23, 26,
41–42, 60–62, 67–68, 76, 90n, 137, 172
   See also Fines and punishments
and Wages
Burawoy, Michael   9, 70, 120, 165

Chan, Anita   170
Chen Yu   19–20
Chinese Communist Party
   Role in industrial policy and factory
management   8, 10, 16, 18–18, 25, 46,
54, 59, 63, 84, 101, 148
   Role in the ACFTU and SWC   35–39, 68,
84–112 (passim), 144–146, 148, 153,
161–162
Cold War   15–16, 28
Company Law (1994)   47, 57, 58
Consumption   15, 95, 166, 168, 174, 183
Corporate social responsibility programs
125–141 (passim)
Cultural Revolution   8, 24, 28, 34–35, 43,
46–47, 103–104
Cultural, sports and leisure activities   13, 28,
68, 105, 115–116, 121, 170–171, 174, 176,
179–180, 183

Education and training (factory-based)   65,
68, 72, 103–104, 109, 116, 120, 171, 174–175
   See also Apprenticeships
Edwards, Richard   66, 67, 70
Enterprise Law (1988)   37
Ethnic relations   99–121 (passim)

Fei Xiaotong   100
Fines and punishments   10, 42, 45, 60–61,
67–68, 72, 82, 87, 90–92, 100, 127, 136,
140, 169, 175
   See also Bonuses and incentives
and Wages
Flexible accumulation   75, 77, 86, 94, 95, 96
Fordism-Keynesianism   75, 77, 95
Foxconn   144, 166–169, 179–184

Gallagher, Mary   76, 84
Gender and employment   38, 81, 109–111, 118,
134, 170
   See also Social reproduction
Global supply chains   125–129, 133–135, 136,
139, 150, 155
   Transnational labor processes and   75,
77, 78–79, 84, 86–88, 95
Globalization   75, 77, 84, 86, 96
   See also Global supply chains *and* Private
and foreign-invested enterprises
Gordon, Milton   100
Great Leap Forward   7–10, 15, 17–20, 47, 55

Health care   13, 68, 106, 115–116, 134
High modernism   7, 15–18, 28
Honda   144, 160, 167–174, 182–184
Housing   12, 13, 42, 47, 68, 71, 92, 110–118, 139,
167–168, 171, 175–176, 178–181

Industrial restructuring and privatization   34,
37–39, 42, 46–47, 52–59, 63, 72, 78,
83–84, 89–90, 95, 103, 106–109, 112,
114–117, 120, 150, 151
Internet   147–148, 166, 167, 169, 171–174, 176,
178, 181, 183–185

Kenichi Ohno   59
Kong Xianghong   146

Labor Contract Law (2008)   92, 148
Labor management methods   8, 14, 17,
20–21, 24–25, 45, 54, 59, 65, 67, 76, 82,
89–91, 93–96, 157, 169–171, 175–176,
179–181, 183

Labor management methods (cont.)
   Simple control model   52, 66–68, 70, 72–73
Labor markets   59, 61–63, 65–67
   Informal   52, 70–73, 75, 81, 84, 88, 96
   Labor shortages   61, 93, 151, 161
   See also Labor recruitment, Labor subcontracting, and Migrant workers
Labor process   54, 75, 77, 85–86, 88–95, 99
Labor productivity   8, 15, 21n, 27, 76, 151
Labor recruitment   99, 105–107, 109, 117, 170
   See also Labor markets, Labor subcontracting, and Migrant workers
Labor subcontracting   62–66, 69–71, 75–77, 80–89
Layoffs   38, 46, 63, 47, 78, 89, 108–109, 111–113
   See also Industrial restructuring
Lee, Ching Kwan   54, 72, 91
Lefebvre, Henri   101
Liu Shaoqi   35

Managers
   Appointment of   42, 59, 63, 103, 106, 109, 120, 156
   Compensation of   43, 59, 60, 62, 175, 177–178
   Election of   42
   Ethnicity of   103, 107, 118
   Power of   54, 59, 66–68, 72, 76, 82–83, 85, 90–96, 158, 175
   Staff and workers congress and   39, 43, 45–47
Meyer, John   48
Migrant workers   54, 64, 66, 69–72, 81, 96, 134–135, 148, 159
   Generations of   147, 161, 165–178, 182–183
   See also Labor markets, Labor recruitment, and Labor subcontracting

Neoliberalism   75, 77, 96
New Institutionalism   33
Non-governmental organizations   129, 132, 140–141, 148–149, 160–161

Ohm   154, 159, 168, 169, 175–179, 183–184
Oi, Jean   54

Polanyi, Karl   76, 84, 91
Private and foreign-invested enterprises   103, 106–121 (passim), 125–141 (passim), 143–162 (passim), 165–185 (passim)
   See also Foxconn, Ohm, Honda, Ricoh and State-owned enterprises
Promotion   26, 27, 41, 70, 107, 115, 120, 156

Retirement and pensions   63, 73, 92n, 94, 106, 107, 108, 112, 113, 116
Ricoh   144, 150, 155, 158
Rural-urban divide   59, 70, 72, 81, 83, 84, 107, 112, 182

Safety and health   15, 46, 60, 65–69, 71, 81, 108, 129, 131, 134, 166
Silver, Beverly   91
Skilled workers   52, 59, 63–66, 87, 104–107, 109, 117, 120, 155
Small teams (in factories)
   Conventional   11, 12, 43, 58, 64, 171
   Japanese-invested factories and   156
   Subcontractor-led   64–71, 76, 80–82, 86, 88, 94–95
Social insurance and welfare   12–13, 15–16, 22, 25, 54, 63, 66, 68, 71, 81–83, 92–93, 107, 115–116, 131, 134, 148, 175, 177
   See also Housing, Health care, and Retirement and pensions
Social reproduction
   Under the work unit system   12–16, 42, 68, 115, 118
   Split mode of   71, 81, 106, 115–116, 166, 169, 178, 182
Soviet Union   10, 56, 87, 102
Spatial adjustment   75, 77, 86, 96
Staff and workers congress (SWC) system   33–49, 58
State-owned assets commissions   60, 92n, 111, 112, 113, 114
State-owned enterprises   7–28 (passim), 33–49 (passim), 52–73 (passim), 75–96 (passim), 99–121 (passim), 144, 152
   See also Private and foreign-invested enterprises
Stock markets   47, 55, 56, 57, 58, 129
Strikes and protests   8, 108, 144, 147–148, 152, 156, 158–162, 165–181

Tao Zhu   10, 19, 20
Technical employees   19, 40, 56–57, 61–63, 66, 70, 72, 86, 87, 103

INDEX

Wages 42, 46–47, 65–66, 70–71, 82–83, 90, 93n, 94–95, 117, 127, 129–131, 134, 140, 147–149, 151, 156–161, 170–172, 174–176, 179–183
   Differences 11, 26, 42, 60–66, 70, 82, 94, 114
   Piece rates 18, 41, 82–83, 94, 138, 139
   Arrears 69, 82, 166
   See also Bonuses and incentives *and* Fines and punishments
Walder, Andrew 8, 54, 89
Walmart 129–141
Wang Yang 144, 149, 150
Work discipline and attitudes 7–28, 42, 81, 89–93, 150, 167–168, 180, 182, 184
Work unit system 12–13, 17, 22, 24–25, 53–55, 61, 76–77, 81, 83, 85, 87, 89–90, 95
Workers' social status 7, 9–14, 37–38, 44, 48, 61, 64, 89–90, 104

Working conditions 18, 28, 65, 93, 94, 108, 129, 166, 175, 176, 179
   See also Health and safety, Working hours, *and* Labor process
Working hours 10, 18–19, 28, 41–42, 58, 81–82, 91–94, 108, 118, 129,–131, 134–140, 171, 175, 179
Workplace participation and democracy 11, 14, 33–48 (passim), 93, 140–141, 156, 169, 176

Ye Jianying 10

Zhao Wei 76
Zhou Enlai 10
Zhou, Xueguang 8
Zhu De 10, 45